GCE Applied

ICT for Edexcel

AS Single Award

John Morgan

D1611117

PAYNE-GALLWAY

Published by Payne-Gallway Publishers Limited
Payne-Gallway is an imprint of Harcourt Education Ltd
Halley Court, Jordan Hill, Oxford, OX2 8EJ

Tel: 01865 888070 * Fax: 01865 314029
E-mail: orders@payne-gallway.co.uk * Web: www.payne-gallway.co.uk

© John Morgan 2006
First published 2006

11 10 09 08 07 06
10 9 8 7 6 5 4 3 2 1

British Library Cataloguing in Publication Data is available from the British Library on request

10-digit ISBN: 1 904467598
13-digit ISBN: 978 1 904467 59 5

Typeset and illustrated by Saxon Graphics Ltd.
Printed by CPI Bath Colourbooks

Ordering Information
You can order from:

Payne-Gallway, FREEPOST (OF1771),
PO Box 381, Oxford OX2 8BR
Tel: 01865 888070
Fax: 01865 314029
E-mail: orders@payne-gallway.co.uk
Web: www.payne-gallway.co.uk

We are grateful to the following organisations for permission to use copyright material:

Microsoft, Excel, Powerpoint, FrontPage, Outlook, Internet Explorer and Windows are either registered
trademarks or trademarks of Microsoft Corporation in the uNited States and/or other countries. This title
is an independent publication and is not affiliated with, nor has it been authorized, sponsored, or
otherwise approved by Microsoft Corporation.

Article on p.89 Copyright © CNET Networks, Inc. All rights reserved. ZDNET UK is a registered service
mark of CNET Networks, Inc.
Article on p.173 ©2002 The New York Times Company. Reprinted by Permission

Screenshot credits
www.dabs.com
www.internetworldstats.com
www.fictionwise.com
Yahoo! screenshots are reproduced with permission of Yahoo! Inc. ©2006 Yahoo! Inc. YAHOO! and the
YAHOO! logo are trademarks of Yahoo! Inc.

Photo credits
Selection of printed reports, letters, brochures and documents, Natalie Gray; Photo of hole in the wall
bank cash dispenser, Harcourt Education Ltd / Peter Morris; Airport check-in desk, Corbis; Selector dial
from a digital camera, Nikon; Self-service supermarket checkout, Alamy; Barcode, iStockPhoto / Melissa
King; Person using a touch screen, Alamy; Magnetic strip on a membership card/train ticket,
Corbis;Cheque reader, Handheld products; Computer keyboard, Getty Images / PhotoDisc; Optical
recognition mark up sheet, Natalie Gray; Chip and pin card, Alamy; Telephone headset, Getty Images /
PhotoDisc; Supermarket delivery van, Alamy, Citroen C4 dancing robot advert, Citroen; Computer on fire,
Getty Images; Space rocket, Corbis; Handshake, Getty Images / PhotoDisc; Bass guitar, Corbis; Surfing,
Getty Images / PhotoDisc; Jetski, Corbis; Open book, Getty Images/PhotoDisc; Computer cable, Getty
Images/PhotoDisc; Computer keyboard, Getty Images/PhotoDisc; Computer monitors, Digital Vision;
Walkie-talkie, Harcourt Eduction Ltd/Peter Morris; Fingerprint, Getty Images/PhotoDisc; Scales of justice,
Getty Images/PhotoDisc; Interview, Harcourt Education Ltd/Devon Obugenge Shaw; Policeman and patrol
car courtesy of Exning Primary School

Contents

The Information Age

1.1

OBJECTIVES

- To be aware of key technologies used to convey information
- To be aware of how technology allows us to present information in different ways
- To understand how information can be shared quickly, allowing people greater interaction with others
- To understand some of the issues and challenges surrounding the use of technology

This unit has been designed to explore how the world we live in is constantly changing as a result of new technologies. We live in an age full of data and information which, in many cases, is crucial to our standard of living and overall quality of life.

Key Technologies

These are the key technologies that help to shape the way we live:

- **Internet**: The global **superhighway** that facilitates the transfer of data and information around the world. Like a spider's **web** it connects us all. Using **email** and **websites**, we can share images, sound files, textual documents and video files with people anywhere in the world as long as they have Internet access.

- **Multimedia**: This is the name given to systems that enable the interactive use of text, images, video, animations and sound. To be part of a multimedia system, the components must be created in or converted to a digital format (for example, sound must be in .mp3, .wav or other digital file format). A multimedia system is one in which previously diverse components converge into one fully **interactive system**.

- **Broadband**: This term comes from the expression 'broad bandwidth' and describes a high capacity communications link that connects the end user to multiple network suppliers. This system utilises **multiplexing** to enable the simultaneous operation of many channels or services on a single cable. This technology is fast and capable of transferring full motion video, voice communication and data over the Internet.

- **Wireless**: A radio-based system which allows the rapid transference of data and information without a physical connection. Wireless systems are becoming more common as people want to connect two or more computers to the same broadband connection but don't want to have trailing wires in their homes. A wireless system allows you to have one broadband **router** connected to your main computer with each additional computer having a small wireless interface

Tip:

Before we talk about some of the key technologies, here is a quick reminder that the work you complete on this course needs to be provided as evidence of your attainment. Look at Appendix A, 'Standard Ways of Working', and familiarise yourself with the section on 'e-portfolios'. This is very important because you need to learn how to collect information in an appropriate format.

adaptor. This adaptor enables the user to access the Internet just as if their computer were connected via a cable. If you have a **laptop** computer, you can even sit in the garden to do your ICT research on the Internet.

● **Digital television** and video: **DTV** stands for Digital television. This technology transmits a TV programme by encoding it in a digital format. DTV can be compressed and features better sound quality and a much higher picture resolution than previous television systems. Digital video refers to the capture, possible future manipulation and the storage of video in a digital format.

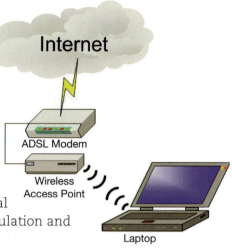

Figure 1.1

Portfolio Builder: **Later in the course you will be constructing an e-book to describe and evaluate five different types of online service. Using the five subheadings from the bulleted list above, start reviewing these key technologies with a view to using your findings in your e-book. As an example, you may like to look at the growth of the Internet and see how this has affected the way we shop for merchandise.**

Opportunities created by the information age

In this section we will take a brief look at how ICT has revolutionised the way we live and work.

Presenting information in different ways

ICT provides a host of features which allow us to present information in exciting and eye-catching ways. For example, our reports might include imaginative text styles, graphics, colour and data presented as graphs and charts. In addition, the Windows environment allows us to switch between applications so we can manipulate data from a variety of sources. These features enable us to provide content-rich documents with a professional appearance. We will be investigating some practical examples later in the book.

Figure 1.2

Sharing information quickly

In the same way that ICT helps us to present our information, it also allows us to share that information more quickly and easily. The fact that our files are stored in a digital format makes the whole sharing process extremely flexible and seamless. For example, large files can be emailed across the world, facilitating collaborative work – colleagues can review important images, documents, sound files or video footage within a short time frame. If you compare sending an email

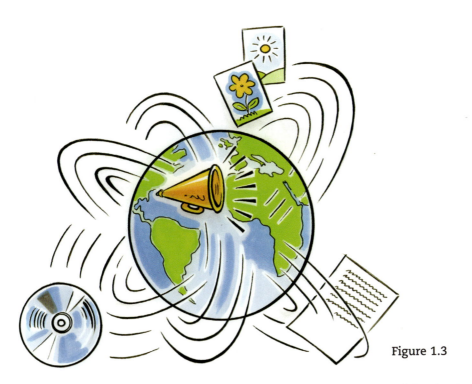

Figure 1.3

attachment and a fax, you can see that a fax would come a very poor second for sharing images and text; and sending sound and video files is simply not possible by fax.

Exercise

Why is it important that our documents look good and have a professional finish? What tools are available to help us achieve this? Make some comparisons between using a typewriter and a word processor to produce a document. What features are available in the word processor that make such a difference?

Exercise

Write a short article explaining why you think a graphic design company can be more efficient today than it was 20 years ago. You may need to conduct an Internet search to find information on this subject. Read the chapter on Internet research if you need help.

Greater interaction with others

Another obvious benefit that comes from using ICT effectively is the opportunity for greater interaction with other people and organisations. There was a time when marketing companies would have to print a full-colour copy of an advertisement, ship it by air to the client, wait for the client review panel to authorise the image and then receive the go-ahead to print. This process would be prolonged if the client had two offices in different parts of the world that both needed to see the proof. Nowadays, of course, this whole process is simplified and streamlined by the use of portable document formats (PDFs) and email attachments.

Business opportunities, large and small

The following article supports the idea that all businesses, no matter what their size, can benefit from the effective use of ICT. Modern application packages such as word processors, databases, spreadsheets, presentation graphics, graphics software and video editing software all contribute to assisting companies with improving performance and efficiency.

'There is compelling evidence to show that businesses using ICT perform better and have more opportunities for growth. The Economist states that Broadband, currently the fastest growing area of ICT, will bring about the biggest behavioural shift since electricity. However there are many businesses in the community that do not fully appreciate the benefits ICT can bring.'

(Source: **http://www.businesslinkwessex. co.uk/xpand/ downloaded 2005)**

Exercise

Write a short article for a newspaper, highlighting why you think that ICT is becoming even more essential for business users than it has been in the past.

Virtual communities

The Internet has brought with it a variety of ways of communicating, including email, blogs, chat rooms, forums and news groups. Each of these services bring individuals and groups together and allows them to communicate more effectively. Like-minded individuals can create and use discussion areas where themes of mutual interest are discussed. For example, a family may have a child with a disability who will need specialist help throughout his or her life. In most cases there will be a specialist help group, whose members worldwide can offer advice and support via a dedicated website. The use of electronic noticeboards for these specialist groups allow people to post and receive messages relating to their queries and concerns. Special interest groups in thousands of areas, ranging from classic cars to the LINUX operating system, are catered for on the Internet. People 'meet' electronically on these specialist websites to discuss topics of common interest.

Exercise

In small groups, discuss how the internet has developed the world of communication. You will need to consider the differences between various communication methods including: email, blogs, chat rooms, forums and news groups.

Mobile technologies

The microchip, which is at the heart of all computers and ICT devices, is getting smaller. This means that previously 'desk-bound' computer systems are now becoming mobile. State-of-the-art batteries with increased capacity and longevity, and highly durable materials including plastics and super-light metals are now being produced in large enough quantities to make them an economic option for use in ICT equipment. Add to this scenario our 'need' to be mobile (as opposed to being desk-bound), and you can see why mobile technologies are really accelerating forward. The creation of more mobile technologies is blurring the distinction between home and work, as ICT equipment from the workplace can be brought home and vice versa.

Exercise

Write a short article for an imaginary company newsletter illustrating how mobile computing has benefited the sales personnel who visit potential customers.

A self-service environment

ICT has revolutionised the way we make purchases and even the way we learn. It has created a self-service culture in which consumers carry out activities and transactions by themselves – these activities include shopping, banking and learning. Many petrol pumps have become automated to the extent that we can place a credit or debit card in the pump itself and avoid going to the service till. We can purchase goods in certain supermarkets by scanning the items ourselves and paying the bill at the same scanning terminal, without the intervention of another human! And the number of people who shop online is increasing all the time – Internet shopping tends to be cheaper and save time. We can also learn using interactive materials that don't involve face to face interactions with a human teacher.

The issues and challenges of the information age

It is important to develop your awareness of the issues and challenges that are as much a part of the information age as the benefits.

The need for lifelong learning

Most technological advances enable us to do things more efficiently; however, there is always a price to pay. In this world of change, it is essential that we continue to learn throughout our lives in order to keep our skills and knowledge up to date. Technology is moving so rapidly that we need to update our skills constantly in order to participate fully in daily life and work. ICT both creates the need for lifelong learning and enables us to do it more easily – providing a variety of learning sources including the Internet, electronic books, CD-ROM technology and interactive video. With every advance in technology we have to learn the skills that go with it. For some, this is a challenge, while others see it as an exciting opportunity.

Figure 1.4

Privacy rights

As we have seen, the digital age brings with it a fast-moving technology, allowing rapid file transfers over long distances – as soon as you click 'Send' it's gone! This ease of communication brings with it the need to respect and protect personal privacy – both our own and other people's. There are now established laws regarding information exchange and we have rights of privacy when using the Internet. But there are always people who will try to break the rules and invade our privacy. For example, fraudsters who send spoof emails claiming to be from our bank and asking us to reveal our personal details and account numbers. These people are not only trying to invade our privacy, but also our pockets!

Copyright and legislation

ICT is making certain products, such as films and books, very portable as they are stored in digital format. Although they are often protected by copyright, it is very easy to transfer the files over the Internet illegally. The same is true for music CDs. When the CD format was invented, no one realised that quite soon most home computers would be equipped with writable CD systems. This has allowed people to make illegal copies of CDs quickly and easily. And now that MP3 files are widely available, a simple right-click and 'Save As' will capture a file from the Internet and store it on a hard drive in seconds. Do you think that the Internet and MP3 file formats could be contributing to increased copyright infringement?

Impact on employment

When ICT systems were first being introduced into the workplace, many people thought it would be the end of their jobs. There was much publicity about computers replacing people and many workers were worried about their future? For people who knew nothing about ICT it was even more worrying. They were the ones who felt the most vulnerable.

As time has passed, ICT has become almost universally accepted in the workplace. Workers know that companies need ICT systems in order to compete with other organisations both in this country and abroad. Companies nowadays are more likely to employ people who have good ICT skills; in addition they often ensure that the existing workforce is updated with new skills. The effective use of ICT within a modern business frees up employees to tackle the 'people intensive' problems and lets the computers get on with 'number crunching' activities.

The digital divide

The **digital divide** is the gap between people who have the equipment and the knowledge to use technology and people who do not have the technology or the education to be able to use it effectively. The digital divide also refers to the difference between different parts of the world – the areas with modern communications infrastructures such as telephone systems and electricity lines and those where such infrastructures are not fully in place. The digital divide will be discussed in more detail in later chapters.

Exercise

What do you understand by the term 'digital divide'?

Online services

OBJECTIVES

- To use the Internet to find different types of online services
- To present a comprehensive description of different types of online service
- To provide an evaluation of each of the online services described
- To present a clear and balanced picture of the current scope and limitations of the Internet

The Internet is a key facility in the information age. It provides the opportunity to expand our knowledge in a variety of different subject areas. In this section of the book we will be finding out about some of the different types of online service that are available. As an ICT student, you will already be familiar with many of those that are mentioned.

In order for us to use the Internet to find information, we must be familiar with one of the key tools, the web browser. There are many web browsers available but the most commonly used is Microsoft Internet Explorer. In the next few sections we will spend some time investigating the browser in order to understand how to use it effectively.

Using the Internet

We are going to use the Internet to obtain information on a range of online services. If you look at the assessment criteria for Unit One, The Information Age, you will notice that part (a) requires that you consider online services. To do this you will need to connect to the Internet and run Internet Explorer. Note that there are many different web browsers available. Internet Explorer is a common browser but Netscape Navigator and Firefox are also very capable browsers.

Figure 1.5 Icons of web browsers: Netscape, Explorer and Firefox

Most schools and colleges will have an Internet connection that is always on, so that whenever you log onto your computer system and run Internet Explorer, you will automatically gain access to the Worldwide Web. If you do not have this 'always on' facility, your teacher can show you how to connect to the Internet using a phone line and modem. Please note: the Internet is constantly changing, so many of the pages used in this book may have changed by the time you view them.

Open your web browser and you will see the default screen, perhaps similar to the one shown in Figure 1.6.

Figure 1.6

In this case the default screen shown in Figure 1.6 is the MSN home page. Your school or college computer probably has a different default screen. This doesn't matter because mostly you will want to move from this screen to one with the information that you are looking for.

Figure 1.7 illustrates some of the important features of the browser that you will need to become familiar with.

The menus and buttons enable us to search effectively for information on the Internet.

Figure 1.7

There are two main ways you can find a website on the Internet.

1. The first way is to use a URL that you already know – by typing it into the browser address box, or by selecting it from your Favourites. (URL stands for 'uniform resource locator' – this is just a fancy name for the address of the page you want to look at. Every Internet site has its own unique URL.) As an example, most people are familiar with eBay – if you enter **www.ebay.co.uk** into the browser address box and press the Enter key, the web browser will take you straight to the eBay UK site and display its homepage as shown in Figure 1.8.

2. The second way is to use a search engine, enter some keywords and then follow the links provided by the search engine. To get to the homepage of the search engine, enter the search engine address in the same way as described for the eBay URL. Here are some popular search engines for you to try:

Google	**www.google.co.uk**
Hotbot	**www.hotbot.co.uk**
Yahoo	**www.yahoo.co.uk**
Ask Jeeves	**www.ask.co.uk**

Figure 1.8

Exercise

Log on to the Internet and use each of the two methods described above to locate information. Then describe the difference between the two methods, using appropriate screenshots to illustrate your findings.

Let's do some research and find out some information about online services. Use the Google search engine to find out some real-time information: in this case we will be looking for weather reports. To do this, type the Google URL into the browser address box (**www.google.co.uk**) . A web page, similar to the one in Figure 1.9, will be displayed on your computer screen.

Tip:

If you are having difficulty finding relevant Internet sites, try using a different search engine with the same keywords. Search engines often categorise information slightly differently and using a different engine may help you to find the information you require. Alternatively, try changing your keywords. These need to be very focused upon your research theme.

Figure 1.9

You are researching the weather so enter some appropriate keywords into the Google search box as shown in Figure 1.10. Check the button labelled 'pages from the UK'. This forces Google to search UK pages only and will enable you to avoid getting links to pages from outside the UK.

Figure 1.10

When you press the Enter key, Google will find pages of information that contain both of the keywords and will present these as a list. Figure 1.11 shows an example of the results that Google might come up with.

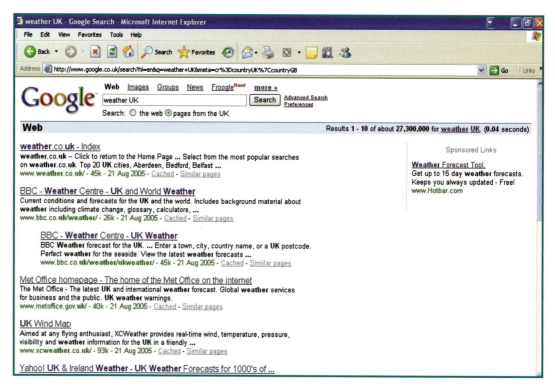

Figure 1.11

You can now review the results, choose the link that looks the most promising, then click on the link to view the page. Figure 1.12 shows the result of clicking on the fourth link in the results list.

As you preview this page you will notice that it is a full of useful information and further links which present an excellent weather information service for the UK.

You are now going to put together some evidence for your e-portfolio that will cover Assessment Criteria (a). The goal here is to aim for Mark Band 3 in order to gain the higher marks. Your teacher or lecturer will tell you where to find up-to-date information about this on the Edexcel website: **www.edexcel.org.uk**.

Now that we have identified a suitable website for weather information, you will need to consider factors such as the target audience, benefits and drawbacks, fitness for purpose, possible enhancements and non-Internet alternatives. Let's review the Met Office website in the light of each of these considerations.

Figure 1.12

- **Target audience:** This site seems to cater for a very wide audience. It is written in a way that might appeal to both adults and young people. It is quite easy to imagine that parents might use this site when planning days out, while school pupils might use it as an additional resource for a school geography project.

- **Benefits and drawbacks:** The benefits of this particular website are clear. The user is presented with unambiguous navigational links. The page is well laid out, with all of the main resources and links presented in an intuitive manner. The site allows the user to enter their own postcode in order to find local weather conditions. The drawbacks are less obvious. The site does appear to have a high graphical content which may be a disadvantage for users with visual impairments and also those with slow modem links. However, the web designers have incorporated a text only version to overcome these possible issues.

- **Possible enhancements:** With a professional site such as this it is very difficult to recommend possible improvements, but you might be able to think of some. Try finding some information using the page. Can you easily find what you are looking for?

- **Fitness for purpose:** This site does exactly what it says it does. It provides a comprehensive online service for people who need up-to-date and accurate (as far as is possible) information regarding weather in the UK and the rest of the world.

- **Non-Internet alternatives:** These include newspapers, the radio and TV, each of which has some advantages. For example, newspapers are a very cheap way of gaining this information, as you do not need a computer, modem and Internet service provider to gain comparable weather information. However, it is likely that most people would prefer the up-to-date and multimedia approach that the Internet provides.

In order to extend your research for this topic area you could refer to some of the user groups who have a special interest in the weather. Use the Google search engine to source some. This time click the Groups button on the Google home page, then enter the same keywords and click Search. A web page like the one in Figure 1.13 will be displayed.

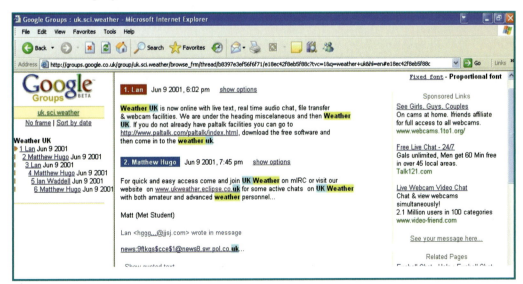

Figure 1.13 Google groups

A quick scan of the second group listed tells us that these people are really interested in discussions about the weather. This group offers 'some active chats on UK Weather with both amateur and advanced weather personnel…', which indicates that these people are fairly committed 'weather watchers'.

If you find some text that you would like to use in your e-book you can either print the page or you can highlight the text, then right-click and select Copy. Then you can Paste the text directly into your word processor. You must keep a note of the exact web page or URL so that you can properly reference and acknowledge the source of text or images from the Internet.

Having reviewed this online service, you need to provide a considered evaluation of it. Try to highlight both the positive and the negative aspects and to provide a clear and balanced picture of the current scope and limitations of the Internet as a whole.

In your conclusion you could say that, as an online service, the BBC weather site provides an excellent weather forecasting and reporting facility. It is accessible, but limited to those people who have access to the Internet.

Exercise

What do you feel are the limitations of the online services provided on the Internet?

How has ICT affected your own life and how would you draw on your experiences to influence how the company progresses with its online resources initiative?

Portfolio Builder: *Use a search engine to find a wide range of relevant information about different types of online services (at least five services are required for your e-book). As you complete this task, bear in mind that you will need to keep evidence of the processes that you go through for your e-portfolio. These processes will be very similar to the stages described in this section. Gather your evidence by keeping an accurate log of each step, including relevant screenshots of all of your steps.*

Having gone through the process of evaluating each of the websites, you then need to provide a concluding comment on the current scope and limitations of the Internet as a whole. Don't forget to keep references of all the relevant materials that you find and quote from them – you must acknowledge all work that you quote.

Note: For achievement in Mark Band 3, you will be expected to find a wide range of relevant information. A wide range should be taken to mean at least six different sorts of information. For example: extracts from websites, screenshots, journal articles, sound clips and quotes from discussion groups, etc. In addition, you could consider examples of the same service supplied by different providers. To continue with the example given in this section, if you were researching websites offering weather information, you could visit another weather website and source some additional evidence to further enhance your e-portfolio.

Case Study

You have been employed as a Marketing Executive for a large internet service provider (ISP). The company has developed a popular service that attracts customers from a variety of backgrounds. The ISP decided from the outset that they would be a content provider and have designed a user interface very similar to that of Wanadoo (**www.wanadoo.co.uk**) and Tiscali (**www.tiscali.co.uk**), etc. which they are now keen to develop. Your manager has asked you to work with the company's web authors to develop the online facilities provided by the company.

As part of this task you will need to prepare a list of at least five online services and describe some of their key features. You will then take these ideas to the web authors and ask them to provide similar services on your company's website. Before you meet the team, you will need to prepare yourself by answering the following question:

● What do you feel are the advantages and disadvantages of each of your chosen sites? (For example: a shopping site with a virtual 'shopping basket' is likely to appeal to the users. But limited use of pictures on the same site detracts from the product and may disappoint customers.)

Exercise

Working in a small group, investigate a website that deals with an aspect of online services. For example, you could choose from **communication** (e.g. email, instant messaging); **real-time information** (e.g. train timetables, news services, traffic reports); **commerce** (e.g. shopping, banking, auctions); **government** (e.g. online tax returns, e-voting). List the different features of the website, including the points that will be specifically measured in your e-portfolio work – factors such as the target audience, benefits and drawbacks, fitness for purpose, possible enhancements and non-Internet alternatives.

Life in the information age

OBJECTIVES

- To use a range of sources to gather relevant information about how ICT affects different aspects of people's lives
- To present a description of how ICT is affecting different aspects of people's lives.
- To identify and analyse the benefits and drawbacks of life with ICT in the information age

ICT is making a huge impact on the way people conduct their personal, social and professional lives. You will see that ICT impacts upon almost every aspect of our daily living experiences. In many homes a microchip ensures that your room is warm when you wake up and that you have hot water as and when you require it. Another microchip may well be monitoring a slice of bread to make sure that it is toasted to perfection. If your family owns a car, it may have a range of computerised systems to monitor the engine temperature, your location, your route, etc.

We will briefly discuss the ways in which ICT affect daily life in the following section.

- **Working styles:** With the advent of modern computer systems, many employees have been able to change the way they work. It's easier for people to work from home using a PC with a broadband Internet service to connect with offices. The use of videoconferencing has reduced the need for expensive and time-consuming travel in order to attend meetings.

- **Communication:** Advances in communication have really accelerated over the last few years. Consider mobile and video phones, email, text messaging …and communications are developing more and more rapidly as time goes on.

- **Education:** In the not-so-distant past we used the term 'talk and chalk' to describe how teachers presented their lessons. How things have changed! The modern classroom is equipped with a state-of-the-art interactive whiteboard that enables the teacher to present lesson topics using multimedia and student interaction. Text, graphics, animations and video are all used to help us to learn more effectively.

- **Entertainment and leisure:** There was a time, again not so long ago, when it could take ages to try to find a music track on a cassette or a scene in a film on a videotape. Those days are almost history. In this information age, CD and DVD technology mean that we can deal with these tasks in seconds. We can even store huge music collections on an MP3 player the size of our thumb. We may not be able to afford a fancy car or even be able to drive, but in the world of a Playstation 2 and *TOCA Race Driver 2*, this is no problem.

- **Banking and shopping:** Certainly ICT has changed the way many of us shop and manage our money. Internet banking allows us to view our account details at any time and we can transfer funds from one account to another. These features give us much more flexibility and enable us to manage our money more effectively. Using Internet shopping we can 'shop around' for the best products and bargains. Many shopping sites show comparisons between prices of the same goods at different stores. It is not unusual to find a large discount when buying online compared with the price of the same product in a conventional store. Shopping online also has appeal for people with disabilities who might find their mobility problems prohibit them from successfully navigating aisles full of busy shoppers. This has been empowering for many people with disabilities, who now have more choice and are no longer dependent on support services to do their shopping for them. At first, just books and CDs were available on the Internet, but now you can even have your groceries delivered following your 'Internet shopping trip'.

Exercise

Working in a small group, produce an A4 poster providing more information about one of the five topics listed above. The poster should be aimed at individuals who have only a rudimentary knowledge of ICT, and who wish to extend their knowledge about the topic chosen. Use the Internet to research your chosen topic and give details of where people can find out more information. Use suitable graphics to enhance your work. Provide appropriate references if you make any direct quotations from the Internet.

- **Decision making:** One area of ICT that has progressed significantly as processor sizes have decreased is the area of Artificial Intelligence. In certain circumstances computers can be trained to give the correct answers when choices are placed before them. This concept was utilised when software engineers decided that they would 'teach' computers to play chess. Chess is a complex strategy game in which the players need to think many moves ahead, always trying to outmanoeuvre the opponent. Computers are excellent at following rule-based algorithms and chess fits the criteria well. Computers can not only be developed to play games but also in other areas where decisions are crucial to the effective operation of a system. For example, computers and their decision-making capabilities are used to monitor and control many modern medical systems.

- **Employment opportunities:** As more companies see the advantages of using ICT, they are expecting a wider range of skills from their employees. Many companies now require 'multi-functioning' staff who are able, not only to carry out their main job role, but to complete it using new technologies. In addition there are many roles which specifically require specialist ICT skills, such as database administrators, software engineers, network administrators, hardware engineers and web designers.

- **Crime and crime prevention:** In recent years, criminals have been quick to exploit the possibilities of ICT for their own purposes. Computers and the Internet provide great benefits for society throughout the world. But not only does ICT help make the modern workplace more efficient, it also allows fraudsters, thieves and confidence tricksters to become more efficient criminals. This high-tech crime has become known as 'cyber crime'. There are two forms of cyber crime:

  1. Modern 'ICT' crimes committed against computers and their associated networks. These include viruses and hacking.

  2. Previously existing crimes that are now committed with the advantages that ICT has to offer. For example, fraud, identity theft and the exploitation of vulnerable people.

  (See also the sections on ICT skills at the end of this unit, where we review crime and crime prevention in detail, as an example of content for your e-book.)

- **Civil rights:** These are the privileges we enjoy as the result of living within a particular country or region. Some civil rights groups might argue that the widespread use of ICT systems has invaded our right to privacy, because computer systems can be used to monitor and store our personal details, what we are doing and where we are: a kind of 'Big Brother' watching all of us. This is an area for heated debate, especially in the light of the terrorist attacks in London in 2005. Some feel there is not enough being done to document criminal activity – they feel that more use of ICT to gather, store and disseminate information on individuals would help to reduce crime in the future. Others feel that it is a breach of our civil rights to have personal information stored on ICT systems – in order for a few criminals to be stopped, we would all have our privacy invaded.

- **Legislation:** One of the key aspects of how ICT has affected legislation is that, since the first Public General Act 1988, the full text of all new Public General Acts is available online. These acts appear in the same format as they were when they were originally passed by the UK Parliament. This gives everyone more access to information and more power to be able to take action if they feel they want to or should do so. Another key piece of legislation has been the Computer Misuse Act 1990 which prohibits anyone from making unauthorised access to a computer system. In addition, the Copyright, Designs and Patents Act prohibits the unauthorised modification of programs or data.

Exercise

In small groups, think about how the use of ICT enables us to work in different ways. You may wish to consider such devices as: portable computers, handheld devices and video phones.

Portfolio Builder: *This section is all about considering life in the information age with all of its advantages and disadvantages. Choose any five of the topics listed on the previous three pages and make some comparisons between the way that we do things today and the way things were done 20 years ago. In order to complete this task, you will need to do some research using the Internet and library materials. In addition, you will find it useful to discuss this with some of your older relatives who will remember what living and working was like before the use of ICT was widespread.*

As you complete this exercise make notes of your findings using the template shown in Figure 1.14. An example of what is required is given in the table.

Technology then	Technology now	Advantages of 'now'	Disadvantages of 'now'	Comments
Pen and paper to write a letter	Electronic document, e.g. email	Quick, informal, no stamp required	Skills required, computer and Internet connection required	email has radically changed the way we keep in touch. It's quick and user-friendly, the message takes seconds to travel thousands of miles

Figure 1.14

After you have collected your data, present an analysis of the benefits and drawbacks of current technologies, including a clear and balanced picture of life overall in the information age. You may find it useful to include some images to illustrate your document.

Exercise

Technology has allowed many company employees to work from home. As a manager within a small company, you have been asked to write a report on why you consider working from home may be beneficial to the organisation. In your report you need to present reasons for why this way of working might benefit both the company and the individual employees. Think about this question as you prepare your report:

Why do you think companies are increasingly asking for ICT skills in their job advertisements?

The digital divide

OBJECTIVES

- To review the factors that cause and influence the digital divide and discuss its impact

- To quantify the extent of the digital divide and discuss the measures being taken to narrow the gap

- To discuss the benefits and drawbacks of the digital divide

In this modern age we may think that all people have access to ICT resources, but this is not always the case. The digital divide refers to the gap between people who have access to a computer (or a computer connected to the Internet) and those who do not. It can refer to individuals, social groups and communities worldwide. The term also describes the gulf between those currently employed people who are able to use ICT effectively and those who are not – due to different levels of literacy, numeracy and technical skills.

The digital divide exists in our own communities and throughout the rest of the world. The purpose of this chapter is to look at some of the factors contributing to the existence of the digital divide.

- **Economic:** Economic reasons are the prime cause of communities and individuals who have no access to a computer or whose access is limited by poor Internet infrastructure, out-of-date computer systems and poor-quality Internet service provider support. Many countries in the developing world struggle to provide adequate telephone lines in certain areas – and purchasing an expensive PC and software is out of the question for many people in the developing world. Companies in such communities may be unable to compete effectively in the marketplace because of a lack of ICT infrastructure within the organisation. This not only has a negative effect but also hinders a company's future growth, thereby reducing the chances of employment opportunities for others.

- **Social:** When the digital divide was first acknowledged, it was Internet access that was cited as one of the key issues and concerns. Nowadays, many people can gain cheap access via community colleges, libraries and Internet cafés. The argument now is more to do with people having appropriate computer skills to enable them to thrive in the information age. It is clear that access to computers and the Internet plays an increasingly important role in education and career opportunities. Without an increase in the availability of ICT resources the divide between the computer 'haves' and 'have nots' will continue to increase. A number of charitable organisations are attempting to help bridge the gap by shipping secondhand PCs to countries in the developing world.

- **Geographical:** Availability of the Internet throughout the world shows large differences between world regions. Visit **http://www.internetworldstats.com/stats.htm**

to see the huge differences in Internet usage between the different continents of the world. You can click on the links within the table to find out the Internet usage statistics for individual countries. In addition to lack of Internet access, there may be issues concerning the language of the majority of the information available on the Internet. Someone who speaks a language that is not widely spoken in the world, and who does not have English as a second language, will have difficulty in finding much accessible content on the Internet. Accessibility to the Internet in rural areas is another contributor to the digital divide, although the increase in satellite services is bridging this particular gap.

- **Fear of technology:** Many people do not use ICT because they:
  - ▲ are not confident in their own ability to learn computer skills
  - ▲ fear that others will laugh at their attempts, therefore it is easier not to try
  - ▲ think that they will cause a computer problem as they experiment and therefore prefer not to try
  - ▲ have heard or read news reports about computer fraud, Internet scams and identity theft, which have exacerbated their fears.

Many of these people are often amazed when they do start using a computer by what it can do for them.

- **Lack of motivation:** Nothing comes to us without work. Many people are not prepared to put in the time and effort required to learn how to use a PC. Others don't see ICT as an advantageous tool that can be used for work and leisure – they might see computers as being linked with games-playing, a waste of time and bad for your eyes. Whatever a person's view on computers, one thing is certain: anyone who wants to use a computer effectively will have to work at it. The Mac and Windows environments were developed to help people have a more intuitive and user-friendly experience of using PCs. Our modern-day computers are worlds away from the machines used as recently as fifteen years ago. In those days you really did have to remember lots of commands even to do the most basic of tasks. But even with the Windows environment, there is still a lot of work to be done to master the basics of effective computer usage.

- **Cultural:** Cultural reasons for not using computers need to be resolved in order to help reduce the digital divide.

The extent of the divide

The digital divide is a worldwide issue and does not just refer to the difference between the people with computers and Internet access and those with no access at all. There are varying degrees of digital disadvantage and some of the other contributory factors include:

- lower-spec PCs
- low-quality Internet connections
- higher-priced Internet connections

- difficulty with obtaining technical assistance

- being a member of a community speaking a minority language

- lower access to subscriber content.

Is the divide widening or narrowing?

The following excerpt from a UK government strategy report gives us some indication that the government is addressing some of the issues raised above and is working towards narrowing the digital divide within the UK.

'This Government has always recognised the impact that information and communication technology can have on our everyday lives, at home and at work. … virtually all households in the UK are within easy-reach of a UK online centre where they can access the Internet in a safe, secure and supportive environment. …we must make sure the whole of society can experience the benefits of the Internet. … We are committed to ending the digital divide for families with children … We have a range of measures to improve accessibility to technology for the digitally excluded and ease of use for the disabled …'

Report prepared by the Prime Minister's Strategy Unit in partnership with the Department for Trade and Industry, March 2005. Downloaded March 2005 from: http://www.strategy.gov.uk/downloads/work_areas/digital_strategy/digital_strategy.pdf

Worldwide, there may be a different picture.

Case Study

In small groups, discuss the following article from the Taking IT Global website. Taking IT Global is an online community for young people around the world to communicate and get involved in local and global issues. As you discuss the article in your group, pay particular attention to the questions raised.

'As both the appeal and reach of ICT's expand, the rift known as the global digital divide continues to get deeper. Because ICT's are dependent upon new, and often expensive technologies, those without resources are often left out in the cold. And as these technologies continue to advance, those on the other side of the divide continue to be left further and further behind.

However, there is much talk to bridging the divide. What people are unsure of is what it will take to bridge the divide. Is this just an issue of access to technology and resources, or is the issue deeper than that?

The global digital divide is one of the top issues and controversies in the ICT world. Although it gives those with access a window into the global world, do ICT's leave those without access on the outside of the window, not even able to peer within?

Many organizations, both public and private, are concerning themselves with the issue. Several governments have set up task forces to deal with the issue, and there is a great deal of talk between developed nations and corporations aiding those with fewer resources. ICT's can be a positive and global force, but not without universal access.'

Taken from: http://www.takingitglobal.org/understanding/ict/digitaldivide

Accessed February 2006.

Organisations such as Computer Aid exist to try and narrow the digital divide. Visit their website for more information: **www.computer-aid.org/home.htm**.

Exercise

In small groups, review the Computer Aid website and then discuss the following questions:

- Do you think it is right for people in developing countries to be given our old computers?
- Can they do anything with these computers?
- Is there anyone there to help them with ICT training?
- Does Computer Aid have enough money to be able to support this ICT initiative?
- In the countries where Computer Aid works, is there electricity and is it reliable enough?
- What is the telecommunications infrastructure like: can people access the Internet?

The information in the Where we work section of the website is particularly useful – follow the links About Computer Aid and then Where We Work. As you answer the questions, use the information you gain as evidence for your e-portfolio.

Exercise

If you were a government minister with the power and authority to make positive changes towards bridging the gap in the digital divide, what would you do?

When you answer this question, make comprehensive notes that are supported with references from Internet and other sources. You will be using this evidence in your e-portfolio.

The benefits and drawbacks of reducing the gap

The benefits of reducing the digital divide really speak for themselves: increased opportunities for personal, educational and employment advancement to name but a few. A quick scan of the job advertisements in your area will confirm that most employers would like their new recruits to have some level of computer literacy skills.

It is possible to gain qualifications in IT by going to day or evening classes at a college or by studying online with organisations such as Learn Direct (**www.learndirect.co.uk**). Such opportunities certainly help to reduce the divide and help people become more able to use ICT technology. You don't have to own a computer with an Internet connection, as most libraries and community centres offer free computer and Internet access. In some areas it is even possible to make use of mobile computer facilities. Specially adapted library vehicles are equipped with PCs and satellite Internet connections so that people in rural areas are able to access the technology.

Are there any reasons why reducing the divide could be seen as a drawback? There is certainly a cost attached and it could be argued that financing increased ICT provision and education may not be sustainable. The initial purchase of equipment is only the start: maintenance and continued education all have to be paid for, as well as replacing outdated equipment while technological advances continue to race on.

By way of comparison, if you bought a new car fifteen years ago, you could expect it to be still running even after another five or ten years use, if you look after it well and don't do more than average annual mileage. On the other hand, a PC that was state-of-the-art just three years ago will be struggling to keep up with the software and Internet uses required of it. The hardware may still be functioning well, but the operating system and application software will have moved forward to such an extent that you need to replace the whole computer.

Exercise

See if you can find anyone who has used a computer with the MS DOS operating system and DOS-based application packages such as WordStar, Dbase II or Lotus 1-2-3. Don't spend too long on this, but if you can find someone fairly quickly ask them if they'd like to go back to using these applications.

Portfolio Builder: *Using all of the material presented in this section, as well as your own Internet and library research, discuss how you think the digital divide can be reduced (if at all). Review some of the measures that are now being taken to narrow the gap and make an informed decision as to whether or not you think these efforts are working. Discuss the benefits of reducing the digital divide and any disadvantages that you can think of. Conclude your work with examples of what you think may still be done to reduce the gap.*

What is an e-book?

OBJECTIVES

- To find and evaluate examples of e-books produced for different purposes, such as: creative writing, reference materials, collaborative projects, for children.

E-books are available from a number of websites. A search engine will return multiple listings from which you can make a selection. Figure 1.15 shows a website called Fictionwise which has a large collection of e-books that can either be purchased or downloaded free of charge. Visit **http://www.fictionwise.com** to see the wide range of books available in a variety of formats. E-books can be read by special reader applications such as Microsoft Book Reader, and some are even available as MP3 files.

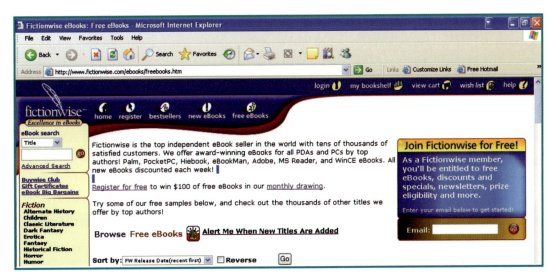

Figure 1.15

Exercise

Take a sheet of paper and write down all of the advantages you can think of for using an electronic book over traditional paper-based reading materials. Using your understanding of the previous section, 1.4 The Digital Divide, present reasons why some people may be hesitant or unable to adopt this technology. Why do you think having the contents of a book available as an MP3 file could be useful?

Locating and using e-books

- Go to **www.microsoft.com**.

- Enter 'ebooks' into the Search box.

- Make sure that the Microsoft.com button underneath the Search box is selected, then click
Search.

- The web browser will then search the Microsoft website for occurrences of the string 'e-book' and give you several links.

Figure 1.16

With the Microsoft Reader installed, you now need to:

- Find a link that offers free downloads of e-books among the search results.

- Follow this link and the subsequent links to locate the free e-books in the e-book catalogue.

Figure 1.17

We will be downloading the Microsoft Encarta Pocket Dictionary.

- Click on the link to the Encarta Pocket Dictionary.

- Then click the Microsoft Free eBooks link to download the dictionary, as shown in Figure 1.18.

- Click Microsoft free e-books to download the Encarta Pocket Dictionary.

- Once you have downloaded the dictionary, Microsoft Reader will automatically open the dictionary.

Figure 1.18

- To open the Encarta Pocket Dictionary next time, open Microsoft Reader, then open the Library and locate the dictionary in the list, as shown in Figure 1.19.

- Click Encarta Pocket Dictionary in the list of e-books to open the book.

- Click on the front page of the book to get to the book reading tools.

Our first step is to try the e-book to see how well it works. We'll try to find information about the word 'digital'.

- Click the Lookup Definition... label at the bottom right of the opening page.

- Enter the word 'digital' in the search box, as shown in Figure 1.20, and press Enter on your keyboard.

- The dictionary will open the page with the definition for the word 'digital'.

Figure 1.19

Figure 1.21 shows a number of the features of this e-book. These have been indicated with arrows for your reference.

- At the top there is a small down arrow next to the Encarta® Pocket Dictionary label. Clicking this opens a drop-down menu with navigational options.

- The dictionary entries often include hyperlinks that you can follow in order to gain more information about the topic. In this case we can see a hyperlink which will lead us to information about a graphics tablet. If we follow the link to the graphics tablet we can return to this page by using the drop-down menu mentioned above and selecting Return.

- The double forward arrow at the bottom of the page allows you to move a page forward in the dictionary, and the double back arrow allows you to move a page back.

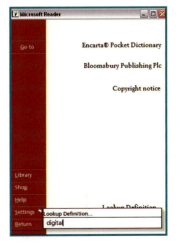

Figure 1.20

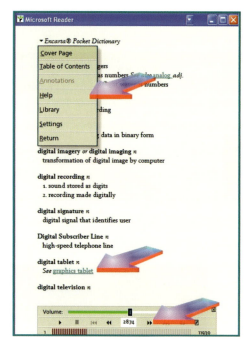

Figure 1.21

Exercise

Using the Internet, find examples of e-books that have been written with different purposes in mind, e.g. for children, hobby enthusiasts, reference, etc.

How would you categorise these books and what features differentiate them from each other?

Portfolio Builder: *Use the Internet to find at least two websites that offer e-books on the subject of history. Download a few samples and make reference to these when you complete your e-portfolio.*

We have reviewed the Encarta Pocket Dictionary e-book in this section; this would be classified as an encyclopaedia or dictionary. If you return to the Microsoft website and go to the free e-book section, you can download more books from the selection on offer. For instance, you could download the English-French Pocket Dictionary. The purpose of this e-book is also reference. Once the book has been downloaded it is stored in Microsoft Reader's Library section. As you download more books in the Microsoft .lit format, your Table of Contents in the Library will increase, as shown in Figure 1.22.

Evaluating e-books created by others

This part of the course requires that you evaluate aspects of others' work. Select an e-book to evaluate and use the criteria and questions below to help you review your chosen e-book. Generally speaking, if you can give favourable answers to all of the questions, it is highly likely that the e-book can be classed as 'fit for purpose'.

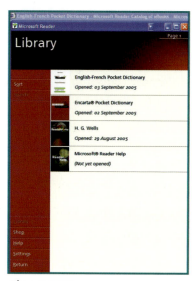

Figure 1.22

Evaluating Information Content

Purpose

- Is the purpose stated or self-evident?
- Has the purpose been fulfilled?
- Is the e-book factual or someone's opinions?
- Are the referenced sources primary or secondary?

Target audience

- Is the target audience clearly identified?
- Does the level of the content reflect this group?

Scope

- Does the breadth and depth of coverage in the e-book match the needs of the subject area?

Objectivity

- Is the e-book biased in any way and, if so, is this acknowledged within the book?
- Are there any conflicts of interest?

Accuracy

- Is the content accurate?
- How have you gone about cross-checking to check that the e-book is error free?
- Are there any obvious inaccuracies in spelling and/or grammar?

Evaluating Information structure

The structure can be thought of as the vessel that holds the content.

Structure and layout

As you review the content, you should also critically consider usability and aesthetics by answering the following questions:

- Is the e-book easy to read?
- Does it have a pleasing look and feel to it?
- Have any graphics used been optimised so that they load quickly?
- Are the pages uncluttered and easy to follow?
- Is there a logical flow from one part of the text to the next related part?
- Are the controls and navigation features in appropriate places?
- Are there any unnecessary distractions on the pages?

Navigation

- Are the pages properly linked?
- Are there any broken links?

- Is there an easy to understand hierarchy or logic to the pages?

- Could the reader become lost within the book?

- Are any instructions clear and unambiguous?

Multimedia components

Which of the following are included in the e-book?

- Artistic text.

- Images, including drawings, photographs and charts.

- Animated graphics.

- Sound files.

- Video files.

Note whether or not these features were used appropriately within the e-book.

Evaluating Information Accessibility

Accessibility of the information within the e-book is of prime importance. Consider the accessibility issues by answering the following questions.

- Was the book easy to download?

- Were there any lengthy registration requirements with user logins and passwords?

- Were there any costs involved and, if so, were these reasonable?

- Was the e-book stable or susceptible to crashes or other glitches in its behaviour?

Portfolio Builder: **Download a children's e-book, for example Treasure Island. Review some of the chapters and comment on the content, structure and layout, format and style, use of multimedia components, navigation, ease-of-use and accessibility. Conclude by assessing the e-book's fitness for purpose. As you do so, bear in mind that you will be applying the same criteria to the e-book that you produce. So see this exercise as increasing your awareness of what is needed to create your own successful e-book.**

Developing an e-book?

6

OBJECTIVES

- To define your intended audience
- To define the content
- To use structure charts to provide a graphical representation of the overall structure of the product
- To use storyboards to present the layout and content of each page
- To create documentation for your e-book

The target audience

Bear in mind that if your e-book is uploaded to a web server you are likely to have many different people reading it. Target audiences are likely to be quite a diverse group. You might start out with a particular group in mind, but you may end up having a different readership entirely. J.K. Rowling may have had young people in mind when she wrote the Harry Potter series, but the books have proven to be hugely popular with adults as well as children.

Exercise

Why is it necessary to know your target audience?
Using the Internet, magazines, TV and other sources, gather information that will help you to establish your target audience. You will use this as evidence to show the examiner that you have considered specific groups of readers.

The purpose of the e-book

The purpose of your e-book is to provide a snapshot of life in the Information Age, illustrating to your readership aspects of our current lifestyle and how ICT affects everyday life. You will be given a specification and asked to produce your e-book accordingly. You must take into account all of the concepts that you have studied so far. Important elements such as content, structure and layout, format and style, the use of multimedia components, navigation, ease of use, accessibility and the e-book's general fitness for purpose should all receive attention as you plan and compile your piece of work.

The prescribed content is set out in the Edexcel syllabus for the GCE in Applied ICT.

You must include:

- A description and evaluation of at least five different types of online service, drawn together to give a picture of the current scope and limitations of the Internet as a whole.

- A description of how ICT is affecting at least five different aspects of people's lives, considering the benefits and drawbacks, drawn together to give a picture of life overall in the Information Age.

- A description of at least three factors contributing to the digital divide and some of the measures being taken to bridge the gap, with an evaluation of the impact/extent of the digital divide, drawn together to give a picture of the current situation.

As you compile your e-book, you must:

- demonstrate an understanding of multimedia design principles
- demonstrate your ability to use software tools appropriately
- include some ready-made and some original multimedia components
- provide an evaluation of your e-book and your own performance in this unit.

The message you are trying to convey

Your message is about life in the Information Age. All of the research you do will culminate in an e-book that will show how ICT affects different aspects of our lives. You may convey this message in any appropriate style. For example, you may choose a documentary-type approach that is factual and very straightforward. The style of your e-book is up to you, but your teacher or lecturer will give you further guidance as you begin work on your project.

The technical specification you must adhere to

Your e-book will resemble a website in its construction. You will present your material, including text, graphics, sound, video and animations, with appropriate navigation tools to assist your readers in accessing the material. As you create your own e-book, you will have a number of software tools at your disposal. All the tools you will need will be discussed in detail within this book.

The deadline for completion

Your assignment work will need to be completed by the given deadline. To do this you will need to divide your work into manageable chunks. One way of keeping track of all the tasks you need to complete is to use a spreadsheet application such as Microsoft Excel. This is an effective way of proving your ability to plan and monitor your work and is also in an easy format to present to your teacher or lecturer as evidence of what you are doing.

Documenting your e-book

Figure 1.23 gives an example of a spreadsheet that has been designed to list tasks to be done, giving details of the tasks and dates by which they need to be done. Notice that you can attach notes (called comments) to your spreadsheet in order to remind yourselves of key features of the work.

Let's get started and create a spreadsheet for keeping track of your work.

- Select Start/All Programs/Microsoft Excel or click the Excel icon on your desktop.

- Highlight cells A1 to E1 in the blank workbook that opens.

- Select Format/Cells.

- Select the Alignment tab and click the checkbox Merge cells and OK.

- Type your title 'Working plan for my e-book' into the merged cells.

- Save your spreadsheet with an appropriate file name.

The next step is to add some headings to each column.

- Type 'Planned Activities' into Cell B2.

- Type 'Week Commencing' into Cell A3.

- Type your task for the first week into Cell C3.

- And so on.

Set up your spreadsheet in a way that makes sense to you and that will be easy to use, and also that will be clear to others reading it what you are doing at each stage of your work.

Now that you have your basic structure, you can enter some target dates in the Week Commencing column.

- Type your first working date into cell A4.

- Continue entering dates down the first column.

Make sure your dates fit in with your school or college's term dates and that the dates you enter allow you to finish all the tasks by the project deadline.

Now you need to think about your planned activities and enter these into the spreadsheet. If you attach comments to cells in your spreadsheet, they can only be seen when the cursor is in that particular cell – this helps to keep your workspace uncluttered. Let's attach a comment to a task in order to give you more information without the clutter

- Click in the desired cell.

- Right-click and select Insert Comment from the menu that appears.

- A yellow text box will open.

- Click inside the box and type any notes, comments or reminders that you think will help you with this task.

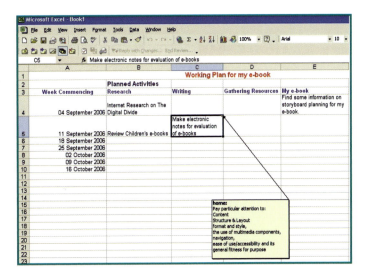

Figure 1.23

- Click in any other cell to close the comment.

- You will notice a red triangle in the top right corner – this is your note tab.

- Clicking in the cell again will open the comment

As you add your tasks to the spreadsheet, make sure you put all the activities in a logical order so that you can clearly see how the tasks follow on from each other to take you to your final destination. Your initial plan may be a little vague, but it will gain clarity as you take part in your lessons and discover more about this unit on the Information Age.

Structure charts and storyboards

Structure charts are diagrams that will help you to define the overall structure of your e-book. The structure chart needs to illustrate how users will navigate from the opening page to other areas of the e-book. It will need to show how the different sections of the e-book relate to each other. Figure 1.24 shows an example of a structure chart.

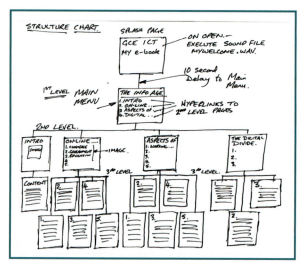

You then need to produce a series of storyboards that present a more detailed view of each page.

In this section, we've talked a lot about the design of e-books and hopefully you will now be starting to get some ideas for your own e-book. For help and advice on creating multimedia components please see the sections on ICT skills – sections 1.7 A to D. You will notice that there are no exercises in these sections. Instead, you will be producing work to contribute to your own e-book as you work through these chapters.

Figure 1.24

See also Appendix A, Standard ways of working, for information on testing, evaluation, assessing the overall fitness for purpose and identifying possible improvements and enhancements.

> **Tip:**
>
> You could generate some pre-formatted blanks for your storyboards in Word. Set out your page with the title and six blank boxes (two columns by three rows). Print out several copies of the blanks and use them for writing your storyboard notes. These charts don't have to be artistic masterpieces, but they must be legible!

ICT Skills
(A – Internet Research)

7

OBJECTIVES

- To perform Internet research tasks, using a browser and search engine.

- To navigate large websites using hyperlinks to locate specific information

- To make informed judgments about the accuracy and reliability of the information you find

- To acknowledge Internet sources correctly

As part of this course you will be expected to develop and use a range of ICT tools and techniques. As part of this, you will be involved in Internet research tasks which will enable you to complete your assignment more easily. You will need to understand the main features of web browser software, including bookmarking and organising favourites. While you may already be using these features, they are covered here in detail for the sake of completeness and to fill any gaps in your knowledge.

Bookmarking

As you carry out your research, you will find many websites that will help you complete your e-portfolio and your e-book. It is useful to be able to know how to quickly locate these sites again for future reference. This can be done using a feature known as bookmarking. If, for example, you were trying to find information about the digital divide and you found a really good website, you could bookmark this site for future reference.

Let's go through the process now by carrying out a search and bookmarking a page we find as a result of the search. We will use the Lycos search engine to find information about the digital divide.

- Open your web browser and type **www.lycos.com** into the address box.

- Type some appropriate keywords into the search box: in this case 'Digital' and 'Divide' are appropriate keywords.

- Click Go Get It – Lycos will do the hard work for us and return a list of websites with more information about the digital divide as shown in Figure 1.25.

Lycos has retrieved about 1.5 million results of pages containing the words 'digital' and 'divide' in the content. Obviously we won't be able to review all of these; we will need to sort through the results in order to locate the information that we require.

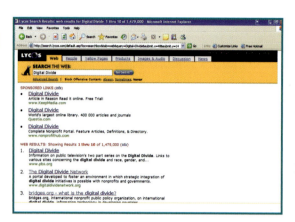

Figure 1.25

You will notice that the search results are split into two categories: the first are sponsored links, to organisations who pay to have their sites at the top of the results page, and the second category contains the general web results. We'll follow the first link under the Web Results category: **www.pbs.org**.

The PBS website is the website of an American TV company, which includes lots of useful information about the digital divide. It would be a good website for you to study in detail because it contains many thought-provoking articles, highlighting how the digital divide is a big concern for society in modern times. Type 'digital divide' into the search box and you will find a wealth of useful information about this.

We will choose item number four in the listing (Figure 1.28) which shows the results of our search for UK sites holding information

Figure 1.26

about the 'digital divide'. As we follow the link, the article will be presented on the **www.zdnet.co.uk** web site (Figure 1.29).

Figure 1.27

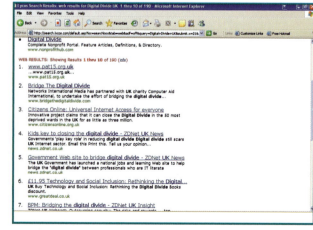

Figure 1.28

The article on this web page containts a detailed account of how BT is working with the younger generation to encourage older people to embrace new technologies.

Now that we've found a website that looks promising for our research, we can bookmark it. To do this:

● click Favourites on the browser toolbar

● select Add to Favourites.

You should then see a dialogue box similar to the one in Figure 1.30.

You will notice that the Name box is pre-filled with the browser title data. In the Create in box, you may see various directories. In this case we will create a new directory or folder.

● Click the New Folder button.

● Type in an appropriate name for the folder, e.g. ICT Project Work.

● Then click OK to create the new folder.

● By default the browser will open this folder, so click OK to store this web page in the ICT Project Work folder.

If you then navigate away from the ZDNet UK web page, for example by clicking the home button or running another search, you can then test your bookmark.

● Click Favourites.

● Scroll down to the ICT Project Work directory.

● You will notice that the ICT Project Work directory now contains a link to the 'Kids key to closing the digital divide' page (see Figure 1.32).

● Clicking the link will return you to the ZDNet page.

Figure 1.29

Figure 1.30

Figure 1.31

Figure 1.32

Portfolio Builder: *Using the tools described in this section, use your favourite Internet search engine to find information about the following: lifelong learning, privacy rights, copyright and legislation, the impact of ICT on employment and the digital divide. As you complete this research don't forget to bookmark important research sites in your ICT Project Work directory. If you want to be even more organised you can create a subdirectory called 'Information Age' for storing each section of this unit.*

Navigating large websites

Most large websites have their own inbuilt search facility, so you can do a keyword search for information stored on a particular site. For example, the Payne-Gallway website contains an inbuilt search engine facility.

- Open your web browser by double-clicking the browser icon.

- Enter the Payne-Gallway URL in the address box: **www.payne-gallway.co.uk**

- There is a search box at the top right of the homepage.

Figure 1.33

- This is the website of a publisher specialising in ICT books, so let's try a search for books on PowerPoint 2003. The search facility on this website uses the same principle as search engines.

- Enter PowerPoint 2003 in the 'Enter search here' box.

- Then click Go!

- Figure 1.34 shows the resulting web page.

- You can now follow the link to find more detailed information about this particular book.

Some larger websites also have a facility known as a site map. This enables users to follow links which will give a text-based overview of the whole site. This view is helpful if you want to scan the page quickly, looking for information to narrow your search.

- Open your browser and type Edexcel's URL (**www.edexcel.org.uk**) into the address bar. Click Go.

- There is a link to the site map at the top of the page.

- Click the site map link and your browser will take you to an overview of the whole Edexcel site.

The site map shown in Figure 1.36 is not a complete overview of the Edexcel site, but a snapshot of the current browser window.

Figure 1.34

Figure 1.35

Exercise

Using both the Edexcel site map and the search facility, find the Student Guide for the Applied GCE in ICT. Which method did you find easier? Is there a place for both of these systems in an e-book or website?

Researching 'Crime and crime prevention'

Let's use the topic from Life in the Information Age (section 1.3 in the Edexcel specification): crime and crime prevention. You will be able to use this material later when you start compiling a sample section for your e-book.

The first thing to do is to have a look at a few sites that have the keywords 'crime, crime prevention'. As we have seen, different search engines handle things in slightly different ways, often returning different results even when you have specified the same keywords as part of the text string.

Let's have a look at how you can refine your searches in order to focus on your target information more specifically. Some search

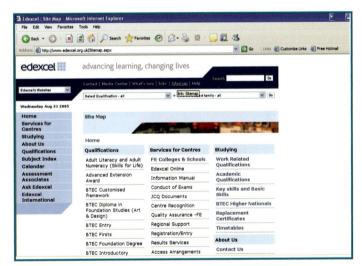

Figure 1.36

engines allow you to use special characters, such as plus and minus signs, to help in this process. For example, if you are searching for 'police' and 'crime' you may also find references to a 1980s pop group called The Police. But if you enter 'police + crime – music', this would find all of the sites with police **and** crime but **exclude** any sites with references to music.

A more intuitive method is to use the advanced options found on some of the search engine sites. We will use Google's advanced search facility as an example.

● Click on the small Advanced Search link next to the search box.

Figure 1.37 shows how an advanced search interface is much more user-friendly than using the plus and minus keys.

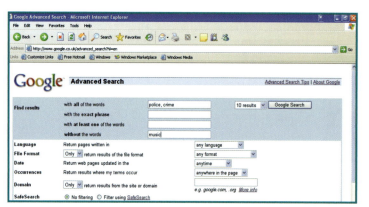

Figure 1.37

Because we need more information about how ICT is influencing crime and crime prevention, we can add computers to the keyword list. One of the results listed by Google was a link to the Metropolitan Police's page on computer crime and how they are combatting it. You might find it useful to have a look at this page (**www.met.police.uk/computercrime/**) if your search doesn't come up with it.

One key site for research concerning ICT is silicon.com.

- Type **www.silicon.com** in your web browser.

- You will need to register on this site in order to access the content.

- Then use the site's search facility to find information about 'police'.

Figure 1.38 shows the resulting screen, with links to pages with the word police as part of the content. We will follow the link that refers to anti-terrorism measures in New York.

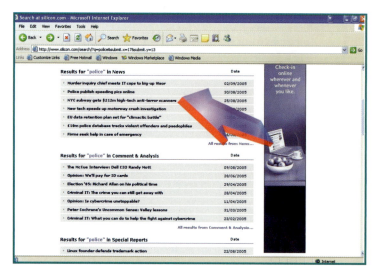

Figure 1.38

This link is to an article called Security Strategy, about how ICT is being used to provide anti-terrorist measures in order to protect the public (see Figure 1.39). The fact that this article relates to the United States does not really matter as we are interested in how ICT is being used as a crime prevention measure throughout the world. Here's one very useful quote from the article: 'Potential security threats such as unattended bags or packages left on platforms will be detected by the network of cameras and sensors, which are able to identify non-moving objects.' To find this article and similar articles, run your own search on Silicon.com.

Portfolio Builder: *Using the* **www.silicon.com** *site, carry out some research to help you with section 1.3 Life in the Information Age. For example, you may find an article that discusses security issues with Internet banking. Make sure that you acknowledge and reference any material you plan to use in your e-book.*

As you continue with your research, try to be aware of the key features of sites which may be of benefit to you. Don't be afraid to surf! For example, following up from the Security Strategy article, try taking a look at some of the photo stories (see Figure 1.40). These may reveal some innovative uses of ICT and contain relevant images for your e-book.

Saving a picture from the Internet

Following the Photo Stories link leads to an interesting news article about security robots. When you find an article like this one, with good photos, you might want to save one or more of the pictures to include in your e-book.

Figure 1.39

Figure 1.40

- Right-click on the image.

- Click Save Picture As.

- Then browse to an appropriate directory on your school or college computer.

- Click Save.

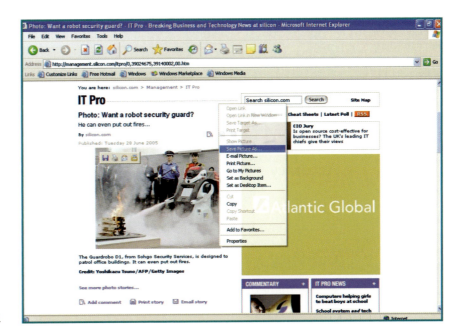

Figure 1.41

References and acknowledgements

The silicon.com website has a Resources link at the top of the page, which will take you to a page where you can access case studies. One of the case studies is an article about police getting extra back-up by linking their computer systems (shown in Figure 1.42). This article could be useful for our research.

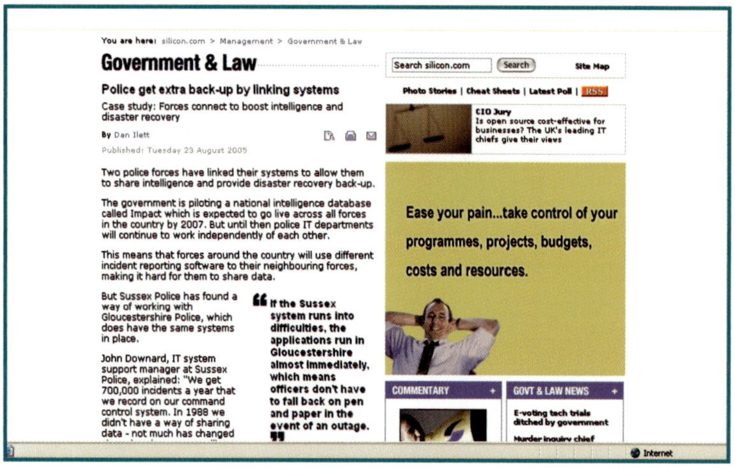

Figure 1.42

You can either print this article or copy and paste the content into another document to save it for future reference. Always remember to keep the URL in order to acknowledge and reference the article if you use information from it or quote it in your e-book.

Set up a references document for storing references to the web pages you have visited. Copy and paste the URL into the references document and type in the date you downloaded the article. This is a quick and easy way of keeping a record of your research. You can then use this information as evidence in your e-portfolio and as an appendix in your e-book.

Make informed judgements about accuracy, reliability and currency

As you surf the Internet it you have to used your own judgement about whether the sites you visit are accurate, reliable and up to date. Try to develop a system that enables you to judge whether or not a site is worth you spending time looking at it. The following are some of the key indicators of the validity of a website .

Authority

- Is the organisation's name clearly stated on the site?
- Does the site have address and phone number details?
- Is the URL sufficiently unique?
- Is there a copyright declaration?

Accuracy

- Does the site include references for factual information?
- Is the site free of spelling, grammatical and/or typographical errors?

Currency

- Are there dates on the pages indicating when the page was written and when it was last updated?

Tip:

You can highlight the URL then right-click and copy it onto the clipboard in exactly the same way as you would any other piece of text. Having done this, open your references and acknowledgements document, right-click and select Paste. This will paste the full URL into your document. Once you have done as much research as you can on one site, you can go back to your favourite search engine. Follow up some of the other links or type in some different keywords in order to find some more text and graphics for the 'crime and crime prevention' part of your e-book.

Portfolio Builder: *Find two websites that you plan to use for researching your e-book. Using the criteria listed above, assess the validity of each website. See how many questions you can answer yes to about each site. Remember, the more yes answers, the more likely it is that the sites fit the bill for accuracy, reliability and currency.*

ICT Skills

(B – Constructing an e-book)

1.7

OBJECTIVES

- **To construct an e-book**
- **To manipulate images for use within your e-book**
- **To implement interactivity with hyperlinks**

Getting started with your e-book

Now you are ready to start developing your e-book. You will be using Microsoft PowerPoint as the main authoring package for your e-book, but other tools will help you to build a feature-rich e-book. The starting point for this work will be to refer to the structure charts and storyboards you developed in section 1.6 Developing an e-book.

The following ideas and examples are intended to give you a picture of what you need to do in order to produce your e-book. They are for guidance purposes only as you will need to use your own ideas and research throughout your project.

Please note: in order to keep a logical structure for the construction of this e-book, all of the screenshots and descriptions will appear in this chapter of the textbook. At certain points we will refer to other parts of the book where you will find instructions on completing certain tasks.

Tip:

If you review the assessment criteria, you will notice that we have taken the description from Mark Band 3. It is a good idea to set yourself high goals on this course. If you do this and lose a few marks along the way, then you will certainly finish with a higher grade than if you aim for the lower level at the start.

In the following section you are going to develop an e-book on one element of the course: Unit 1, The Information Age. You will be presenting a comprehensive description supported by a range of well chosen examples of how ICT is affecting at least five different aspects of people's lives.

Let's get started by opening PowerPoint. Either double-click on the PowerPoint icon on your desktop or select Start/All Programs/Microsoft PowerPoint. Depending on how your computer is set up, you may see a different default layout when you first open Microsoft PowerPoint to the one shown in Figure 1.43. Your teacher or lecturer will guide you through these initial differences.

Setting up the design

At this point, you could choose a themed approach and let PowerPoint do a lot of the design work for you. However, your teacher/lecturer may well want you to set your own layout right from the start, including choice of font, font size, font colour and background colour. For the background follow these steps.

- Select Format/Background.
- Select Background fill using the down arrow.
- Select a background colour using the down arrow, and choosing from More Colors.
- If you would like a different background effect, select Fill Effects (see Figure 1.44).
- Select a gradient of your choice with a second merged colour.
- Select Apply to All.

You can change the font style by selecting Format/Font and making your selections in much the same way.

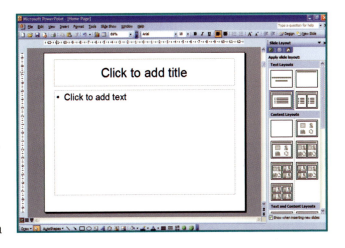

Figure 1.43

Creating your opening slide

The slide showing in PowerPoint is the default slide for the first Auto Layout Slide template. Each of the slide layouts have 'placeholders' for text, images, graphs and charts. These help you to format your pages.

- Click the title placeholder and insert the title for your e-book.
- Click the subtitle placeholder and insert your subtitle and your name.

This will be the opening page of your e-book. The next page you design will contain the main menu for the e-book.

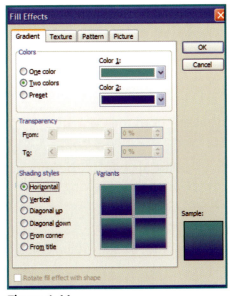

Figure 1.44

Figure 1.45

Típ:

If you would like a font, font colour or graphic to appear throughout all of your slides, select: View/Master/Slide Master, any alterations you make here will appear on every slide in your presentation.

Exercíse

Open the Slide Master and experiment with different design features to see if you can come up with a theme to use throughout your e-book.

Inserting slides

To insert the next slide:

● Select Insert/New Slide.

● From the Text Layouts available in the Slide Layouts on the right of the screen, select the Title and Text template, as shown in Figure 1.46.

Figure 1.46

This slide will be the menu page of your e-book. Now you can use the titles from the storyboards you created in the last chapter to create your menu. Figure 1.47 shows an example of this. When you type text into the placeholder boxes, the text is automatically formatted to a standard font and size. The text box automatically adds bullet points to whatever you type in, and a new bullet point appears each time you press Enter on your keyboard.

The next step is to produce the title page for each of the four topics. To do this insert four new pages and type the title onto each to match the text of the bullet points on the menu page.

Adding hyperlinks

At this point the main menu page has no interactivity. You can make each of the bullet points into links which will take the user to the relevant content. So, for example, when the user clicks Introduction, they will be taken to a page containing the introduction to your e-book. We will start the work on interactivity later in the book.

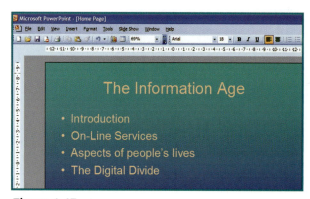

Figure 1.47

● Select Insert/New Slide.

● Go to Slide Layouts on the right of the screen.

● Select Title and Content from the Content Layouts.

Notice that each new slide appears in the left column of the PowerPoint window, giving you an overview of the slides you have generated so far.

When you have created a new page, type the title into the top text placeholder as shown in Figure 1.48.

Inserting graphics

Here's how to add an image to your e-book pages.

● In the centre of the title and content page you have just created, there are six icons for inserting content.

● Click the Insert Picture icon.

- The insert picture dialogue box will open.
- Browse to the graphic you want to insert and click on it.
- Click Insert.
- Your graphic will be placed in a position below the heading on your slide. Using left-click and drag, place your graphic in the desired position.

Figure 1.48

Típ:

For assistance with locating suitable graphics, please go to page 65 of section 1.7 ICT Skills (D – Multimedia Content).

Using animation

You can make your page a little more dramatic by having the graphic make an animated entrance onto the page. To do this you can use PowerPoint's animation features to make the graphic 'fly' into the page.

- Right click the graphic.
- Select Custom Animation.
- The Custom Animation window will now display on the right of your screen.
- Select Add Effect/Entrance/Fly In.

You can set the animation parameters by using the options in the Modify:Fly In menu on the right of the screen. Set the animation parameters to:

- Start: After Previous
- Direction: From Bottom
- Speed: Medium

Try out these parameters then experiment to get the effect you would like.

Having completed the title slide for the first topic, you can apply the same processes to produce the other slides at the same level in our structure chart hierarchy. See Figure 1.51 for an example of how they might look.

Típ:

As you use material that you have sourced from the Internet or elsewhere, copy the reference/author details to the references document you have set up. You will use this as an appendix for your e-portfolio. It is much easier make a note of all references as you are going along rather than to backtrack at the end.

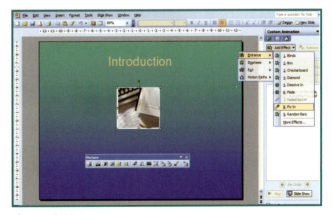

Figure 1.49

Portfolio Builder: **Using the information from the previous section, complete all of the second level slides for your e-book. Second level slides are those which are one level below the main menu – i.e. the title pages for the topics. Don't forget to create an animated graphic for each slide.**

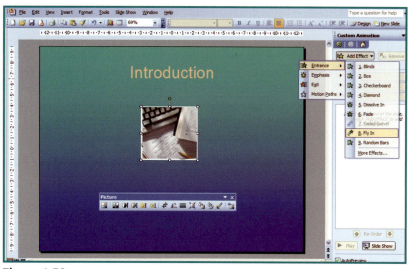

Figure 1.50

Image manipulation in PowerPoint

The images you want to use may benefit from some improvements. For example, an image may need adjustments to its brightness or contrast, it may have parts that need removing by cropping, or it may be in colour when you need it to be in black and white.

There are many graphics packages available that allow you to manipulate graphics – and there is quite a significant price difference between the packages.

At the higher end of the scale, applications such as PhotoShop are used by professional designers and have all of the facilities and features that you would ever need. For the purposes of our e-book we are going to keep it simple and use the picture editing software that is in-built into Microsoft PowerPoint.

Check whether the picture toolbar shown in Figure 1.52 is displayed at the bottom of your PowerPoint screen. If not you can make it display by checking on View/Toolbars/Picture.

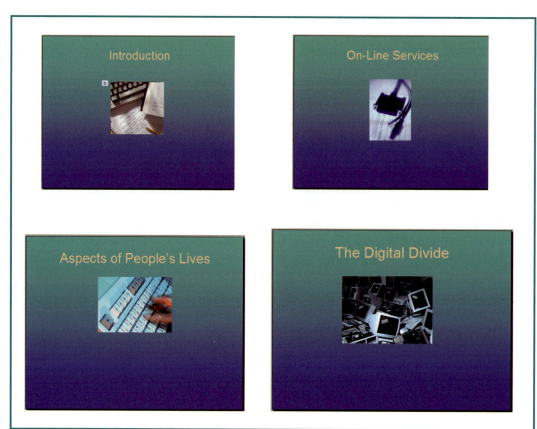

Figure 1.51

Figure 1.52 Microsoft Picture toolbar

Let's use the picture toolbar to make an improvement to how a graphic looks. We'll change the white area of the book graphic to transparent so that the screen background goes right up to the edge of the image.

- Click on the image to select it.
- On the Picture toolbar, click the Select Transparent Color tool.
- A wand-like tool will appear.
- Position the tool over the graphic, making sure that the tip is over the white area.
- Click the white area of the graphic.
- This white area will now be set to transparent.

You can see the difference in Figure 1.53.

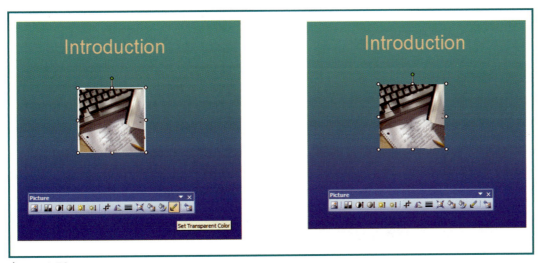

Figure 1.53

If you would like to preview the finished slide:

- Click the Slide Show button.
- Select View Show to run the slide show.
- Press Escape on your keyboard to return to the PowerPoint editing mode.

The other features of the Picture toolbar include: cropping, brightening or darkening the image, increasing or decreasing contrast, rotating and formatting.

We will use the Picture toolbar to manipulate a photograph that we will use later in the e-book. In this case, the graphic needs to be brightened in order to improve the picture quality.

- With the picture selected, click the More Brightness button, the one with the bright sun symbol.

- Keep clicking until you are happy with the level of brightness of the picture. Figures 1.54 and 1.55 show the improvements made.

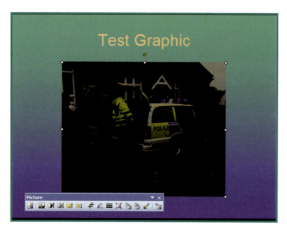

Figure 1.54

Figure 1.55

Let's now crop the image to remove the unwanted area of the image to the left of the police car.

- On the Picture toolbar, select Crop.
- Left-click on the bottom left picture handle.
- Drag the handle towards the centre of the image to the point you would like to crop the image.
- Release the handle and the image will be cropped.
- With your mouse pointer on the centre of the graphic, left-click and drag the image to so that it is positioned centrally again.

The cropped image is shown in Figure 1.56.

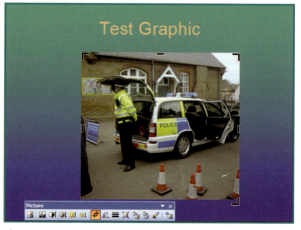

Figure 1.56

Exercise

Select an image of your choice and, using the PowerPoint Picture toolbar, experiment with some of the available tools. Keep a record of your work using screenshots and descriptions to store in your e-portfolio.

Resizing graphics

While we're on the subject of graphics, let's take a quick look at how to resize graphics within a Windows environment. As you can see in Figures 1.57 and 1.58, when you select any picture a set of 'picture handles' appears on the image. These handles allow you to resize the image to fit the space you have available.

With the second level slides completed, you can continue by designing the introduction, which will be created in much the same way as the previous slides.

Working with text

Now you can create some slides containing the text of your e-book, starting with the introduction. You can see in Figure 1.61 that we have called the first page of the introduction, Introduction (a) – this is because there is too much content for one slide and we need to extend it over a number of slides. The introduction will be a series of slides designed to set the scene and introduce the readers to the content of our e-book.

Let's animate this text to come onto the page in the same way that we did with the image of the book.

- Right click the text.
- Select Custom Animation.
- The Custom Animation window will now display on the right of your screen.

Tip:

The handles on each corner allow you to proportionately stretch or shrink your image when you drag them. This means that your picture will not be distorted when you complete this operation. The handles on the top, bottom and sides will allow you to stretch or shrink your image only on the side you choose to drag. This will distort your image. You can see the difference in Figures 1.59 and 1.60.

Figure 1.57 Corner handles

Figure 1.58 Side handles

Figure 1.59
Proportional reduction using corner handles

Figure 1.60
Non-proportional reduction using side handles

- Select Add Effect/Entrance/Checkerboard (or whatever effect you wish to create).
- Change the Start and Speed settings to the ones that you would like.

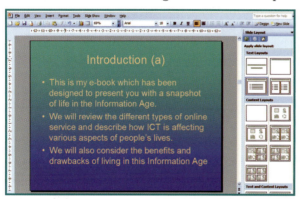

Figure 1.61

We will now continue with our introduction and add more content to slides which we will call Introduction (b), Introduction (c) etc.

The remaining slides in your introduction need to contain background information and context for the audience – we must assume that the audience is not familiar with life in the Information Age. The last slide needs to give the reader the details of when the e-book was produced, where and by whom.

Portfolio Builder: *Continue to use PowerPoint to complete a set of slides to introduce your e-book. Please bear in mind the guidelines on what your introduction needs to include. Make sure that you keep track of each step in this process. You will be expected to provide not only a completed e-book but also an e-portfolio which provides evidence of your understanding of all the processes involved in producing an e-book. This can be achieved by providing annotated screenshots in much the same way as has been done in this book.*

Adding content to the e-book

Let's take a look at the part of the e-book that will discuss aspects of people's lives. Here you have the opportunity to describe and evaluate the role of ICT as it affects each one of us. The Edexcel syllabus states that you should describe how ICT is affecting at least five different aspects of people's lives. You must also consider the benefits and drawbacks and then draw these features together to give a picture of life overall in the information age.

For the purposes of covering some of the skills needed we will consider one aspect of people's lives: crime and crime prevention (covered in section 1.3 of this book). You will need to research this topic thoroughly prior to being able to include it in your e-book. This will be one of the topics in our section on Aspects of People's Lives.

Let's start by adding a title slide for this topic:

● Select Insert/New Slide.

● Select Title Slide from the Text Layouts available on the right of your screen.

● Enter your heading in the title placeholder. We will enter 'Crime & Crime Prevention'.

● Enter your subheading in the subtitle placeholder. We will enter 'The Impact of ICT'.

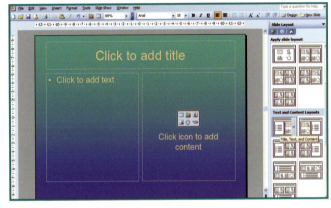

Now let's create some content slides for the topic.

● Select Insert/New Slide.

● Scroll down to the layout you require. (We scrolled down to Other Layouts and selected Title, Text, and Content, as shown in Figure 1.62.)

Figure 1.62

● Change the Default setting to Title, Text, and Content (you will need to scroll down to Other Layouts for this. See below)

Transitions between slides

We're now going to add some hyperlinks between the pages of the e-book. First we're going to set the title page (or splash screen) of the e-book to move automatically to the main menu page after ten seconds.

● Select the main menu page (this should be the second slide in your e-book) by clicking on it in the list on the left of your screen.

● If necessary, use the scroll bar to get back up to the top of the list.

● With the slide open, right click on the slide and select Slide Transition (see Figure 1.63).

● On the right of the screen, under the Advance slide heading, check the Automatically after box.

● Use the up arrow to set the timing to: 00:10.

● Select Blinds Vertical under the Apply to selected slides heading. (This is the type of transition – you can experiment with different ones.)

Click the Slide Show button at the bottom right of the screen to test that your transition works. After 10 seconds the opening slide should automatically move on to the main menu.

> **Típ:**
>
> For assistance with researching the information you need for this section of your e-book, please go to page 37 of section 1.7 ICT Skills (A – Internet Research).

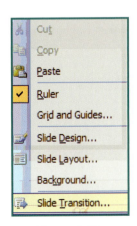

Figure 1.63

Creating navigation buttons

Home button

The first button we will place will be a Home button to return the reader to the first slide in the e-book. We will use an Action Button and gridlines to help position the button accurately.

First we will set up some gridlines to make it easier to position the button accurately.

● With your main menu page open, select View/Grid and Guides.

● Select View\Grid and Guides.

● Click the checkbox Display grid on screen.

● Set the spacing to 1 cm.

● Click OK.

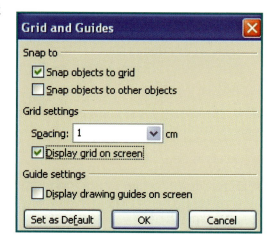

Figure 1.64

You will notice that a series of gridlines has appeared on your slide. As you drag a button into position on the slide it will automatically align itself to the nearest gridline.

Now we will add the button.

● Select Slide Show/Action Buttons, as shown in Figure 1.65.

● Choose the button that looks like a house.

● In the top left of the slide, click and drag the image to the size you want.

● As you release the mouse button the home button will appear on your slide and the Action Settings dialogue box will open.

● Notice that the dialogue box is open at the Mouse Click tab. This is what we want, so leave as it is.

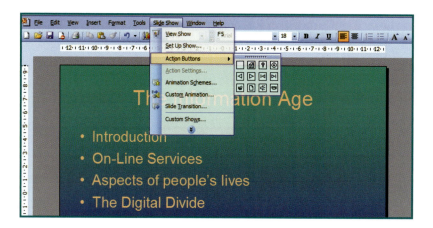

Figure 1.65

Figure 1.66

- The default setting for the Hyperlink is to the First Slide (which is the action we want), so we leave this as it is.

- Click OK.

Back, forward and main menu buttons

The next step is to add navigation buttons that will allow us to travel between the pages of our electronic book. Let's add a back button first.

- Select Slide Show/Action Buttons.

- Select the back arrow button.

- Place this button somewhere in the bottom left of the slide.

- As you release the mouse button the Action Settings dialogue box will open.

- Select the Hyperlink radio button.

- Select Previous Slide just below the Hyperlink to label.

Figure 1.67

Add your forward button in the same way, selecting Next Slide in the Action Settings dialogue box. You can reposition buttons at any time.

Text hyperlinks

The next step is to turn each of the bullet points on the main menu page into links to the different sections of the e-book.

- Highlight the first bullet point by clicking to the left of the text and dragging the mouse button to the right until the whole phrase or word is selected.

- Right-click the selected text.

- Select Hyperlink and the dialogue box shown in Figure 1.68 will appear.

- Select the left-hand button Place in This Document.

- Click on the page you want in the list of available slide – in this case we want slide 3. Introduction.

- You will notice a preview of the selected slide in the Slide preview box.

- Click OK.

Repeat these steps with the other bullet points on the main menu page until you have made hyperlinks for each of your main heading items.

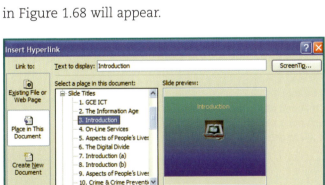

Figure 1.68

Replicating navigation buttons

Our next step is to copy and paste the three buttons we have designed to all of our subsequent pages or slides. As we copy and paste each button, not only will the button be duplicated, but also its properties. Therefore, as we copy and paste our home button the link that makes this button work will be copied also. You can try this out.

- Right-click on the home button.
- Select Copy.
- Select the slide headed 'Introduction' from the list of slides on the left.
- Click anywhere on this slide and paste.
- The home button will be placed in the exact position on the Introduction slide as it was in the original.

Figure 1.69

Follow this same procedure to duplicate the Back and Next buttons onto the Introduction slide, as shown in Figure 1.69.

Reassigning the properties of buttons

We need to make it possible for the reader to jump back to the main menu at any point while reading our e-book. To do this we can adapt our existing Home button, by repositioning it and reassigning its properties so that it links to the main menu page instead of the splash screen.

- Left-click on the Home button.
- Right-click and choose Edit Hyperlink – this will open the Action Settings dialogue box.
- Set the Hyperlink to: Slide… in the drop-down menu.
- In the Hyperlink to Slide dialogue box, choose your main menu page (in this case it is the slide called The Information Age).
- Click OK and OK again.
- Drag this button to its new position – we have put it to the left of the back button, so that all the navigation buttons are together, as shown in Figure 1.70.

Típ:

You will need to document this process for your e-portfolio. You will be making adjustments to your design as you progress with your e-book. This is a valid and necessary part of your work and as such must be recorded.

Figure 1.70

ICT Skills
(C – Organising your e-book)

OBJECTIVES

● **To organise the pages of your e-book**

Rearranging slides in PowerPoint

When we first started setting up our series of slides it seemed intuitive to input each slide in order of its level in the hierarchy. This however, is not how readers will be using the book. They will need the slides (or book pages) to follow each other in a more linear manner. To rearrange the slide, we will use the Slide Sorter view.

● Click on the Slide Sorter button down at the bottom left of the PowerPoint screen.

● Alternatively select View/Slide Sorter.

● You will then see your slide show as the view shown in Figure 1.71.

To move a slide you need to:

● Click on a slide to select it.

● Then drag and drop it to the desired position.

● To move more than one slide at once, hold the Ctrl key down and click all the slides you want to move.

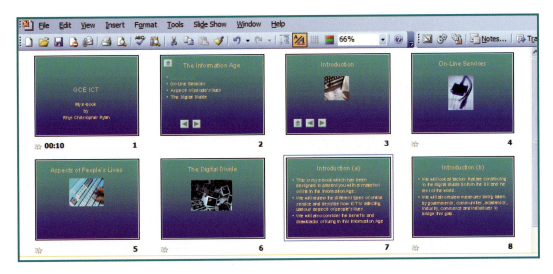

Figure 1.71

Rearranging the e-book like this will change the slides the navigation buttons link to. For example, we moved slides 7 and 8 from our e-book to just after slide 3. Now, when we press the forward button on slide 3 of our e-book, the next slide will the first page of the introduction: Introduction (a) – see Figure 1.72.

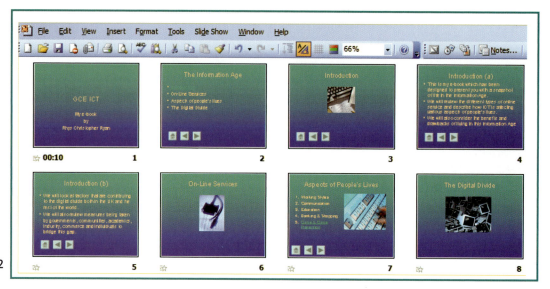

Figure 1.72

We will need to use the same process as we used previously of copying and pasting to transfer our buttons to both pages 'Introduction (a)' and 'Introduction (b)'.

Copying and pasting several navigation buttons

Now would be a good time to add navigation buttons to all of the pages in the e-book. As well as copying and pasting navigation buttons individually, you can use the Ctrl key to select multiple buttons.

- Select Normal View using the small button in the bottom left or by going to View/ Normal.

- Go to a slide that already has all the buttons in place.

- Hold down the Ctrl key on your keyboard.

- Click on each navigation button in turn to select them all.

- Right-click the buttons and select Copy (see Figure 1.73).

- Go to the next slide.

- Right-click anywhere on the slide.

- Select Paste to paste your buttons onto the selected slide in exactly the same positions as on the original.

Repeat these steps until you have copied the buttons onto all of your slides.

Figure 1.73

Filling in the gaps using Slide Sorter view

When you are in Slide Sorter view it is easy to spot gaps in the content that you will need to fill in later. For example, Figure 1.74 shows that in our e-book, we need to add a menu to the title pages for the sections On-Line Services and The Digital Divide, in the same way as has already been done for Aspects of People's Lives.

Figure 1.74

While we are in Slide Sorter view, we can move all of the crime and crime prevention slides we have created so that they come in the correct section – just after slide number 7. At a later point we will then add content for the other four chapters of this section which will be inserted before the crime pages. We will also add content pages for the On-Line Services and The Digital Divide sections.

Adding hyperlinks to the section menus

We can now create a hyperlink for 'Crime & Crime Prevention' on our 'Aspects of People's Lives' page, to each of our sub-pages. The procedure is the same as the one we used before.

- Highlight the Crime & Crime Prevention text (see Figure 1.75).

- Right-click and select Hyperlink.

- Select the Place in This Document button.

- Select the page you want to link to (in this case, screen 8, as shown in Figure 1.76).

- You will notice a preview of the selected slide in the slide preview box.

- Click OK.

Now when the user follows the link we have just constructed they will go straight to the first page of the Crime & Crime Prevention chapter.

Figure 1.75

> *Note that even if we subsequently change the order of the pages or add more pages, the hyperlink from the menu page will still go to the Crime & Crime Prevention page, no matter what number slide it becomes.*

The forward arrow from this opening page leads to a further sub-menu which lists the case studies featured in the chapter. We now need to construct three further hyperlinks so the reader can choose between the options:

- PITO in the UK
- Fighting Terrorism
- A Japanese Security Robot

We won't go through how to add these hyperlinks as the process is exactly the same as that described above.

Making adjustments as you go along

As you test your e-book, you will find yourself making small adjustments and improving your work as you progress. You will notice that developing an e-book using PowerPoint is a fairly intuitive process. The great advantage is that you can make mistakes and correct them very easily. For example, in our book we wanted to add an extra hyperlink to discuss benefits and drawbacks as part of the sample e-book. It was a simple matter to add another bullet point and then create a hyperlink to the appropriate pages, as shown in Figure 1.76.

Figure 1.76

At any time you may discover that certain aspects of your project may have to change due to unforeseen circumstances. In the case of our e-book, we've chosen a graduated background which is a light green colour towards the upper half. As it happens, the default text for a hyperlink is also a light green colour.

When we added hyperlinks to one of our Crime & Crime Prevention pages, we discovered that hyperlinks in the top half of the page are not very visible – as you can see in Figure 1.77. One way to fix this is to change the graduated background colour. Remember to describe what you have done and why in your e-portfolio. Provide screenshots with annotations at appropriate points.

Here's how to change the background colour.

- Go to Format/Background.
- Select the colour you would like.
- Then click Apply to apply the new background colour to the slide you are on.
- Or click Apply to All to apply the background colour to all the slides.

You can also change the font colour to improve legibility. Figure 1.78 shows the improved legibility of the links after the background and font colours had been changed.

Putting in additional features

As you progress with your e-book you may find that you need additional features that you had not considered in your planning. For example, in our e-book we realised that the reader might need to jump back to the previous menu page, rather than simply to the previous page. Adding this feature could save the reader doing a lot of unnecessary clicking of back buttons.

To do this we needed to add an additional button that would enable the reader to jump back to the previous menu. It will work in much the same way as the up arrow moves between directories in Microsoft Explorer, as illustrated in Figure 1.79.

We simply chose another action button, in this case the Beginning button, and set its properties so that it returned to a named slide, 'The Impact of ICT'. We then copied and pasted the button onto all the pages in the section – in this case the two pages shown in Figure 1.80.

We then went on to add buttons linking back to the next level up in our hierarchy to all the pages in our e-book.

Figure 1.77

Figure 1.78

Figure 1.79

Figure 1.80

Figure 1.81 shows the completed section of our e-book on 'Crime and Crime Prevention', with the background and font colours changed to overcome problems with hyperlink colours.

Figure 1.81

Using FrontPage to create an e-book

We've included a fairly detailed overview of PowerPoint and how to use it for building your e-book. It is a useful application for building an e-book, though it does have some limitations.

It would be good to present a comprehensive range of authoring tools in this book, enabling you to choose a favourite for constructing your e-book. Unfortunately we don't have the space to look at every application, but we will take a quick look at FrontPage 2003. This application has been primarily designed for building websites, but it can also be used to generate your e-book.

One of the key aspects that you need to become familiar with is the concept of **frames**. An e-book designed around frame technology enables you to have a contents page which is always visible as readers navigate to different pages in the e-book.

Let's get started and use FrontPage to build the basic structure for our e-book. We won't go too far with this because once you have the structure working, adding content works in a very similar way to using a word processing application.

- Click Start/Programs/FrontPage.
- Click File/New/More Web Page Templates.
- The Page Templates dialogue box will open (Figure 1.82).
- Select the Frame Pages tab.

This will enable us to choose a suitable frameset for our e-book. We'll choose the Footer frame, which will enable us to have our table of contents along the bottom of our book.

- With the Footer selected click OK.
- You should see a screenshot similar to the one shown in Figure 1.83.

Notice that the page is split into two: the top section is where our reading materials will be displayed and the bottom (smaller part) is where we will put our table of contents (which will eventually contain links to the appropriate pages in the book).

- Click the New Page button in the upper section.
- Click the New Page button in the lower section.

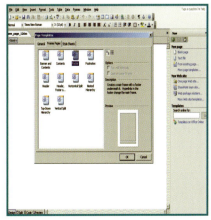

Figure 1.82

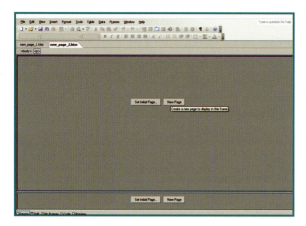

Figure 1.83

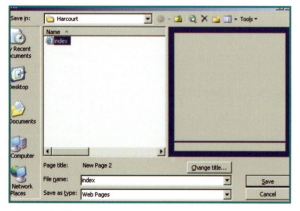

Figure 1.84

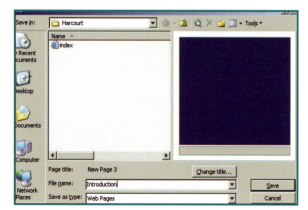

Figure 1.85

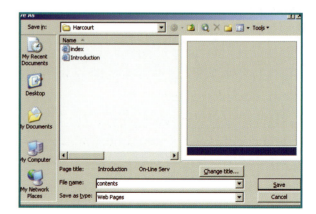

Figure 1.86

- This will generate new pages using FrontPage's default filenames (which are fairly meaningless and not very helpful in terms of identifying what each page contains).

- We can start saving the pages now, giving them meaningful names.

- Click File/Save As to open the dialogue box shown in Figure 1.84.

  Notice the thick dark blue border on the right – this is 'containing' the whole of our page and as such is called the frameset. This file must be called 'index.html' as it will be the opening page for our e-book. This frameset will provide the control mechanism for the rest of our pages.

Having saved this page, you will then be prompted to save one of the book's content pages. Call this 'Introduction' and click Save.

Our next prompt shows the blue highlight around the bottom frame. This is our Contents list. Call this 'Contents' and click Save.

Enter your table of contents list in the lower section, using the tab key to separate the list (Introduction, On-Line Services etc.).

We will now turn the word 'Introduction' into a link that will open our Introduction page when clicked.

- Highlight the word 'Introduction' in the table of contents.

- Then right-click it.

- Select Hyperlink.

- The Insert Hyperlink dialogue box will then open.

- Select Introduction.HTML from the file list that you've already created.

- Repeat this for 'On-Line Services'.

- Save your work.

- Click File/Preview in Browser

Figure 1.87

Figure 1.88

Figure 1.89 shows how our page will be presented in the browser window. We then repeat this process for the remaining items in the table of contents.

As you can see in Figure 1.90, the Introduction page is shown in the browser window with the contents frame visible across the bottom of the screen. If we were to Click the 'Online Services' link this would take us to the appropriate page whilst leaving the contents frame unchanged. The advantage is that the user will always have a visible reference point on the page in order to jump quickly to the main chapters of the e-book.

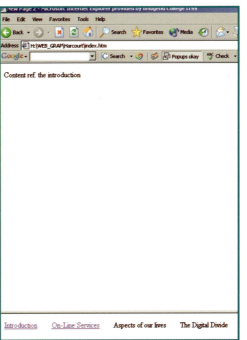

Figure 1.89

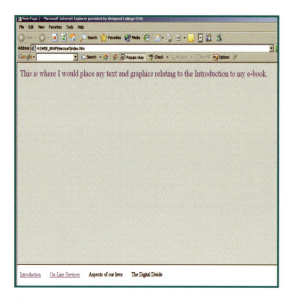

Figure 1.90

Don't forget that the previous pages are not meant to illustrate the full authoring capacity of FrontPage. If you choose to use FrontPage or DreamWeaver to create your e-book as a website, you will need to experiment in order to find out how to edit text and backgrounds and generally design the overall appearance of your e-book.

ICT Skills
(D – Working with Multimedia Components)

7

OBJECTIVES

- To be able to use ready-made multimedia components
- To use a digital camera and scanner to capture images
- To capture screen-based images

Ready-made multimedia components

The Internet has a wealth of multimedia materials that can be used in your e-book. Many web-based companies offer free samples of graphics, comprising still images, animations, photographs, video clips and sound files. In addition application packages such as Microsoft Word and Microsoft PowerPoint have inbuilt libraries of multimedia material. As you build your e-book you will make use of this type of online resource, as you do so it is important for you to acknowledge the source of this material.

Clip Art

Let's use the Clip Art feature in Microsoft Word to find an appropriate graphic to use in our e-book.

- Select Insert/Picture/Clip Art.
- On the right-hand side of your screen, the Clip Art search dialogue box will automatically appear (see Figure 1.91).
- Enter the word 'computer' in the search box and click Go.
- The Microsoft Clip Art facility will search its folders to find all images that have the word computer as part of their description.
- You will then get a list of results as shown in Figure 1.92.
- From the choice of Clip Art shown, you can choose one of the images in the following way.
- Click to select your chosen image.
- An arrow will appear to the right of the image.
- Click the arrow and a number of options will appear.
- Select Insert to insert the Clip Art item into your document.

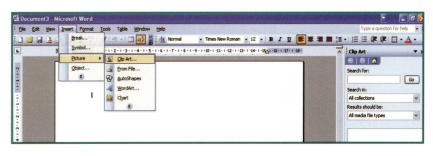

Figure 1.91

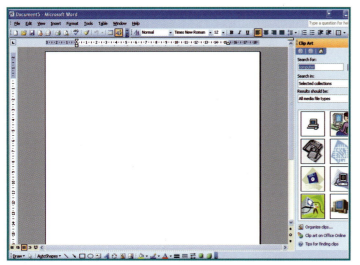

Figure 1.92

Sometimes you won't be able to find an appropriate piece of Clip Art. In this case select the link Clip Art on Office Online. Clicking on this link will take you to the Clip Art section of the Microsoft website – this massive online Clip Art library which provides a much wider selection of Clip Art than is available on your PC.

Notice that the Clip Art is organised into categories such as Occupations, People, Academic, etc. Other word processing applications, such as Star Office and WordPerfect, will also provide access to Clip Art libraries.

To continue our search we will enter the word 'computer' into the online search box.

We have chosen the image of a couple checking in at an airline terminal (see Figure 1.93). We could use this image in our e-book to illustrate how ICT influences people's lives.

There is also a facility to select multiple images (by checking the small box underneath each image). This allows your to place the images in a Selection Basket for download once your selection is complete.

You will notice that we have checked three images which have been added to our Selection basket on the left-hand side of the browser window. All we have to do now is to click on the 'Download 3 items' link to download these images to our computer, in the Microsoft Clip Organizer. We can then insert them into our document at the required point.

Sourcing graphics from the Internet

Let's use an Internet search engine to try and find some suitable graphics for our e-book. We will try to find an image which reflects one aspect of how ICT affects people's lives – computers in hospitals.

- Open your web browser and type in the URL of the Google search engine: **www.google.co.uk.**
- Select Images on the Google main page.
- Enter: 'hospital computer' in the search box.
- Click Search Images.
- Google will display a range of images that fit your search criteria.
- Google has a nice feature for displaying the images as thumbnails, which allows you to judge very quickly whether an image is suitable for your project. They are low-resolution images which, if clicked, will load a new page showing the full-size image (Figure 1.98).
- Click on the picture or on the link See full-size image – this will open the new window.
- With the new window open, right-click on the image.

Figure 1.95

- Select Save Picture As…
- The Save Picture dialogue box will open.
- Select the directory where you would like to save the image.
- Click Save.

Tip:

If you right-click and save the thumbnail, you will have a very low-resolution image. If you use this in your e-book it will look very poor quality when you enlarge it and will detract from the professional appearance of your project. So you must open the full-size image.

Portfolio Builder: *Spend some time doing Internet research to find graphics sites which contain images that you could use as part of your e-book. You may wish to illustrate, for example, a point you are making about how elderly people or people with disabilities use a computer system to purchase groceries online, thereby overcoming mobility problems. It is important to give some thought to the type of images you will use because these will play a key role in your e-book.*

Having saved a picture with the intention of using it in your e-book, you need to acknowledge its source.

In the previous section we have seen how to capture images from the internet for use within our publications. As we work through the following section we will discuss how we can create our own image content via a digital camera, scanning and the use of video cameras.

In each of these cases it is very important for us to understand the implications of file sizes and how large files may be detrimental to our e-book website. The larger the file, the longer it takes to appear on our computer screen as an image. We have all experienced this when we've visited a website containing large images which take a long time to load; this often results in us becoming impatient and moving on to another website which may not have this limitation.

For further information on compression, please see page 73 in this chapter.

Tip:

There is an expectation by Edexcel that students limit the size of their e-portfolios. It is therefore important that any digitally produced images are 'fit for purpose' to maintain viewing quality *and* images are of an appropriate size.

Digital cameras

It is beyond the scope of this book to give a detailed account of colour photography and the use of digital cameras. However, we can give a brief overview – even though there are many different digital cameras on the market, the principles of use are very similar.

The basic idea is that you:

- capture the required image with the camera
- transfer the image from the camera to a computer
- use graphics editing software to manipulate the image
- save the image in a file format suitable for use within your e-book.

In this information age you don't have to be a brilliant photographer to take an excellent picture. With a digital camera you are able to take the photographs, preview the images on camera and only keep the images you think you would like to use in your e-book.

Taking photographs

Visit **www.kodak.com**/ and follow the Consumer Photography link. Here you will find some excellent tips on taking good photographs.

Downloading pictures to a PC with Windows 2000 or XP

In order to demonstrate the processes involved, we've taken a photograph of a card reader to use as an example. You should put any photographs you take to use in your e-book into your e-portfolio as supporting evidence to show how you transferred an image taken with a digital camera to a PowerPoint application. You will need to take your own photographs for your e-book (see the Portfolio Builder activity at the end of this chapter).

Note: The following section assumes that your school or college technician has already installed the camera drivers and software onto your computer. In most cases the technician will be the only person who has the required authority or permissions to install new software onto your computer network.

Your pictures can be transferred to the PC by one of the following means:

- connecting the camera to the computer via the USB or FireWire port
- connecting a special card reader to the computer via the USB port.

Whichever method you use, the computer 'sees' the card reader or camera as an additional disk drive. This means that the folder or directory structure that you are familiar with will be viewable as soon as you attach one of these devices.

As soon as you have connected the camera or the card reader to the computer you will see a window appear as shown in Figure 1.99.

As you can see, the desktop shows a number of devices available, including a Fuji card on drive H. You can open this drive just as you would any other disk drive on your PC. If you are using a Sony, Minolta, Olympus, Kodak or other make of camera, then your disk drive will show the manufacturer's name accordingly. For the purposes of our example we will refer to a Fuji camera.

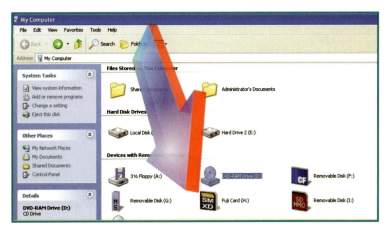

Figure 1.99

- Double-click the Fuji card drive.

- A new window will open showing a folder called DCIM.

- Double-click the DCIM folder.

- You will then see a sub-folder bearing the name of the camera manufacturer.

- This folder contains the photographs as shown in Figure 1.100.

The next steps are as follows.

- Click Edit/Select All.

- This will highlight all of the images shown within the cameras directory.

- Drag and drop these images into your chosen directory on the school or college drive.

- This will copy the images into the directory. (You will see a file transfer dialogue box appear as this process takes place.)

Figure 1.100

- Figure 1.101 shows how we have opened two directory windows. One contains the removable camera card (source drive) and the other is a folder or subdirectory in our computer's disk drive (destination drive). The process of drag and drop is more easily accomplished if you set the source and destination windows in this manner.

- Having successfully transferred your images from the camera's card to your computer, you can then delete the images from the picture card.

- Choose Edit/Select All to select the images in the card reader folder.

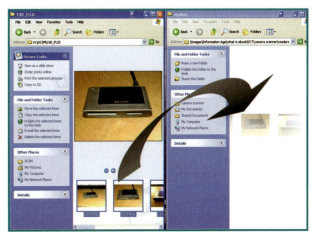

Figure 1.101

- Then select File/Delete.

- You may then remove the camera card from the reader and place it back into the camera.

Using movie clips

Many digital still cameras also have a movie mode. This will enable you to capture short clips of video to enhance your e-book. For example, you could include a clip of a fellow student being interviewed about an aspect of our e-book. This would enrich the content and help to set it apart from paper-based alternatives.

Figure 1.102 shows a close-up of the mode dial on a Nikon camera.

To make a movie clip, you set the dial to 'movie' (the icon that looks like an old-fashioned movie camera); then press the shutter to start filming and again to stop. You can transfer the movie clip to your PC in the same way as described for digital still images. The only difference is that your file format will now be an MPEG video file instead of a JPEG.

You can now easily integrate the clip into your e-book.

- Select Insert/Movies and Sounds/Movie from File... as shown in Figure 1.103.

- Select your movie clip from the appropriate directory.

- PowerPoint will then ask you if you'd like to have it play automatically when the page is opened or wait for a mouse click to start it.

- If you would like to experiment with video, you can also use a video editing application to modify your clip prior to integrating it into your e-book. Windows Movie Maker may be available in the Accessories of Windows XP. This software is very easy to use and enables you to capture video (either from a camera or an existing file); You can edit the movie by adding effects, transitions, titles and credits; then save to your computer or CD.-ROM

Use a scanner to capture images

Scanners work in a similar way to the image capture device on a photocopying machine. However, instead of the scanner printing the page, it makes a copy of the image and stores it as a file. There are two different ways of using a scanner.

- Running the scanner software to scan the image and thereafter saving it as a file.

- Running a graphics application and using the File/ Import command from within the application to scan the image directly into the same graphics program. (This relies on the software and the scanner being TWAIN compliant.)

Figure 1.102

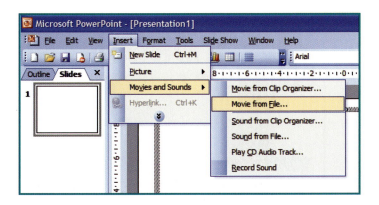

Figure 1.103

Figure 1.104

Portfolio Builder: *If you have a video facility on the digital camera, make some short video clips of students participating in a course-related activity. For example, you could make a short clip of a student describing a range of online services with which they are familiar. Or, even better, ask a friend to film you presenting this description. If you are shy, just place the camera on a stable surface or tripod, let the camera run and edit afterwards with Movie Maker to keep the parts you need.*

Scanner import from within PowerPoint

We are going to use a photograph from Computing magazine (their website is **www.computing.co.uk**), which appears in an article about SchoolNet in Africa, and which is credited to Mark Samuels.

Here's how to scan in an image from a printed page.

● Place the page under the scanner, face down.

● Select Insert/Picture/From Scanner or Camera.

● A dialogue box will open (as shown in Figure 1.105).

● Select your scanner from the drop-down menu (you only need to choose if you have more than one device).

● Select Web Quality (this will store a lower resolution image suitable for screen viewing).

● Click Insert.

● A timer will appear indicating that scanning is taking place.

Figure 1.105

The scanned image will display, in its uncropped condition, as shown in Figure 1.106.

You will notice that the image has handles and the PowerPoint Picture toolbar is visible.

Tip:

If you connect a digital camera or card reader, you can follow the same process within PowerPoint.

● Select the Crop tool.

● Drag the corner handles to crop the image.

● Click the finished image in the centre.

● Drag so that the image fits centrally on your slide as shown in Figure 1.107.

Figure 1.106

That's it; image scanned, cropped and positioned in a few easy steps, all from within PowerPoint.

Capturing screen-based images (screenshots)

Capturing screen images (screenshots) is a simple task using a combination of keyboard shortcuts. This technique is useful when you want to show how you completed certain tasks. For example, if you wanted to illustrate folders on your disk drive, you could use the screen capture process to do this.

● Open the required directory or folder.

● Capture the image by pressing the Print Screen (Prt Scr) key on your keyboard.

● Open your e-portfolio document.

● Select Edit/Paste or right-click and select Paste, of press Ctrl V.

● Your full screen image will be pasted into your document as shown in Figure 1.108.

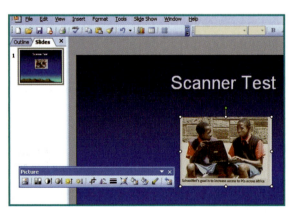

Figure 1.107

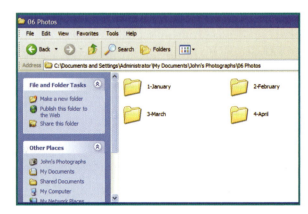

Figure 1.108

You can also crop a screenshot to show just the area you want.

● Click to select the image.

● Handles will appear at each corner and at each side.

● At the same time the Picture editing toolbar will be displayed.

● If the Picture toolbar does not display, go to View/Toolbars/Picture to open it.

● Select the Crop tool and drag your image by the handles to crop so that only the desired area is showing.

Figure 1.108 shows our image after we have cropped away the unwanted parts.

That's the process for capturing screenshots. This is a very effective way for you to show your assessor how you have mastered appropriate skills for the GCE in ICT.

File types

It is essential to use files of an appropriate type as you construct your e-book and e-portfolio. Files are identified by their three-digit extension: for example, an image of a house may be called house.jpg. In this case 'house' is the filename and '.jpg' is the file extension.

JPEG: Probably the most useful format to use in a multimedia application is the file type known as JPEG. JPEGs use highly efficient image compression algorithms to reduce file sizes without noticeable loss in image quality. These are especially useful if you want to transfer files over the Internet or if you have a size limitation on your e-book. Images for screen viewing do not need to be as high a resolution as for print.

GIF: This format is used for images containing 256 colours or fewer. Images of cartoon characters for example would fit this category. These are also used as a format for animations if a number of individual GIF files are presented as one file. The browser then takes this composite image file and plays the animation when it is loaded into a web browser.

HTML: This format is used by web browsers. Most websites you visit will be using files in this format (or one closely related to it, such as DHTML, XML etc). When you have completed your e-book you will be able to export it to the HTML format so that a web browser will be able to present it to the outside world.

Most scanners will allow you to save your image in a file format that you want to use. Cameras mostly use JPEG images, which are ideal for our purposes and no conversion will be required.

Combining and presenting information

We could write a whole book on this small element of the scheme. However, we will investigate only a few areas in order to get you started. The following section reviews some of the features available within Word which you may find useful as you document your progress on this course.

Presenting information can be a daunting task. If we consider our word processing application package, we will find many features that enable us to present information in a variety of ways. We will investigate a number of these, but for a

> **Tip:**
>
> Changing the file's extension by renaming won't change its format. You have to use appropriate software to modify the structure of the file to change its file type.

more detailed account there are many specific titles in the Payne-Gallway series that cover these aspects in much more detail.

Page Setup

Most of your work is likely to be word processed in what we call portrait (vertical) format. However, there are instances where the landscape (horizontal) view is preferable. For example, you may be setting up a table of data which is much wider than it is long and landscape view would allow all the data to fit on the page more easily.

● Choose File/Page Setup.

As you can see from Figure 1.109, you can set margins, paper size and other layout features from the Page Setup dialogue box. To change the page orientation to landscape:

● Select Landscape.

● Select Apply to: Whole Document to change the whole document to landscape format.

● Or you could select Apply To: This point Forward. (You can always change back to portrait format at a later point if necessary.)

Bullets and Numbers

● Type in your list, for example:

Privacy rights

Copyright and legislation

Impact on employment

The digital divide.

● Highlight the text.

● Select either the Bullets or Numbering button on the Formatting toolbar.

We want to number our list, so we will select Numbering. Our list is then presented appropriately numbered as requested:

1. Privacy rights

2. Copyright and legislation

3. Impact on employment

4. The digital divide.

If you press Enter twice after the last item in the list, your document text will revert to left justified, with numbering (or bullets) switched off.

Figure 1.109

Tables

Tables are an important design feature you can use for presenting information. The table consists of a series of cells in rows and columns, in which you can store text and graphics.

Here's how to create a table.

- Click the Insert Table button on the Standard toolbar, or select Table/Insert.
- Left-click and highlight the appropriate number of rows and columns (in this case 3 by 4).
- Release the left mouse button.

The following table will be displayed on screen:

You can now enter data into your table structure. To move from cell to cell, either select the required cell using the mouse pointer or move through the cells in sequence using the Tab key.

Add components created in another piece of software

Very often you will have created a document in one application package which you then need to insert into a different application. For example, we are using a document, Appendix C, to gather research information and to keep track of references. At some point we may wish to use a paragraph from this document and place it directly into our PowerPoint slide show. Using this as the example, we would complete the following steps.

- Highlight the text (and/or graphics).

- Right-click and select Copy.

- Go to the target application (in this case a slide in PowerPoint).

- Right-click and select Paste.

This will place the selected text in our PowerPoint slide.

In the following example, we have found an Internet site containing a PowerPoint presentation giving useful statistics about the digital divide. We can take a copy of the slide as follows.

- Right-click the slide in the browser window and select Copy.

- Right-clicking in our target application and select Paste.

- Figure 1.110 shows a web page with some interesting statistics on world Internet usage. We can copy this data into our document.

- Click and drag to highlight the data.

- Right-clicking and select Copy.

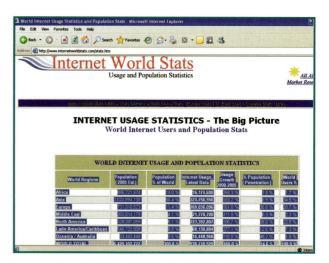

Figure 1.110

- Go to the target application (in this case Excel).

- Right-click and select Paste.

Figure 1.111 shows how the pasted statistics appear in our document.

You are now free to manipulate this data to suit you own purposes. For example, we may like to output a part of this as a graph or a chart for use in our PowerPoint presentation. This procedure for copying from a source application and pasting into a target application can be followed with a variety of Windows applications. Remember to always reference and acknowledge all materials that you have not created yourself.

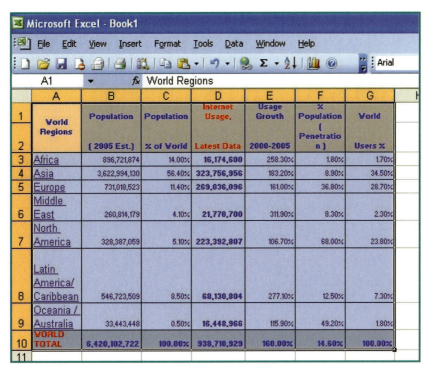

Figure 1.111

Work hard on your e-book and aim for the Mark Band 3 criteria to achieve top grades. In the next chapter we will investigate the power of Internet shopping sites as a result of database technology.

UNIT 2 – THE DIGITAL ECONOMY

The Information Needs of Organisations

2.1

OBJECTIVES

- To review how organisations communicate using ICT, including: data capture methods, data processing, presenting and exchanging information
- To investigate the marketing of goods and services, distribution and transaction processing
- To review the management of customer relations
- To examine just-in-time stock purchases

Organisations range from one-person businesses to multi-million pound corporations. Whatever the size, all companies rely on accurate **data** to provide reliable **information**. Effective communication is vital in this process. Increasingly, businesses are replacing paper-based communications with email, web-based forms and secure financial transfers. ICT plays a key part in the way 20th century organisations function.

Capturing and Processing Data

Data can be thought of as related raw facts, numbers or measurements. When this data has been processed it can be presented as information. Data capture refers to the process of obtaining the data, usually via some form of input device, such as keyboard text entry. Data capture is a rapidly evolving field of ICT, organisations are investing much time and money in order to increase speed and reduce input errors.

One example of a data capture device is the barcode readers that are used in supermarkets to speed up the shopping process. As you will probably know from your trips to the supermarket, a barcode reader can scan goods much faster than we can pack them into bags!

The data captured by the barcode reader can be processed and used in whatever ways the supermarket needs, for example:

- to create the bill for our shopping
- to keep track of how fast items are selling so that more items can be reordered when stocks get low
- to inform the supermarket's buyers which goods are selling well and which are not.

The word **inform** is key here – it highlights the fact that data is processed into information.

Figure 2.2 gives details of some of the data capture devices that are in current use.

Effective data capture must be followed by accurate data processing. If we take the supermarket example, each item that passes the scanner will have its price 'read' and added to a running total by the computer. The computer will also process any special offers and amend the bill accordingly. As the last item passes the scanner, and the final total is requested the computer will calculate the final total and then print the bill. As this process is taking place,

Figure 2.1

the computer will also compile stock records for the warehouse to make reordering more precise. The barcode reading process has now advanced to such a stage that self-service checkouts are now possible. Here the customers scan and weigh their own goods with the aid of a touch-sensitive screen and then make their payment.

Figure 2.2a Barcode readers

Figure 2.2b Touch screen

Figure 2.2c Magnetic strip

Figure 2.2d Magnetic ink character reader (MICR)

Figure 2.2e Keyboard

Figure 2.2f Optical mark recognition

Figure 2.2g Smart card

Figure 2.2h Headset

Exercise

Make a list of the ways in which we record (capture) data, both manually and using computers. Report back to the class, describing each different method you've thought of and including images of each particular type.

Presenting and Exchanging Information

There is a difference between **data** and **information**. Data is the raw material (that has been captured) and information is the finished product (that has been processed). Figure 2.3 shows an example of how data is processed to become information. Each separate piece of data is combined with the other data captured and processed to present us with information – in this case the finished payslip. You will notice that each separate data item isn't of much use until it is processed and the payslip produced. For example, knowing the number of hours worked and the tax code won't be very informative unless we also know the rate of pay.

Data	Information
Hours worked Rate of pay Tax code Number of overtime hours Overtime rate	**Pay Slip** ~ ~ ~ ~ ~ ~ ~ ~ ~ ~ ~ ~

Figure 2.3

In a world of ICT-enabled devices, presenting information is sophisticated and takes a huge variety of forms. For example:

- our electricity and gas bills are computer printouts

- at the travel agent we see various holiday options on the VDU

- after we've chosen our holiday we will receive a printout

- at a bank service till we can view confirmation about our transaction on screen and we may also choose to have a printed receipt of the transaction

- when buying cinema tickets, we may see a pictorial view of our seat locations on a computer screen

- a sales manager can present a performance review, using graphs and charts of the year's sales

Exercise

In groups of three, discuss the different ways in which information is presented in your daily lives.

In our digital world the exchange of information is rapid. The sales manager in the previous example could make the same presentation to colleagues on the other side of the world using the same ICT tools, together with a webcam and Internet connection. This allows the company to make huge savings in terms of time, money and employee fatigue.

Within any organisation the exchange of data and information is vital. Organisations that develop effective communications systems are likely to survive in a market which is becoming increasingly more competitive, as companies are not only competing nationally but with companies worldwide.

Companies consider large stock piles of unsold goods as wasted money. Unnecessary use of storage space and purchasing too soon from suppliers has cost implications. Many companies have become bankrupt as a result of investing in too much stock that hasn't sold quickly enough. ICT solutions make keeping stocks at the right level much easier. Supermarkets use data from their tills at the end of the day to compile stock lists. These lists are sent to central warehouses so that goods can be sent overnight to replenish the previous day's used stock, thereby minimising on storage space. Accurate information exchange is vital in this process.

Conducting Transactions

The Internet has become an essential vehicle for online transactions, together with the widespread use of 'electronic money' – online shopping is only possible because of the credit and debit cards with which we make payments. (Imagine a shopping website that required you to send a cheque or postal order to make a purchase – you'd very likely give up and find one that would accept a card payment.) But buying online also raises security issues. Companies need to ensure that they are offering safe forms of payment to their customers. Without customer confidence, companies would not soon lose their opportunity for e-business.

A few years ago online shopping transactions were limited to items such as CDs and books which could be posted easily. Now there are companies selling almost everything over the Internet, with a growing army of customers willing to enter their card details and make the purchase.

Marketing Goods and Services

While glossy brochures still have their place, they are very expensive to produce and, once they have been printed, they can't be updated without printing a whole new batch. A website on the other hand is relatively cheap, easily amended and updated and is more accessible to a much wider audience.

Goods and services can be presented in a feature-rich, multimedia environment that is easily accessible by many. (See the section on the digital divide in Chapter 1 for exceptions to this.)

To see an online video demonstration of the latest high-tech gadget can inspire people in a way that could never be achieved using traditional printed brochures.

Distributing Goods

ICT has revolutionised the way we deliver goods from one place to another. The real bonus is not so much the actual transportation but rather knowing precisely what and how many units to deliver. We've already stated that stockpiles of goods are a waste of money. ICT allows effective distribution by informing warehouses of exactly how much stock is likely to be required by each individual store. This refinement allows organisations to keep costs down by reducing expensive storage time and waste.

Managing Customer Relations

The more an organisation knows about its customers, the better it is able to serve them. ICT enables companies to keep databases of customer details, including records of previous purchases, allowing the company to make personalised suggestions for future purchases. The use of the database also means that the customer only has to enter their personal details once, saving them time and effort and making them more likely to reuse a shopping site.

ICT can also enable a company to track the status of an order and present the information to the customer – details such as whether the order has been processed or dispatched yet. The company can also give the customer an expected delivery date, which all helps to keep them reassured and happy. If problems do arise, this useful information can assist in keeping the customer informed of why there is a delay and when this will be resolved. The lack of such information can very often lead to a deterioration of customer relations, which ultimately weakens the business.

Just-in-Time Stock Purchasing

As already stated, excess stock = lost money. Modern ICT systems can provide relevant, up-to-date information that enables stock managers to ensure that as goods arrive they will be sold within a short space of time. This is known as 'just-in-time' purchasing because the goods are not kept in a warehouse for very long.

An organisation's computer system processes data about how quickly an item sells by combining it with data about how many are left in stock. The processed data provides information that is used to order new stock. The data will be regularly updated, making the prediction as close as possible to how many items will actually be sold. Obviously this is not an exact science; the stock control computer is trying to predict the number of items to reorder based on past events. But consumers might behave unpredictably and buy more or less of an item than has been stored – in response to a food scare, for example. The stock control computer can never predict exactly how many items will be required.

Exercise

Research a well-known company (for example, Tesco, Marks & Spencer, Dixons or any other company of your choice) and try to establish how they manage each of the functions described in this section:

- capturing and processing data
- presenting and exchanging information
- conducting transactions
- marketing goods and services
- distributing goods
- just-in-time stock purchasing.

Present your findings in the form of a short PowerPoint presentation.

From Brick to Click

OBJECTIVES

- To investigate the underlying principles of Internet shopping, including worldwide customer base, low running costs, 24/7 presence

- To consider the possible advantages (and drawbacks) to both the e-business and the customer

The online shopping revolution has made huge differences to the way many companies do business. In this chapter we look at some of the advantages of running an Internet shopping business.

A Worldwide Customer Base

It's not too difficult to see that, once on the web, the world becomes a much smaller place for a company. No longer is the number of potential product sales restricted by geographical location. Overseas sales that previously couldn't be made because of the expense, time or labour involved now become possible. A website is instantly accessible to any individual, company or organisation with access to a computer, phone line (or alternative) and an Internet Service Provider (ISP).

Low Set-up and Running Costs

Exercise

In small groups, discuss your requirements for setting up an online music store selling second-hand CDs. What would be your minimum outlay in terms of the equipment you would need and other set-up costs, including technical equipment, storage space, external communications facilities, etc.?

Although the purpose of this exercise wasn't for you to give up your part-time job and become an e-commerce millionaire, it should have helped you to realise that the Internet really does allow individuals to set up shop very economically. As you will have seen from doing the exercise, it wouldn't take too much for you and a couple of enthusiastic friends to set up a small online business. You would need some equipment, but you may have most, if not all, of what you would need in place already. You would also need some finances to buy some stock. Following that, a quick route into e-commerce would be to use a well-established commercial site to kick-start your business, such as eBay.

The table in Figure 2.4 lists some of the differences between online and traditional shops, and highlights how much cheaper it is to set up an online shopping business.

	Traditional shop	Online shop
Premises	Suitable customer-friendly building	Doesn't matter – the customers won't see it!
Location	Good high street location to maximise customer exposure	Premises can be located anywhere
Fixtures and fittings	High-quality fixtures & fittings to convey an impression of quality	Cheap racking to hold products
Presentation products	Presentation products for display	Not required. Use high-quality images for the website
Customer expectations	Expects that the item they want will be in stock (size, colour, brand, title, etc.) – this has storage (and therefore cost) implications	Expects that there may be a delay before delivery – this gives some leeway in terms of what you need in stock
Heating costs	Running costs include adequate heating for the whole shop in the winter	No premises to heat (unless you are selling a product that needs storing at specific temperatures)
Parking	Customer parking might be required	Not required
Security	May need security personnel to prevent shoplifting	No shop to secure

Figure 2.4

Exercise

In a small group, draw up a comparison chart of the start-up costs for selling trainers in a traditional shop and as an online business – include actual costs in your chart. Assign tasks with the group to research the set-up costs, including the following:

- Review estate agents' websites in your area to establish typical rents for commercial properties.
- Think about the number of pairs of trainers required for display and stock (sizes, colours, brands etc.)
- Research the costs of display stands for the shop versus racking for the online facility.

As you will notice while doing your research, the costs for the traditional facility are much higher. Think about how you might fund each of these business ventures.

Look up the term 'drop shipper' on the Internet. Would you consider using this arrangement for your online facility?

Extension of Product Range

We've already seen how the start-up costs for an online business can be negligible compared to traditional methods and that an Internet business can reach a wider potential customer base. Another advantage of e-commerce is the possibility of extending the product range. This range extension has occurred in at least two ways:

1. By supplying an existing product range direct to people's homes via online shopping.

2. By extending the range of products on offer.

Supplying an existing product range via online shopping

This is the most common approach, where companies that have relied on traditional brick-based selling (i.e. have traditional shop premises) have extended their services to attract the online buyer. Examples include supermarket chains which are offering home shopping facilities so that customers can purchase their shopping from the comfort of their own homes. Customers log on to the supermarket's website with their user name and password and then fill their online shopping basket with the items they want in their weekly shop. They then go to the online checkout, pay using a cash card and select a delivery time to receive their goods.

Extending the range of products on offer

Some companies have extended their existing range by offering products online which are difficult to offer in-store. For example, large supermarket chains now offer additional services such as home insurance, ISP services and loans. Before the advent of the Internet they would have found it difficult to offer such services as they don't have the facilities for sitting down with customers and discussing these services. The Internet provides them with a vehicle through which they can market and sell these services.

Companies do have traditional call centres where this business can be accommodated but these centres are expensive to run and require skilled telephone personnel to advise and sell the products. Some companies have tried to 'outsource' this work to countries such as India with variable success. The Internet then, seems to be a way forward for this type of product or service.

Figure 2.5

24/7 Presence

One of the greatest advantages of an online shopping facility is that web servers don't have to close down at night, take holidays or other breaks and they don't cost double for working through holiday periods.

There aren't many shops (if any) that you would find open 24 hours a day, 7 days a week. In the world of the Internet, however, that is a reality. If you feel like adding a new CD to your collection, you can do so at any time of day or night. If you've received money as a Christmas present, you can even go online on Christmas day to make a purchase.

Instant purchases

With some products you can even buy your product and receive it immediately. Music and e-books in the form of MP3 files are two such products. For example, imagine it's 2 a.m. on a bank holiday Monday and you feel like listening to the Arctic Monkeys track 'I Bet You Look Good on the Dancefloor'. You have four options:

1. Forget about it and go to sleep.

2. Wait until the morning then go out and buy the whole album.

3. Phone a friend. Ask if they have it and if they will they bring it over. At 2 a.m. you don't stand much chance!

4. Log on to a music site and do one of the following:

    a. Listen to a 30 second sample for free.

    b. Play the whole track once for as little as 1p.

    c. Purchase the track in MP3 format for less than £1.

    d. Purchase the whole album as an MP3 download (no covers or case) for much less than the cost of a CD.

Figure 2.6 shows an example of one of the websites you could use to do this.

Although it might seem tempting to download music tracks illegally without paying for them, there are stringent copyright laws against this. The cost of a court case with a record company certainly makes such an illegal saving seem less attractive! See also the section on Copyright and Legislation in Unit 1.

Buying software and video online

In the same way that music and books are instantly accessible, so is software. We are able to download software in the same way as with music. After making our payment, we will receive the authorisation serial numbers via a secure link, all without stepping away from our web-enabled PC.

Figure 2.6

As broadband increases in speed, memory-intensive media such as video is increasingly becoming a download option. Soon we will be hiring films from video websites as simply and easily as we now download MP3 files. No need to leave your home, just log on to a video hire store's website and 'hire' your film, downloaded direct to your PC.

Case Study

As long ago as January 2000, the video hire business Blockbuster started planning streaming video. All they need now is faster broadband systems to make this a reality. Read the article taken from **www.silicon.com**.

Blockbuster and MGM to explore streaming

'Video rental chain Blockbuster has signed a deal with Metro-Goldwyn-Mayer to make the studio's films available over the Internet in the future.

Both companies said they will investigate digital streaming, downloading and other potential home delivery technologies. The deal is non-exclusive – both companies can look at other partners – and covers MGM's library of old films as well as new releases.

The two companies will share any revenue made by the agreement.'
By John Oates
Published: Thursday 20 January 2000

Exercise

Choose two Internet shopping sites that sell something tangible (as opposed to a service) and see if either mention an opening or closing time. Extend your research to see if they have any limits on delivery. List the advantages you feel the Internet company has over traditional bricks and mortar shops. Are there any disadvantages you could mention, too?

Fast Response Times

A transactional website is very likely to be cost-effective, especially one that is able to:

- present goods or services to the customer
- facilitate a purchase
- collect customers' details
- receive payments electronically
- dispatch goods following the receipt of a valid order.

From the company's perspective, the response time for the transaction is very fast. This is because they haven't actually had to do very much. Think about the steps involved in making a purchase and notice how much of it you do for them.

1. **You** search for the product.
2. **You** place the order.
3. **You** enter your method of payment and card details.
4. **You** enter your personal details, including name and delivery address.
5. **Their computer** automatically prints your order.

6. **They** collect the item from stock, pack it and post it.

7. **Your** purchase influences their next order of stock.

Exercise

Visit **www.pcworld.co.uk** and research the saving you make when purchasing online as opposed to visiting the store. Such savings are know as 'web exclusives' versus 'in-store price'. From what you have learned so far in this chapter, give reasons for the difference in price.

Real Time Sales Information

As we mentioned above, the customer's order informs an important step in the sales process. When a customer purchases something, the stock level in the warehouse is going to reduce by one item. So each customer's order enables the warehouse system to update its reordering needs precisely. In addition to this, the data may be used to keep stock purchasers informed about which product lines are selling well and, just as importantly, which lines are not.

Customer Expectations

An area that is receiving more attention from companies is that of customer expectations. Many customers who use the Internet for their shopping have an expectation that they will get the goods cheaper than in a high street store. There is also an expectation that they will have to wait for their goods to arrive and that there may be a delivery charge to consider. Many customers also understand that if they make purchases over the Internet, they might only have email as a communication method should things go wrong. Even with the disadvantages, more and more people are using the Internet for their shopping and presumably they feel satisfied that they are getting a good deal without the inconvenience of having to go out whatever the weather to a traditional store.

We've just mentioned price and how many people believe that the Internet will offer the best deal available. This is frequently true and to prove it, let's go shopping! We've just decided to log on to the PC World website to check out those cool-looking (and excellent-sounding) multimedia PC speakers, Harman Kardon Soundsticks II. If we click a few buttons we can buy them online from PC World for £101.37. Alternatively, we could jump in the car and queue up in PC World to purchase them for £139.99.

You don't have to be a brilliant mathematician to realise we've just saved almost £40 for sitting on a swivel chair, clicking a few buttons and ordering online. With the money we've saved, we could log on to an online music store and purchase around 48 MP3 tracks of our choice. And there isn't even a delivery charge – the speakers will be delivered to the door free of charge.

Portfolio Builder: *Using the Internet research skills you developed in Unit 1, find and investigate a suitable transactional website. The site will need to offer a comprehensive service so you may like to choose one of the market leaders.*

Give a detailed description of the site including what you would consider to be the main features. Provide examples, including screenshots of these features – for example: order status, wish list, account details, sorting features, reward programmes, etc.

Evaluate the overall design of the site, highlighting the features you find effective and indicating areas where you feel there could be improvement. Put yourself in the position of a customer so that your overview is from a 'customer experience' viewpoint.

Portfolio Builder: *One of the big issues with online transactions is the perceived security risk, such as identity theft and the loss of money by fraudulent means. Using the information in this chapter, online materials and other information that you find or that your teacher/lecturer supplies, describe several of these potential threats. You should clearly describe how customer data collected by organisations may become compromised.*

Your discussion should also indicate measures being taken by e-commerce companies to protect data and how customers must act responsibly as you disclose your personal information.

You will need to assess the effectiveness of the measures already in place to protect data and investigate how legislation supports them. Provide a conclusion, indicating your personal feelings about the risks attached to e-shopping, given all of the positive and negative aspects that you've researched.

Transactional Websites

OBJECTIVES

- To investigate the purpose of transactional websites
- To examine the structure, what is offered and ease of use
- To investigate methods used for capturing customer information
- To review the techniques used to maintain a customer base

In the first part of this chapter we will be looking at a typical transactional website and making some observations about it. The intention is for you to become familiar with the processes you need to go through with a number of websites in order to meet the objectives of this section of the course.

For each of your chosen websites, you will need to investigate and report on the following points:

- the purpose(s) of the site and how successfully it meets its objective(s)
- how the site is structured
- the goods and/or services it offers
- the product information provided
- ease of use.

As you review your chosen sites, you will need to collect and store your findings in your e-portfolio. Remember there is an e-portfolio requirement for each chapter and this must be no larger than 15MB in size. You will need to ensure that graphics (one of the biggest offenders in terms of the memory required) are optimised for the screen, and are therefore a manageable size.

Let's start by looking at a typical transactional website. We have chosen Dabs, a website that sells computer equipment and other electronic goods. We started by typing the URL (**www.dabs.com**) into our browser address bar and got the Dabs homepage as shown in Figure 2.7.

Purpose of the site

We can gain a great deal of information about this site from the homepage. The name Dabs doesn't give much of a clue as to the purpose of the site but as soon as we look at the website, it becomes clear that Dabs = technology.

How the site is structured

Now let's look at the structural features of the site.

Layout

The site looks very professional and, although tightly packed, the screen area is clean and well presented. The company logo and motto (as shown in Figure 2.8) reassure the customer of the company's values and mission.

Navigation

One of the first things to notice is the wide range of features available to the Internet shopper and the ease with which you can navigate between

Figure 2.7

them. The site is divided into departments which are presented using a tab layout, as shown in Figure 2.9. This enables the shopper to go quickly to their chosen department.

Figure 2.8

Figure 2.9

Shopping features

If we are just browsing, we can add articles to a wish list, which keeps track of our potential purchases. It is then easy to move items into the shopping basket by clicking the 'Move to Basket' icon on the wish list page. Or alternatively, to remove the item from the wish list by clicking the 'Remove' icon. The site also has the standard shopping basket and order status features we have come to expect from Internet shopping websites. We will be looking at the shopping basket feature in more detail later. Help is available and we can also view our account position by clicking the 'my account' link. Figure 2.9 shows the links to these features, which appear at the top right of the screen.

The goods and/or services offered

On this website we can search for products in several ways:

- using the department tabs at the top of the screen and then refining our search using sub-categories

- using the sub-categories listed under the department headings in the left-hand menu

- clicking on the links to the products featured on the home page

- carrying out a search using the search facility.

We wanted to search for pen drives. As we would expect from a large and well-structured website, there is a search facility which works in a standard way, so there is no problem using it. We decided to use the search facility to carry out our search. We entered the search terms Pen Drive, as shown in Figure 2.10, and then clicked GO.

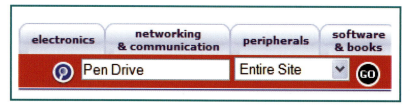

Figure 2.10

Figure 2.11 shows how the results are displayed. In this case the database has found so many items that we are invited to refine our search further.

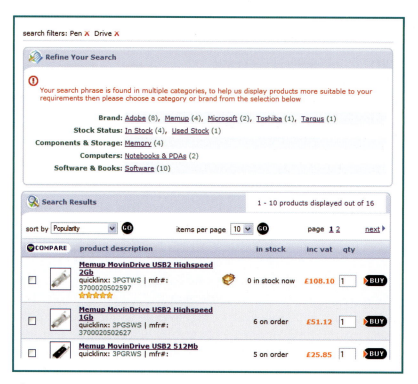

Figure 2.11

We can choose to look through the list, which can be sorted in the following ways:

- by popularity
- in alphabetical order (ascending)
- in alphabetical order (descending)
- by price (ascending)
- by price (descending).

Alternatively, we can refine our search by clicking on a category such as Brand or Components & storage.

The product information provided

Once we have located a product that looks promising and clicked on its link, we can find out further information about it by clicking the 'description', 'specification' or 'customer reviews' tabs at the bottom of the Product Information panel. The customer reviews option is a very nice feature of the Dabs website. It enables customers to provide a review and star rating (1 to 5) of any products on the site. If the item we are thinking of buying has received reviews, we can read what others thought and view their rating for the product overall, its ease of use and value for money.

Another feature of the Dabs website is the Compare feature, that allows us to make comparisons between two or more brands before making our selection. We're going to make a comparison between two different scanners. First we click the Peripherals tab, then Printers & Scanners in the submenu, as shown in Figure 2.12.

Figure 2.12

We could then have refined our search further using links to the various sub-categories. Instead we scrolled down to the product listings as shown in Figure 2.13. We decided to sort the scanners in ascending price order using the drop-down sort menu.

Figure 2.13

We then selected two scanners for comparison (the Canon Canoscan and the HP ScanJet 2400) by checking the box to the left of each product image (see Figure 2.14).

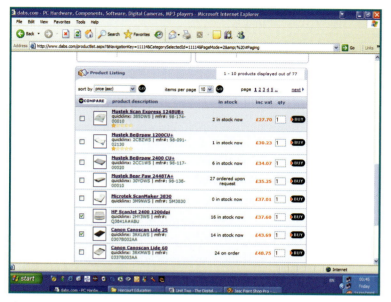

Figure 2.14

We then clicked on the Compare button at the top of the column and the Dabs web site presented us with a side-by-side comparison of the two products. The screenshot in Figure 2.15 shows the comparison of two scanners.

Figure 2.15

Note: By the time you read this book, this particular comparison may well be unavailable. If this is the case, just select two similarly priced products and do your own comparison.

Ease of use

Buying a product

To buy a product, we simply had to click the Buy button next to our chosen item. Immediately the product appeared in our shopping basket, which is visible on the right-hand side of the screen (see Figure 2.16).

This was the only item we wanted to buy so we clicked the Checkout button straight away. However, we could of course have continued shopping and adding items to the shopping basket before getting to this stage.

At the bottom of any page on this website, you can see the Thawte, Visa and Mastercard logos, which show that the Dabs website has signed up for the security standards of these organisations. This offers us reassurance that it is safe to enter our credit card details on this website.

Figure 2.16

Modifying a purchase

As with other shopping websites, we had the option to modify the contents of our basket at any time until we confirmed our purchase. To do this we had to click the 'edit/view basket' link in the My Basket box at the top right of the screen. Figure 2.17 shows the resulting screen.

This screen gave us the opportunity to:

- check the number of this item in stock

- check the item price and the total price

- amend the quantity

- delete a product we didn't want to buy

- move a product to the wish list if we weren't sure about it

Figure 2.17

That was a very quick tour of a website that makes armchair shopping a reality. We have presented some of the main features of this transactional website, but there are many other aspects of the site we could have discussed.

Some of the advantages of using a website like Dabs are:

- No pressure from sales people
- No problems with bad weather, parking, etc.
- No queues
- The likelihood of better prices
- The chance to read other purchasers' opinions about selected products

Exercise

In our review of the Dabs website, we highlighted what we consider to be the positive features of the website. But what are the drawbacks of a site like this?

Using the website featured here or one of your own choice, write a short article from the point of view of a person who has had a bad experience with Internet shopping. What went wrong? Which features of the site were difficult to use or find? How could the shopping experience be improved?

Capturing customer information and authenticating customers

Customer information may be collected with our knowledge (overt) or without our knowledge (covert).

Overt data capture

Whenever we visit a transactional website, we will almost always be asked to leave our personal details by completing a web form. This is an **overt** form of data capture because we are aware of exactly what data the website is capturing. The data is collected by the company so they can:

- understand the likes and dislikes of their customers
- place customer details on their mailing list
- monitor browsing and buying activities
- authenticate identity to avoid criminal activity.

Covert data capture

Cookies are a **covert** way of capturing data, used by websites to track your surfing habits, often without your knowledge. A cookie is a small data item sent by a **web server** to a **web browser** so that it can be read back at a later point with the user information it has collected.

In this way, the website 'knows you' when you return to the site. Cookies help company websites with their targeted marketing. They keep track of which products and adverts you viewed and build up a picture of the types of products you are interested in. On your return to the website, the selection of goods offered to you will be personalised to your interests.

Exercise

In small groups, visit a number of transactional websites and investigate the type of data the companies are seeking to capture. You might like to try the following or other sites of your own choice: www.dabs.com www.pcworld.co.uk www.next.co.uk www.tesco.co.uk

Answer the following questions as you carry out your research:

- Are any benefits offered to encourage you to register?
- Does the company guarantee that your details will be safe with them?
- Do you feel all the questions are relevant to you?
- Having registered, would you return to the site?

Make a list of your findings and report back to the main group.

Techniques to engage, entice and retain customers

If a company is selling an established and popular brand over the Internet, engaging and enticing customers is not such an issue. However, if the product is not already a brand name, how does a company establish and keep its customer base? The answer lies in building customer loyalty. A website needs to nurture this through continued interaction with its customers. In order to achieve this it must:

- offer goods and/or services that the customer perceives to be of high value
- provide easily accessible information about your products and/or services
- make the selection and purchase process easy and hassle free
- charge a fair price, which is perceived as good value by the customer.

A customer's perception of the service offered by a website is based on a number of important factors, including:

- the level of service
- the product features
- the total cost of the transaction (including any carriage costs)
- the perceived level of security in purchasing from the website.

Because customers can change suppliers easily, the company must provide a service that will make them reluctant to leave.

Exercise

Think about a recent purchase you have made (online or in a store) and analyse how you felt about it. Take into account some of the points raised above. Did your purchasing experience make you want to return or did it present concerns or frustrations?

Portfolio Builder: Visit a website of your choice and take a critical look at the site as you go through the process of making a purchase of at least four items.

- Be careful to stop the process before you have to enter any personal or credit card details.

As you do this task, document each step in the process and provide screenshots as evidence for your e-portfolio. Ensure you make a few mistakes along the way so that you can review how easy it is to go back or make changes. For example, choose the wrong product and quantity and then edit your choice, noting any difficulties or problems that you encounter. Try to put yourself in the position of an inexperienced Internet shopper, as this will help you to find any weaknesses in the site.
Make notes on the following:

- how the website captures customer information
- the techniques used to engage and entice the customer
- usability and accessibility
- the overall customer experience.

As you work on this portfolio building activity, ask your teacher or lecturer to give you a copy of the Edexcel standards. Be particularly aware of the criteria for the Mark Band 3 grading criteria. This will help you to focus on producing materials that will gain higher grades.

Back Office Processes

OBJECTIVES

- To understand the concept of back office processes, including virtual shopping baskets, CustID and authentication, customer tracking, payment processing, stock control, despatch and delivery

- To draw diagrams that illustrate:
  - the chain of events leading to online purchases
  - the back office chain of events triggered by the purchase
  - the flow of information into and out of the organisation as a result of a purchase

The term **back office processes** refers to all the events that take place 'behind the scenes' of the website. These processes are invisible to the customer but are essential to complete the transaction.

Maintenance of the virtual shopping basket

The virtual shopping basket (also known as a shopping cart) works just like a regular supermarket trolley (but with additional features). The virtual shopping basket allows you to:

- add and remove products

- view the contents of the basket

- view a subtotal of the cost so far.

The virtual shopping basket is based on a model of a real supermarket system, but it includes more advanced features. Imagine being able to get a subtotal of the cost of the shopping at the click of a button before you get to the checkout!

In practice, the web-enabled shopping basket is actually a data capture device. Behind the shopping basket there is a powerful database that records all the items in the basket. When you click the 'buy' button, the product details are copied from the appropriate record in the website's database to a list of purchases. This list includes the product name, an image of the product and the item price.

As you continue shopping and adding to the cart, the 'virtual invoice' keeps track of your purchases and provides a running total.

<blockquote>

Exercise

Go to www.dabs.com and go through the process of adding a DVD recorder, a USB2 pen drive and a digital camera to your shopping basket. At each step in the process use the 'edit/view basket' link to keep track of your purchases.

Write some brief notes to a friend who is an inexperienced Internet user, describing the process of shopping in this way.

</blockquote>

Identification and authentication routines

When you enter an online shop with the intent to purchase, you have to make yourself known to the system. This requires the first-time customer to register their details with the online company. As part of this registration process personal details will be recorded, including name, address, postcode and telephone number. At some point in the process, the customer will be asked to select a user name (often their email address) and a password.

These details will then be used for all future visits to the store:

- the user name to identify the customer
- the password to authenticate the customer (i.e. confirm that they are who they say they are)

Note: This password is crucial to your security. You should not divulge it to anyone or send it via any unsecure means such as email.

<blockquote>

Exercise

Using the Internet, search for articles on the following:
Phishing (fake branded websites)
Identity theft
Spam emails

Write a definition of each of these terms and describe how it represents an abuse of customer information and identity.

</blockquote>

Real time tracking of customer actions

Real time tracking of customer actions can be accomplished using cookies, which we will discuss in more detail in section 2.5. Customers who have logged in to a website can also be effectively monitored by the system. Such monitoring can help the company as they try to target appropriate advertising materials at the potential customer. For example, when the customer logs in, the system database will have a record of all previous sales. It can then send a pop-up advertising a discount on an appropriate product for that client. The discount will often only be valid on that day, which encourages the client to make an immediate purchase and increases the chances of customer loyalty by providing such a personalised loyalty bonus.

Payment processing

As we've already discussed, the advent of online shopping meant that methods of making online payments had to be developed. For companies just starting out it can be expensive to set up an online payment system. Linking in to the major banks and having the facilities to accept credit card payments involves an initial set-up charge as well as ongoing monthly subscriptions. A less expensive alternative is to register with an online facility such as PayPal and pay a percentage of the payment received for every transaction.

Websites that are able to take credit card details must have safe facilities that are clearly advertised as secure. Any failure here will inevitably lead to the loss of customers and place the future of the online business in jeopardy.

Stock control

The great thing about an e-commerce site is that almost everything is automated. The database keeps track of all of the products, customer details, order pick lists (see Despatch and delivery section below), prices and supplier details. This makes it very easy for the system to manage stock. Tight stock control is very important, because too much stock means that the e-shop has expended money before it needed to. The case study below includes an exaggerated example of poor stock control to illustrate the point.

Case Study

An e-shop had an inexperienced buyer who ordered 500 LCD displays. Reviewing the history of sales for the e-shop reveals that the company sells a maximum of 50 LCD displays per month. This means that the company have 10 months worth of stock that has to be paid for up front and that takes up valuable space in the warehouse. There is a one month delivery turnaround from the supplier, which means that the most LCD displays the company needs to order per month is about 55 (this includes a 10% leeway in case of additional orders being requested). Each LCD display costs the company £340. We can work out the value of the excess stock in the first month by subtracting 55 from 500 and multiplying by the cost (£340).

500 − 55 = 445
445 × £350 = £155,750

So the company has £155,750 tied up in stock! Realising their mistake, the company won't order any more LCD displays until the stock level has reduced to about 50.

You can see from this scenario that the company is tied to this stock. If they have other financial needs, they won't be able to use the money that is tied up in the excess LCD display stock. The stock does have a value but only after it has been sold, at the rate of 50 displays per month. The company also runs the risk of the LCD display becoming less popular as newer models are introduced, and they may not sell their stock at all.

Despatch and delivery

Despatch and delivery is one of the most labour-intensive elements of the online shop, as it involves warehouse and delivery staff rather than automated database systems. For each order the warehouse staff will receive a 'pick' list which identifies:

- the customer name and address
- the alternative delivery address if one is specified
- the items for delivery
- any special instructions, such as next day delivery, insured delivery etc.

With this information, staff are able to go to the appropriate storage shelves, pick the items, wrap them, address them and send them to the despatch area to await collection by the courier.

Diagrams that Describe Events

You will need to draw several diagrams for your e-portfolio as evidence of your understanding of electronic processes. You might like to try using the drawing tools available in Microsoft Word to assist you with this task. Chapter 2.9 provides a step-by-step guide to using some of the drawing tools within Word.

The process of making an online purchase

Let's draw a diagram to represent the process of a customer making an online purchase. First we need to list each of the events in the chain in the order in which they occur:

- customer logs on to the website
- customer enters a user name and password
- computer system authenticates the customer
- customer searches for a product
- customer makes a selection and adds the item to their shopping basket
- customer confirms the order
- customer enters valid credit card details
- computer authenticates the customer's ability to pay
- customer logs out.

This is a very basic chain of events but it does give a good idea of how the system works. Once we have written the list, we can use it as the basis for creating our diagram. As you can see in Figure 2.18, we need to include alternative scenarios, such as the customer leaving the site without making a purchase. We also need to make distinctions between the different types of events in the process, which weren't apparent in our original list.

You will notice that three different shapes have been used in this information flow diagram:

- a rectangle to denote a **process**
- a rhombus to denote **data entry**
- a diamond to denote a **decision**.

The chain of events triggered by the purchase

Now let's try drawing a diagram to represent the chain of events that the online purchase triggers within the organisation. Here's a possible list of the events in the order they occur:

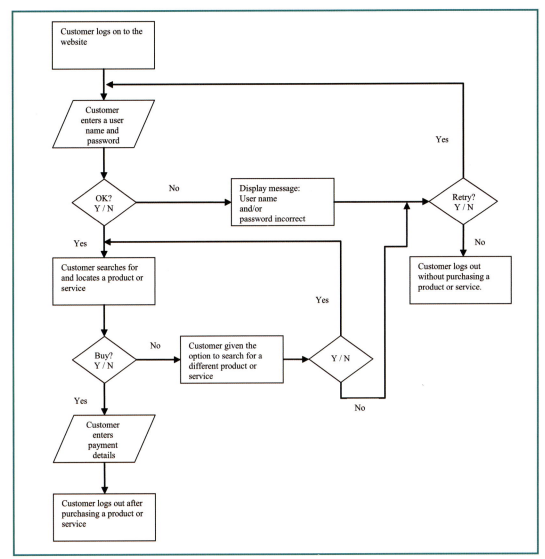

Figure 2.18

- The customer places an order.
- The system checks that:
  - ▲ the customer's details are correct
  - ▲ the customer's means of payment has been validated.
- The system checks that the item is in stock.

- The system debits the database by the number of items purchased.

- The system also checks whether the purchase has taken the number in stock to below the reorder number. If so:

  ▲ the system places an order with the suppliers.

- The receipt is printed for the customer.

- A pick list is generated for the warehouse.

- The goods are packed and despatched.

Now let's place these steps in an information flow diagram, as shown in Figure 2.19.

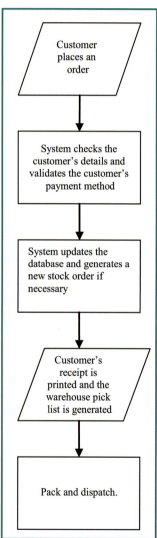

Figure 2.19

Notice that we've used the term 'receipt' here and not 'invoice'. An invoice is a document that asks the purchaser for payment, usually within 30 days of the purchase date. An e-commerce site selling to the public does not offer this 30 day account facility – the customer is expected to pay up-front, before receipt of the goods. That is why a receipt of purchase is produced to be sent with the goods to the customer, instead of an invoice.

The flow of information into and out of the organisation

Let's consider the information that flows around the whole organisation as a result of the purchase. First we'll make a list of the groups of people involved and how they interact with each other.

Customers	These are key players who keep the company solvent by placing orders and paying for goods and/or services.
Accounts	This department ensures that the financial aspects are taken care of: they pay suppliers for the goods supplied to the e-business; they take money from customers; they pay the company's staff.
Warehouse	This department receives order details from customers and despatches the goods. They receive goods from the suppliers.
Suppliers	The suppliers send out goods to the warehouse in response to orders made by the warehouse staff.
Sales	The sales team receives and processes orders from the customers and liaise with the warehouse.

Figure 2.20 shows how this whole process can be represented in a flow diagram. In this diagram we have used a rectangle to denote company departments and a rhombus to denote external agencies.

In practice, and depending on the size of the e-business, some of these departments might not be quite so clearly defined. For example, if you were to set up your own website selling second-hand CDs, you and your friends might double up on some of the responsibilities to save money.

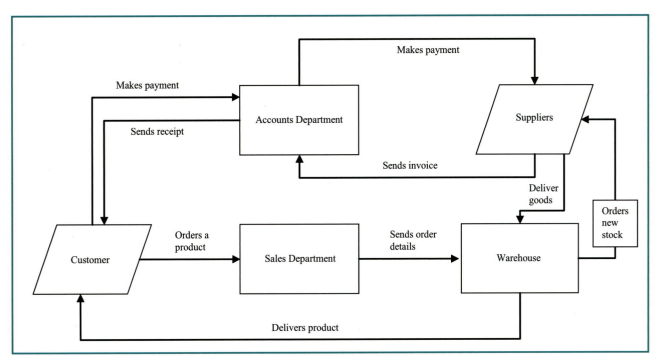

Figure 2.20

Portfolio Builder: *Using these diagrams as a guide, produce your own flow diagrams following the e-portfolio instructions. You will need to consult your teacher or lecturer before you attempt this task. Make sure you sketch out your ideas on paper first. Then, when you are sure you've covered all of the criteria, generate your diagrams. Be accurate and ensure you label the diagrams correctly. Your arrows must show the flow in the correct direction.*

e-customers

OBJECTIVES

- To understand how e-shops hold information about us in order to influence our purchasing decisions

The first task of any e-shop is to persuade the customer to make a purchase. This chapter reviews some of the methods used by transactional websites to find out about us and our shopping habits.

Purchase history and sales information

History always serves a purpose. As we look back at the mistakes of others (and ourselves), we can resolve not to make the same mistakes again. For the e-shop business a customer's purchasing history is a gold mine of information, as it informs the company about what we like to purchase. With this information, the company knows which product advertisements to target us with.

The fact is that, no matter how catchy the advertisement, unless the product is something that is of interest to us, the advertisement will fail to attract us and may even discourage us from returning to a particular website.

Case Study

Have you ever seen a dancing car? Perhaps not, but most of us have been entertained by the advertisement for the Citroen C4. The 30-second TV commercial was conceived by the Citroen creative team at ad agency Euro RSCG's London office. They hired Justin Timberlake's choreographer Marty Kudelka and used the music of electronic dance outfit, Les Rythmes Digitales. They 'cyber scanned' a Citroen C4 with lasers and created a perfect 3D model.

Marty Kudelka was then hooked up with motion sensors over his whole body to capture the moves of his dance. In this way he provided the movement which high-powered computers transferred to the digital images of the car. Two months later and Citroen had a multi-million pound marketing campaign underway.

You can find details of the advertisement by going to **www.theembassyvfx.com** (look in the Portfolio section). As things change so quickly on the Internet, you may need to do your own search to find details and images from the advertisement.

Exercise

Hold a survey within your class. Download a QuickTime version of the ad and play it in class – use the interactive whiteboard if you can. You will find a good quality video on www.theembassyvfx.com or use a search engine to find the video. The Embassy is the company that created the special effects part of the advertisement.

Carry out a vote to find out:

1. How many people really liked the ad?
2. How many people think of a C4 every time they hear the 'Jacques Your Body' track?
3. How many people bought the C4?

The results of the exercise will probably give positive results for questions 1 and 2 but less so for question 3. The reason for this is in the targeting. Although lots of people like the ad and think of that 'robot car' every time they hear the music, most will be just 'window shoppers'. They look, they like but they don't purchase.

Despite all this, it is still highly likely that this advertisement for Citroen has been extremely successful and resulted in increased car sales – it will have reached its target audience as well as many other people. It would be very difficult to target the advert at just drivers, so it was distributed to all TV viewers, a proportion of whom are drivers wanting to buy a new car of the Citroen C4 type.

Target advertising is all about finding out what your audience likes and then tailoring your presentation to suit.

Figure 2.21

Online shops are able to be much more focused in targeting their adverts, based on the data they have gathered about us. Have you ever filled in an online survey to try and win a desirable object? As you answered all the questions about your likes and interests, you were in fact contributing to a massive database that in the future could be used to send you adverts (emails, newsletters, etc.) that are targeted to your particular likes and interests (unless you checked the box requesting that the company doesn't send you emails).

Loyalty schemes

As you hand over your supermarket reward card at the till, you are participating in a loyalty scheme. The more you buy, the more points you gain which results in you getting more vouchers. Here are some more examples of loyalty schemes:

- a free DVD or computer game after you've had your card stamped 10 times at the DVD rental shop

- vouchers at the petrol station: collect 10 and you get £5 off your fuel

- a clothes catalogue offering £10 off your next order if you spend £150 today.

All of these schemes require that you return to the shop a number of times before you gain your reward – encouraging you to make more purchases.

Online shops can do the same. That's why you get emails from time to time advertising special offers. As you spend more time with a particular online shop, you will be giving more information about your likes and dislikes. Sometimes this happens covertly, in other words without your knowledge. The system can detect and record which areas of the site you frequent and whether you make a purchase or not.

Surveys

As has been mentioned previously, e-shops need to get to know their customers. The big disadvantage for an e-business is that they will never meet their customers and they are highly unlikely to ever speak to them over the phone. One way to get around this is to get customers to complete surveys. This is the online way of 'getting to know you'!

Companies often encourage us to fill in their surveys by offering the chance to win prizes if we participate. The following questions are typical of online surveys:

- What is your age?

- Which newspapers do you read?

- How many children do you have?

- Do you smoke?

- Which of the following holidays appeal to you?

All of these will provide the company with information about the products we are likely to be interested in.

The survey commissioner will then pass your details and the results of the survey to associated companies who may then target you with certain products. For example, in the example survey shown in Figure 2.22, if you select 'Family holiday', you can expect to receive emails with details of family holidays to France that you can buy.

Competitions

Competitions work in a very similar way to surveys. People are persuaded to complete surveys because there is the lure of a new car, holiday or other high-value prize. The cost of the prize is seen by the company as simply an expense to be set against their marketing budget.

The lure of the prize is often enough to persuade potential customers to part with their email address, telephone numbers and other personal data such as their hobbies and interests.

Figure 2.22

Cookies

Cookies are small text files which the 'visiting' web server sends to our computer's hard disk. The cookie is used to make a relationship between our computer and the website we visit. It enables the site to build up a profile of our preferences in order to make our continued visits more efficient.

For example, a cookie can store information about the options we select on a site. The next time we visit the site, the cookie indicates our preferred options without any intervention from us. We may indicate a language preference on our first visit which, on all subsequent visits, will not have to be offered as an option – the cookie will make the decision for us.

Figure 2.23

An e-commerce site can 'interrogate' the cookie to find out how many times we have visited the site and which pages we have viewed. Their system can then change facilities in order to accommodate our likes and dislikes for all future visits.

Spyware

Spyware is not the same as a cookie. Spyware is an executable file which is sometimes added to sample software. It can also be downloaded when we add another facility, like a toolbar to our web browser. Spyware can monitor your computer system and send back information to the originating computer, hence the term spyware. It secretly views our actions and in its mildest form sends back marketing data so that we can be targeted in future with focused advertising. In a more ruthless format, spyware can monitor our key presses and capture such things as user names and passwords, which may be used for fraudulent activities.

You can take action to protect your computer from spyware by installing anti-spyware software. Adaware is a popular spyware 'zapper'. A word of caution: some anti-spyware software actually contains its own spyware with which it monitors your computer use, so beware!

Customer relations

A personalised service

When you visit an e-commerce site and make a purchase, you are essentially faceless – there is no one who knows you. You don't get the personal service you might expect from a shopping trip to a traditional store, such as:

- a friendly greeting
- a helpful assistant
- an adviser who can tell by your body language how you're feeling about a product
- someone to say 'Thank you for your purchase, please call again soon'.

How can a website substitute for this personalised service and add the human touch to the customer's experience? We've seen how cookies can help with this. However, cookies can be deleted or we can set our browser to reject them, thus foiling the e-shops plans for investigating our browsing habits. Alternatively, user registration can provide the website with all the details it needs to offer a personalised service.

Exercise

Go to an e-commerce site and register with them as a prospective customer. After browsing for a minute or two, log out and then return to the e-shop. Do you receive a personalised service (for example, does the website welcome you by name, offer you products based on the pages you visited, etc.)? What suggestions could you make for improving the personalised service of the website?

Persuading customers to spend more

For centuries shop keepers have been in the business of helping us to part with our money. It is not enough for us to fill a large trolley of shopping at the supermarket, they still want us to purchase a couple of packs of sweets on the way out as we pass the checkout. They want us to act on impulse. We probably don't need that pack of chocolates or chewing gum, but it does look inviting as we are waiting in the queue next to the checkout.

Online shops are in an ideal position to assist us with impulse buying. The power of suggestion works very well in the online environment.

If you log on to eBay with your user name and password, all of your previous selling and purchasing activities are made known to you. If you purchase an item and then make a payment with PayPal, the system knows who you are and doesn't need you to type in a delivery address or credit card details as it already has these on file.

Having successfully registered with an e-shop, you can expect a trickle of emails (or perhaps a flood), addressing you by name and highlighting special offers for that particular day or week.

All of this works towards building that vital seller/purchaser relationship.

Offering other products

As an example of this, have a look at **www.play.com** – a website that sells CDs, DVDs and games. If you look at a music CD, the site will show a list of other CDs, using the line, 'Customers who bought XXX also bought YYY'. They are hinting that we should also consider buying one or more of these other CDs as well.

Many transactional websites use similar techniques to encourage additional purchases: for example, the Dabs website use the line, 'Customers who bought this item were also interested in XXX.'

Email shots

Email shots are often used to 'remind' you to return to the shop. They will often be the vehicles for fantastic special offers that they want you to believe are too good to be missed.

Figure 2.24

As we have seen in this chapter, the business of dealing with e-customers can be quite complex. In the next chapter we will be investigating this customer relationship in more detail.

e-consumer awareness

OBJECTIVES

- To discuss the electronic storage and distribution of personal information
- To discuss how this data might be misused
- To investigate measures that can be taken to protect this data

As you've probably noticed throughout this course, it is very easy to copy data when it is in an electronic format. Just consider the copy and paste facility within Microsoft Word: a couple of clicks of the mouse button and the text or image is yours! The same is true of our personal information stored on computer systems. If it is not safeguarded, then a few mouse clicks will allow it to be copied for potentially malicious purposes.

In this information age, we need to be very careful with the way in which we store and transmit personal information. This chapter will discuss the principles involved in safeguarding data.

What information is held about you by organisations?

There are many governmental, business and social organisations that may hold data about us. It is understandable that the government needs to have information about us: where we live, what we do for a living, how much we earn, etc. This information enables them to charge us taxes in order to pay for essential services. It also allows them to compile data on national trends in order to inform future policies.

Businesses and other organisations also need a certain amount of information from us for legitimate purposes. This is not limited to the world of the Internet. Wherever we go companies and organisations are anxious to gain quality information from us in order to gain future sales.

In terms of e-commerce, a business website needs to know our name, address, telephone number and email address, which they will collect when we register on the site. They may also collect other information about us which they will use to target their advertising, for example: the newspapers we read; the TV programmes we watch; our favourite food; our favourite holiday destinations; the types of books we like to read.

When we get to the point of making a purchase, the online business will require bank account or credit card details in order to fully process our order. In some instances we will have to present this information every time we log on to make a purchase. In other cases this data will be permanently stored on file, saving us having to re-enter the data.

In some instances, the company might retrieve some of the data from other sources. For example, depending on the value of the purchase, the company may take up references in the form of a credit report to check if we are likely to be able to pay for the purchase. This information will be given to the company by other financial organisations.

The more we use the Internet to make purchases and for other financial reasons, the more companies will have access to this important information.

How is this information protected?

We discuss the protection of information fully in chapter 2.7. In this section we will briefly outline some of the essential features in any data protection system. These are:

- physical security
- user ID and access rights
- encryption
- secure and electronic transactions
- firewalls
- virus protection.

Physical security
Physical security is put in place to prevent loss of data from computers by protecting the computer hardware from damage by fire, flooding, theft, etc. Physical security also includes the use of backup systems which physically copy data and store it in locations well away from the originating data source. In this way, if the building catches fire and the hardware burns, the backup data will still be available in the remote location.

User ID and access rights
People are the weak link when it comes to security. People who don't safeguard their user names and passwords may well encounter security problems at some point. People who choose obvious passwords such as a pet's name are also at risk. Many companies make provisions for lost passwords by holding other security data about clients, such as a mother's maiden name or a favourite pet's name. Writing down a password is an easy way of giving an opportunist criminal the chance of free data access.

Encryption
Encryption of data involves jumbling the data at one end of the system, sending it over the Internet and then reconstituting the message at the receiving end. This sounds very simple, but encryption is a highly specialised field and one which the criminal underworld is continually trying to master.

Secure and electronic transactions (SET)
SET is the process by which electronic money can be transferred relatively safely over the Internet. With the advent of electronic communication in the information age, this area of technology is advancing very rapidly. As computers become bigger and faster, so their 'code cracking' power increases. As technology advances, the need for secure electronic transaction systems becomes even greater.

Firewalls and virus protection

Firewalls include both hardware and software solutions which stop harmful data being transmitted via the Internet onto our machines. Combined with good virus protection software, these systems are invaluable in our fight to keep the 'bad guys' out.

Exercise

Ask your teacher or lecturer if you can make an appointment with the computer lab technician at your school or college. Prepare some questions to ask him or her regarding the security of the systems used in your establishment. Think about issues such as physical security and how passwords are used for network access. After the interview, write a short report indicating the types of security measures in place and how you as a user are expected to assist with these measures.

How accurate is this information?

It is quite difficult to establish just how accurate the data held by organisations is. One of the reasons for this is the huge amount of time it would take to check all the data. Because of the security issues, companies and organisations are very strict about who they give access to, and this would include you if you contacted them in order to check your own data for accuracy. You would undoubtedly have to fill in some forms and provide proof of ID in order to access your data. (For example, if you wanted to check your medical record.)

With the advent of the Internet, there is a good chance that you will have entered at least some of the data the company holds about you yourself. Just think of the number of times you have been asked for your personal information as you've applied for different Internet-based services. In all of these cases, you will have typed this information yourself or used an automatic form filling facility such as that found on the Google toolbar.

What is the data being used for?

Most companies use the data they collect for the purposes of running their business and providing their customers with a better, more efficient service. For example, we would be very frustrated if we had to enter all of our personal data every time we made a purchase at our favourite online shop. We would probably all agree in this instance that it is reasonable for the company to hold this data.

Where problems arise is when unscrupulous companies then take the data and sell it to other interested parties. If you ask your parents, they will confirm that they have been telephoned by sales personnel offering them services that they certainly didn't ask for or want. It is often hard to work out where these companies have gained the phone numbers and other personal details.

Who has access to this data?

There is a great deal of information freely available to anyone who has the time to go and find it. Here are some examples:

- If people get into trouble with the law, details of their crimes may well be published in local newspapers.

- The electoral register contains details of all the people who are old enough to vote and is freely available.

- If we submit details of plans to alter our homes, anyone can go to the council offices to view our designs.

- You can even log on to certain websites and find out how much your neighbours paid for their homes (as long as they purchased after 1st April 2000). Try it out for yourself on **www.ourproperty.co.uk**.

Are identity theft and identity fraud a real concern?

There is legislation in place which aims to control the way organisations and individuals are able to exchange information. There is specific legislation regulating online transactions, and there are strict rules and guidelines which companies and individuals must adhere to. These rules cover:

- data protection
- civil rights
- distance selling.

Exercise

Visit **www.silicon.com** and search for recent articles about identity theft. Use the information you find to support your e-portfolio work for this chapter.

Portfolio Builder: Use the Internet to find information on the laws governing data protection, civil rights and distance selling.

Visit *www.informationcommissioner.gov.uk* and follow the links to find information on data protection, including the eight guiding principles. (Use the Data Protection link on the left-hand menu, then click on the Guidance link, then on The Data Protection principles.)

Visit *www.businesslink.gov.uk* to gain information about the distance selling rules and guidelines for the UK. Use the website's search facility to search for 'distance selling and online trading'.

Visit *www.internetrights.org.uk* to find information on how our civil rights are affected by ICT and the Internet. (Follow the ICT Policy links on the left-hand menu.)

When you have gathered your information, produce an article on current legislation. You can use this work for Part (c) of the Assessment Criteria.

Security

OBJECTIVES

- To review possible security threats to an organisation
- To evaluate a range of risk minimisation strategies

Security has always been a significant concern for individuals and organisations who use computers. A quick scan of a professional IT journal will reveal articles covering security failures of one type or another. In recent years examples include military personnel leaving a laptop containing secret information in a car, and major online companies inadvertently allowing customer accounts to be breached because of unknown flaws in their systems.

A growing number of organisations have installed wireless networks that do not have the appropriate security features enabled. Anyone with a wireless-enabled laptop or palm computer could stand outside their premises and gain free access to their Internet connection. This might seem harmless enough, just someone getting some free bandwidth. But what if the individual is a criminal and using your traceable IP address for illegal activity?

This chapter reviews security issues and solutions in some detail. At the end of the chapter you should have a good idea of what is required in order to implement and maintain a secure computer system.

Risk assessment

A risk assessment is a procedure used for identifying potential risks and then putting in place measures to minimise the likelihood of them occurring. Before conducting a risk assessment it is worth considering the value of the data and information that is stored on a company's system. A company database containing all of its customer contacts can be stored on a CD costing 50p, but what is the real value of the CD?

Exercise

Think about the real value of the CD mentioned in the above paragraph. If the CD was the only copy, how much would it cost to replace? You should consider the time and number of people that would be needed to collect all the data again, as well as the availability of the information from other sources.

Now that we've established that the value of the data is high, let's start our risk assessment by identifying some possible threats to data files stored on computers. These include:

- physical risks from fire or flooding
- attacks from hackers and other malicious sources such as viruses
- human error, for example, staff might delete or corrupt important files by accident
- security weaknesses in system software or application packages

Having established the possible risks, we then need to list and grade each one with a risk factor of high, medium or low. Grading the risks helps us to prioritise our resources to minimise the risk. Notice the use of the word 'minimise' – usually it is impossible to eradicate the risk completely; often the best we can do is to ensure we have a recovery plan in place so that in the event of mishap we can retrieve the situation fairly quickly with minimum damage.

Physical security

Most of us think of computer security in terms of anti-virus software, logins, passwords and firewalls. These are all essential features of a good computer security system, but are no good at all if someone steals your computer!

Physical security is concerned with robust measures that protect your PC and its data from:

- theft
- accidental damage such as fire and flood
- intentional damage.

Physical threats can be minimised by ensuring that computers and their data are:

- stored in secure locations, preferably out of public view and behind locked doors – some companies try to prevent easy theft by having no computers on the ground floor of their premises
- protected with the aid of fire and burglar alarms
- equipped with backup systems that are stored in another building, away from the main computer room
- secured with wires and locks, effectively fastening computers to desks to avoid theft.

Exercise

The Carnegie Mellon Software Engineering Institute has an excellent website on computer security, known as the Cert website. Visit this website (www.cert.org) and find the article on home computer security – scroll down the home page to the Articles section and click on the Home Computer Security link. Make a list of the nine tasks that are recommended for securing a home computer.

User ID and access rights

Most work places and educational establishments have large computer networks with many users. To safeguard the security of the system it is necessary to ensure that each user logging on to the system is who they say they are. This is achieved by requiring each user to enter a user name and password in order to log on. If the user name and/or password do not match those stored in a secure file on the system, they will not be allowed entry.

On many systems the user is allowed up to three attempts at entering their details. If after three attempts, they fail to enter the correct details, the system will allow no further attempts until a system administrator has provided authorisation. In addition, systems can require users to change their password monthly to ensure higher levels of security. The weakness in this system is the human element – users may tell others their password or write it on a post-it note which they then stick to their computer monitor!

In order to overcome such risks to the system, other methods of identifying users are being developed, including:

- fingerprint scan

- retinal scan

- face scan

- hand (vein structure) scan

- voice recognition (although this is vulnerable because people can alter their voices).

All of these methods can be used to allow authorised users access to physical areas (such as areas of a building) as well as to secure computer systems.

Exercise

Write an article comparing and contrasting the security of electronic communications (using the material in this chapter to help you) with the traditional alternatives, for example, fax, telephone and post. Think about the number of people involved at each stage in these processes and about the opportunities for breaches of security.

Encryption

When we are sending files over the Internet we need them to be secure. This can be achieved by encoding the information in such a way that only the person with the right 'key' can decode it. Cryptography has been around since Roman times, and is seeing a new use in our digital age.

Exercise

A code has been applied to the following message. What do you think the message says? Because you don't have the 'key', you may find this difficult. However, if you persist using trial and error, you may be able to crack it.
PDA ZECEPWH AYKJKIU

There are two main types of computer-based encryption systems available today.

1. Symmetric key encryption

In symmetric key encryption, each computer involved in a communication, both the sender and the receiver, must have the code installed. This secret code provides the key to unlocking a message. The sending computer encrypts the message before sending it over the Internet; the receiving computer uses the secret code in order to reconstitute the message in readable form.

As a very simple example, you may decide to create a coded message by substituting each original letter with the letter that is 3 letters further along in the alphabet. (Note that this is a clue to the encryption system used in the exercise above – plus or minus a digit.)

A variation of this method, instead of shifting individual letters, is to group the message into blocks which are then shifted. Letters within the blocks are then shifted by variable amounts; this can be very complex for the human mind to solve.

Even though this does seem complicated, modern computers have rendered these methods useless for secure communications. For example, a computer could be programmed to try all of the shift variations until the code is cracked. In addition, it is essential that you have a secure system for passing the encoding key. What happens if a third party intercepts this transmission and intercepts the key? For these reasons, symmetric key encryption is not effective in today's information age.

2. Public key encryption

Public key encryption uses two keys: the public key, as the name suggests, is known to everyone, while the private (or secret) key is known only to the recipient's computer.

If we wanted to send a secure message using this system, we would use the recipient's public key to encrypt the message, the recipient's computer then uses the private key to decrypt it. Both keys are related in such a way that only the public key can be used to encrypt messages that the private key will subsequently decrypt. Even if you know the public key, it is virtually impossible to calculate the private key from this.

Let's take a look at an example of how the public key system is implemented. You may be familiar with the term **secure socket layer** (SSL). This is an Internet security protocol used by browsers and servers to transmit confidential information. SSL comes under an overall network security protocol known as **transport layer security** (TLS).

Figure 2.25

Whenever you enter a website that's using a secure protocol such as TLS there will be some subtle changes in the browser. Let's look at the NatWest bank website as an example.

Figure 2.25 shows that the URL for the NatWest website looks just the same as any other website. Now let's see what happens as we enter the secure area for personal banking. To get to this area we need to log in using our customer details.

Figure 2.26 illustrates the fact that, as we attempt to go to a secure area, the **http** address prefix changes to **https**, indicating that the browser has entered a secure mode of working. In addition, the status bar on the bottom of the browser window (bottom right) will show a small padlock. This indicates that a secure session is now taking place.

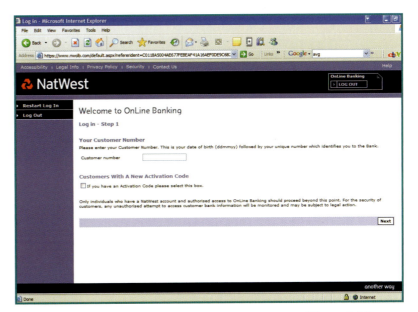

Figure 2.26

Public key encryption relies on a system that uses hash values. A hash value is a number that has been calculated by applying a mathematical formula to the original input number. Here is an example of this concept:

input number	algorithm	hash value
57342	Input × 221	12672582

Imagine how difficult it would be to work out the original input number if you were given just the final hash value of 12672582. Of course, the task becomes very easy if you are also given the algorithm used to generate the hash value.

This is a simple example of what is a far more complex system in practice. Public keys are generated by using very large hash values. It is not unusual for a 128-bit

Portfolio Builder: **In a small group, discuss security threats to businesses and how these will impact on the safety of customer data. Extend your discussion to the use of laptops by employees and how this introduces further security management issues. Write up the main points of discussion for inclusion in your e-portfolio.**

number to be used – 128-bit numbers have a very large number of unique possibilities, making the code extremely difficult to crack.

Secure electronic transactions

SET is the secure electronic transactions protocol developed by MasterCard and Visa. This system enables credit card transactions to be managed securely over the Internet. SET allows both the buyer and seller to authenticate themselves via a digital certificate. Digital certificates are issued by the Certificate Authority (CA) which verifies that the public key attached to the certificate does actually belong to the person/organisation already stated.

Firewalls

The firewall takes its name from the physical firewall used by firefighters to help prevent large fires from spreading from one area to another.

The firewall on a computer network acts in a similar way by filtering incoming data from the Internet and blocking potentially harmful Internet data. Rules are set up by the network administrators to establish exactly what types of data the firewall will or will not allow through. Firewalls are entirely customisable and can also be set up to impose additional restrictions on certain computers, for example preventing selected computers from sending and receiving attachments. In this way the company has a high degree of flexibility in how it manages its flow of data in and out of the organisation.

The Internet uses protocols such as IP, HTTP, FTP, SMTP, etc. A firewall can be customised to block or allow any for these. For example, you could set up your firewall to only allow certain computers to use the FTP (file transfer protocol). A server enables Internet data access via numbered ports. For example, a web server uses port 80 while an FTP server uses port 21. As a network manager within a company you may decide to configure your firewall to block all port 21 activities except for perhaps one PC. It will then be much easier to monitor and manage that if you have 20 PCs with this facility.

A firewall provides a certain level of protection from the following:

- known operating system bugs
- email bombs – these are multiple copies of the same email designed to 'clog' your account
- viruses – although virus software should also be used
- source routing – this allows hackers to mimic data packets coming from certain sites

Exercise

Using the Internet, research four of the items in the list above and write a detailed report describing the type of threat, what it does and how a user can defend their PC against it.

- macros containing malicious source code

- remote login – where someone tries to control your computer from another PC on the Internet.

- service attack – this is when a server is inundated with a series of bogus requests: the server tries to respond but can't locate the issuing (hacker's) system; eventually the server will crash through overload.

A firewall should be viewed as only part of the security measures adopted by an organisation. Here is a priority list for the security measures that need to be implemented on a system:

1. Choose an ISP that offers 'server side' virus and spam filters.

2. Install a hardware router that has a built-in firewall between your modem and computer network.

3. Make sure you keep up-to-date with your 'antis': anti-virus, anti-spam, anti-spyware and anti-phishing software – many of these are freely available from such sites as **www.download.com**.

Virus protection

On January 27th 2004, the Internet version of the Times newspaper, the Times Online, reported that the MY DOOM virus had affected an estimated 200,000 to 300,000 computers, some of which were voluntarily shut down to prevent the virus spreading. This is one illustration of the serious problems that can be caused by a well-designed virus. Viruses come in many different guises, and each has its own peculiar traits that are designed to infect our computers. Terms such as Trojan Horse, boot sector virus, worms, macro virus and email virus are all names that have been given to virus-type threats to our computers.

It is possible to avoid problems with viruses by installing virus protection or anti-virus software on your computer. This software is designed to monitor the computer system, checking that no abnormal activity is taking place. This software normally has routines for detecting and immobilising viruses. It is vital that the software is kept up-to-date and most anti-virus software is designed to make regular request to the company's home page for updates.

A company called Grisoft distributes anti-virus software and has a free edition which is for home and non-commercial use. Go to **www.grisoft.com**, click on the AVG Products link in the left-hand menu and select AVG Free Edition. This free software provides adequate protection for home computers.

Tip:

In this life, things go wrong when you least expect them to. A hard drive may crash due to mechanical failure; a virus may attack your computer and render it useless; you may leave your disk on the bus or lose your pen drive. And for some inexplicable reason these catastrophes always seem to happen when you're working on a large project that has taken many hours of hard work and you haven't taken the time to make regular backup copies.

You can save yourself a lot of hard work and headaches by following the security guidelines in this section.

Exercise

If you have a firewall-enabled router at home, or perhaps a software equivalent, try the following. Go to www.grc.com and try their ShieldsUP security test. Scroll down to the ShieldsUP link on the website's home page, then click the Proceed button. You may then choose options such as File Sharing, Common Ports, etc., as shown in Figure 2.27.

Figure 2.27

The program will check your computer while you are online and give you a report indicating how well your firewall is protecting your PC.

The Database

8

OBJECTIVES

- **To examine how the database supports e-commerce applications**
- **To understand how a database may be structured**

In any e-commerce application a database is used to store:

- products and prices
- stock levels
- customer details
- orders from customers.

Database Principles

Before you start to design and build a database there are a few principles that you will need to familiarise yourself with.

- A database is a collection of related data: for example, a hospital database stores data about its patients.
- A database is very much like a filing cabinet but much more efficient in terms of its capacity for storing and searching for data.
- Database users can **search**, **sort** and produce combined **reports** very quickly.

Exercise

Make a comparison of using a database and using traditional filing techniques. Make a list of the advantages and disadvantages of each. You may use the Internet to gather information.

A database file consists of a number of **related records** and each **record** consists of a number of **related fields**. For example, the hospital database file will contain many hundreds of patient records. Each record identifies one individual patient and contains a number of related fields, such as: First Name (field 1), Middle Name (field 2), Surname (field 3), Date of Birth (field 4) etc.

Every patient record will have the same number of fields, but not all of the fields need to contain data. For example, a patient called Ben Jones does not have a middle name, therefore the Middle Name field in his record would not contain any data. The field names (such as 'First Name', 'Middle Name' etc.) are labels for the 'containers' which hold the data. Each of these containers must be of a certain size (character length) and **data type**. For example, the First Name field in the hospital database example has been set up so that the data type is text (that is, alphabetical characters) and is a maximum of 15 characters long. Databases allow us to specify a whole range of different data types in order to simplify our job as database designers. Some of the data types available in Microsoft Access include: Text, Date/ Time, Number, Currency, Yes/No, Memo.

A database consists of four main elements or features.

Tables: This is where the data is stored. The table consists of a number of fields, each of which is a label for the individual data item stored. Each field is assigned properties, depending on the type of data which will be stored.

Forms: Data can be typed directly into the database table, but designing an input form makes the database look more professional, more user-friendly and less prone to **transcription errors**. You can also view information via forms, but **reports** are much better suited for hard copy viewing.

Queries: As the name suggests, queries allow you to extract information from your database. For example, in a police database, if you needed a list of the first names and surnames of all officers who held an advanced driving certificate, a query would enable you to achieve this (if the database has a field to contain this information of course).

Reports: Tables, forms and queries can all be printed. They do, however, look very basic. Creating a report will make the presentation of your data more professional. Reports can be set up to represent a complete table or a query. Reports are very flexible and allow you to use many different formatting features to improve the appearance of the printed output.

Validation rules

As one might expect, validation helps to ensure that our data is valid both when it is first entered into the database or edited at a later time. For example, if we want a user to enter a percentage score into a student grades database, then this data item must be a number greater than or equal to zero, and less than or equal to 100. Any number outside of these bounds is invalid. If a user entered 101, for example, it would be desirable for the database to generate an error message for the user.

Validation rules can be used for the following purposes:

● Range checks: This is used when the number entered must be within a certain range, as in the percentage score example above.

● Presence checks: This is used when a data item must be present; for example, an e-commerce website needs the customer's postcode in order to send them the goods, so the Postcode field must have an entry.

● Length checks: A validation rule can limit the length of string that may be entered by the user. For example, you may set the maximum length of string for the Surname field to 20 characters.

- Format checks: This is useful when we want the database to restrict the user to a certain data entry format. For example, a Telephone Number field may have an input mask that insists that the number is in the format (00000) 000000, with the actual data being a valid telephone number, for example (01792) 768334.

There will be more on validation rules in chapter 2.9.

In small groups discuss the concept of validation rules and come up with some examples of validation rules that could be applied to database fields. Think of some examples of data that would not be valid according to your rules. For example, one rule that you could apply to a Surname field is that it cannot contain any numbers – if it does, then an error message should indicate that the data entered is invalid.

Types of database

When a user visits a transactional website, all they see is what is known as the 'front end' of the process. This is the part that allows the user to interact with the website and make purchases. In the background there will be a database which is presenting the products, keeping track of purchases, and generally managing the whole process.

Flat file databases

The simplest form of database is the electronic equivalent of a **card file system**. Sometimes known as a **flat file**, this type of database is good for keeping such things as names, addresses and telephone numbers. It is effective for minimal database requirements, such as a client list held by a beauty salon or hairdresser, but this approach has many limitations.

Let's look at an example of a flat file and investigate the limitations. Imagine you've been asked by one of your friends or relatives to set up a database to manage the loans made by a Video/DVD library. A flat file solution might look something like the table of data shown in Figure 2.28.

Code	Title	Cert	Hire Cost (£)	Member Number	Member Name	Address	Post Code	Telephone Number	Date Hired
V005	Lord of War	15	2.00	M007	Peter Lamont	28, Halt Street	BS5 6AT	01983 773244	20/09/06
D009	Pride and Prejudice	U	3.00	M051	Ruth Ness	30, Tree Green	BS5 4AS	01983 704211	21/09/06
V051	Goal!	12A	2.00	M051	Ruth Ness	30, Tree Green	BS5 4AS	01983 704211	21/09/06
V067	Domino	15	2.00						
D065	Four Brothers	15	3.00	M010	Hugh Davies	41, Bristol Way	BS5 3AT	01983 721111	21/09/06
D068	Serenity	15	3.00						
D069	Wallace and Gromit	U	3.00						

Figure 2.28

The main problem with this database is duplicate data. A flat file database forces repetition – for example, there is no way of avoiding typing in the name, address and postcode of a library member for each DVD borrowed – this gives rise to errors and inconsistencies when data is both entered and updated. And how tedious for the database user to have to enter the member's full details for each additional title they borrow!

Think about the problems that would occur with a database on a much larger scale. A hospital database holds thousands of patient records. Each patient is assigned a doctor/consultant. Of course a doctor/consultant will be assigned numerous patients. In this case, a flat file approach is a recipe for disaster. Every time the same doctor was assigned to a patient his/her name, surgery address, contact phone number and any other details held would have to be entered into the system – a very laborious task and one which is prone to transcription errors.

Relational databases

In order to overcome the problems of flat file databases, we can set up a **relational database**. All but the most basic of databases will require the designer to set up relationships between the data tables, and a relational database will certainly improve matters for our video/DVD library. The first step is to split our database into two tables: a Member table and a Video file, as shown in Figure 2.29.

Videos

Code	Title	Cert	Hire Cost (£)	Member Number	Date Hired
V005	Lord of War	15	2.00	M007	20/09/06
D009	Pride and Prejudice	U	3.00	M051	21/09/06
V051	Goal!	12A	2.00	M051	21/09/06
V067	Domino	15	2.00		
D065	Four Brothers	15	3.00	M010	21/09/06
D068	Serenity	15	3.00		
D069	Wallace and Gromit	U	3.00		

Members

Member Number	Member Name	Address	Post Code	Telephone Number
M007	Peter Lamont	28, Halt Street	BS5 6AT	01983 773244
M051	Ruth Ness	30, Tree Green	BS5 4AS	01983 704211
M010	Hugh Davies	41, Bristol Way	BS5 3AT	01983 721111

Figure 2.29

Creating one-to-many relationships

We are going to use a 'one-to-many' relationship to link the Videos table to the Members table. In other words, each membership number can appear many times in the Videos table but can appear only once in the Members table.

The Member Number field is used to link the two tables together. In the Members table, this membership number is called the **primary key** and allows each member record to be uniquely identified. In the Video table this same Member Number is known as the **foreign key**.

Now all we need to do for each video loan, is enter the Member Number and date into the appropriate field of the Videos table. This solution is not the most elegant, but it does show how two tables can provide a neater way of doing things and avoid some duplication of data. In a relational database it is not unusual to have solutions with many different tables. Each table stores specific, related information and common fields provide the links between the tables.

Exercise

Write a short report presenting two reasons why a relational database can be a better choice than a flat file system. Use some data tables to illustrate your report and to highlight valid reasons.

Other Database Features

Importing data

Very often the data to be stored in a database already exists in another format. For example, a shopping website manager may have been keeping customer records in a spreadsheet before the fully enabled e-shopping site was created. This spreadsheet data may easily be **imported** into the database, saving time and effort re-typing the data and avoiding any possible transcription errors.

Sorting

The sort facility is one of the many powerful features of a database. As you already know, data doesn't get entered into a database in alphabetical order or by order value. If patients became ill in alphabetical order of surname then the sort facility in a hospital database would not be required – but this, of course, is not the case. But the hospital administrators may want to sort patient names alphabetically for any number of reasons.

Similarly, customers visiting a shopping website might want the data they view to be in a specific format: for example, they might want to see possible alternative purchases listed in ascending price order. This will allow them to see the cheapest products first. Databases are capable of sorting data from multiple fields with exceptional speed and accuracy. Figure 2.30 shows an example of the sort facility in

Figure 2.30

action – on the PC World website, we did a search for MP3 players and then used the 'Refine your Search' option to see the results in ascending order of price.

Searches

Another essential database feature is the 'search' facility. An online store catalogue can contain around 5,000 different items so it's crucial that the website has an effective search facility, allowing the customer to quickly locate the desired product.

Reports

As mentioned earlier, reports are used to help present the data stored in a database. Reports do for databases what graphs and charts do for spreadsheets. They take ordinary-looking information generated as a result of a search, query or sort and turn the results into documents that can make a presentation look really professional. The concept of grouping allows you to further enhance your output by, for example, grouping all orders received from individual customers on your e-shopping site; thus making your reports much more easily read and user-friendly.

Now that we've looked at the principles of a relational database, the next step is to use some software to build and implement a working model. To do this we will use Access, which is part of the Microsoft Office suite of applications software.

ICT Skills

OBJECTIVES

- To create diagrammatic representations of systems, events and information flows
- To use a range of tools and techniques within the Access database environment
- To create a database that will fulfil the course requirements

In this unit we have been investigating e-commerce-enabled websites and the services that they offer. The work you complete in this section will enable you to build an Access database for your e-portfolio. In this chapter, we will go through all of the practical skills you need to complete this task, from producing the initial designs right through to building the database. We will be using the example of a typical e-shopping database to present the ICT skills you will need to build your own database. The database will be designed to manage the website's customers, goods, prices and orders.

Planning the Database

Diagrams of systems, events and information flows

As part of your work on this topic you need to be able to generate diagrammatic representations of the systems and processes involved. These diagrams will help you to plan an effective system and to pre-empt potential problems before they arise.

In chapter 2.4 we looked at diagrams showing:

- the chain of events leading to online purchases
- the back office chain of events triggered by the purchase
- the flow of information into and out of the organisation as a result of a purchase.

We're now going to draw a diagram to represent our database design.

Creating simple relationship structures

The first step in designing a relational database is to decide on the tables that we will need and the relationships between them. As we mentioned above, the database will be used to manage the customers, goods, prices and orders. So these would be a good place to start. The names you choose for your tables should reflect their data contents.

Let's start with the Customer and Orders elements of our database, and draw an **entity relationship diagram** (ERD) to represent the **relationship** between them. In this case, we have a customer who can make many purchases. This idea is represented in our ERD as shown in Figure 2.31.

Figure 2.31

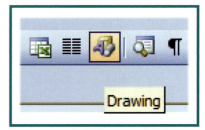

Figure 2.32

When you produce your ERDs, you can use a specialist application such as Microsoft Visio, or you could use the drawing tools within Microsoft Word. To use the tools in Microsoft Word, the first step is to click the Drawing button on the top toolbar, as shown in Figure 2.32.

This will activate the Drawing toolbar at the bottom of the screen. To draw the simple ERD shown in Figure 2.31, first select AutoShapes/Flowchart/Flowchart: Process, as shown in Figure 2.33.

● The cursor will change to the 'cross hairs' and you will be able to drag a rectangle on the screen for the Customer box.

● Right-click and select Copy (this will ensure that both your rectangles are the same size).

● Right-click and select Paste (this will be the Orders box).

● Then drag and drop the second box to the right of the first box.

We now need to use a connector to join the boxes together and show the relationship. In this case we have one customer who can make many purchases. This is our one-to-many relationship. The 'many' side can be represented with an arrow in the ERD. In the Access database, it will be represented by the infinity symbol '∞'.

● Select AutoShapes/Connectors/Straight Arrow Connector (as shown in Figure 2.34).

● Left-click and drag to add the connector between the two rectangles.

Add colour to the rectangles as follows.

Figure 2.33

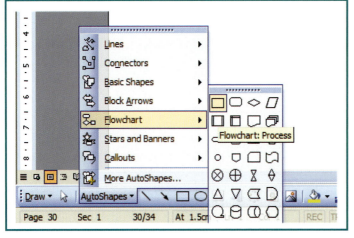

● Right-click the shape and select Format AutoShape.

● Click Fill Colour and select an appropriate fill colour.

● Repeat for the second rectangle.

Finally enter the text.

● Right-click the first rectangle and select Add Text.

● Type in the label Customer and format the text as required.

● Label the second rectangle in the same way.

This ERD is fine as a starting point, but we need to extend it to accommodate all of the data and relationships.

We've already seen how the Customer is linked to the Orders in a one-to-many relationship. In the case of Goods and Orders, an Order may consist of many Goods (or products) and a Goods item might appear in many Orders. In order to accommodate this many-to-many relationship we will use a linking table called OrderLine. We need this table to show the individual lines in each order – if we don't include this table, we will only be able to enter one product per order, which wouldn't be very helpful for customers wanting to order several items and will be bad for our business! (Note that the prices will be held in the Goods table, so we don't need a separate box for them.)

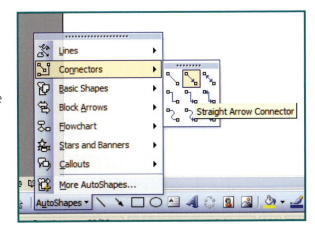

Figure 2.34

The final ERD is shown in Figure 2.36.

Exercise

Using the drawing tools available in Microsoft, reproduce the diagram shown in Figure 2.36, using different background colours and text formatting to the ones used here.

If you have time, have a look at the Northwind Database sample that comes with Microsoft Access. You will quickly get an idea of why companies employ whole teams of database designers, programmers and administrators, just to keep the company records straight!

Exercise

Set up a database structure of four related tables for a video hire shop. You should include the following tables: Customer, Rentals, Videos and Rental Line. Make sure that your arrows point in the correct direction and that you label your boxes correctly.

Típ:

Whenever you draw a rectangle or other flowchart shape that needs to be repeated, draw it once then copy and paste for all future instances. This will ensure that all your shapes are of a uniform size and will make your diagram look neat and professional.

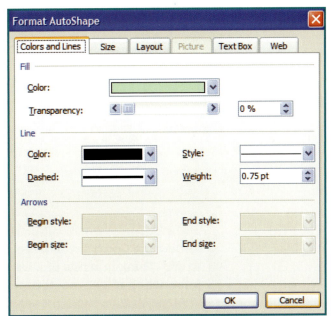

Figure 2.35

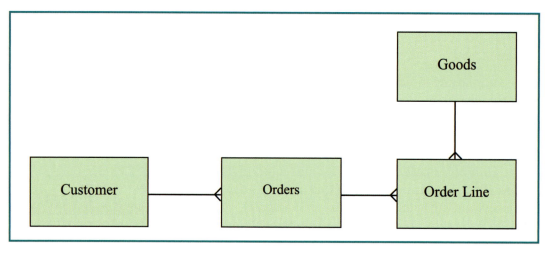

Figure 2.36

Portfolio Builder: *Discuss the database requirements for your e-portfolio with your teacher or lecturer, then draw an entity relationship diagram of your database using appropriate tools. You could start with a pencil and paper and some rough sketches first. Discuss your ideas with your classmates; talking about the concepts involved will help to clarify them.*

Defining the data fields

So far we've decided on our table names and defined the relationships between them using an ERD. The next step is to identify the fields that each table will need in order to hold our data. The fields in Figure 2.37 show the minimum that might be required. As you start building your database in Access you may decide to modify these somewhat.

Customer:	Goods:
Customer ID	Product ID
Title (Mr, Mrs, Dr, Prof, etc)	Product Name
Surname	Description
Forename	Price
Address 1 (e.g. 45 Sanderling Lane)	Number available
Address 2 (e.g. Wellingborough)	
Address 3 (e.g. Northamptonshire)	
Postcode; Telephone; Mobile; Email	
Orders:	**Order Line**
Order ID	Order Line ID
Customer ID	Order ID
Date	Product ID

Figure 2.37

Exercise

Review the Goods list and see if there are any additional fields you would like to add. Think in terms of a warehouse storing these items. What additional information might you need to know?

Building the Database

We now have a good idea of the direction our database is heading in, so let's get started by opening Access and commencing the build. Start Access in one of these two ways:

- Double-click the Access icon on your desktop.

- Select Start/All Programs/Microsoft Access.

You will be given the option to create a new file.

- Do this by clicking 'Create a New File'.

You will then see a screen which offers a number of choices for new databases, as shown in Figure 2.38.

- Choose 'Blank database'.

This will open the 'File New Database' dialogue box. This is where you will name your database file and also choose a location for it on your disk drive. (You may need to check the 'Standard ways of working' section in the Appendices for assistance with directory structures.) The default file name is 'db1'.

- Change the name to the one you want for your database (we chose the name 'Economy_db').

- Click the Create button and Access will create the structure of the database.

Figure 2.38

Figure 2.39 shows the default view, which is Tables view (you can see this under the heading 'Objects'). You will also notice Queries, Forms, Reports, etc. which we will come to later.

Setting up the tables

We're now going to create our first table.

- Click 'Create table in Design view'. This will give us the flexibility we need to design our database. With Design view highlighted, click Open.

- The screen shown in Figure 2.40 will be displayed.

Figure 2.39

This is where we design our initial table structure. At this point we need to refer back to our plans to check what tables we need. We need four linked tables – let's start with the Customer table and set up the fields that we need in this table (see Figure 2.37).

- Type in 'CustID' as the first Field Name.

- We'll ensure that each customer is given a unique number by allowing Access to automatically increment the CustID by one every time a new customer is added to the database.

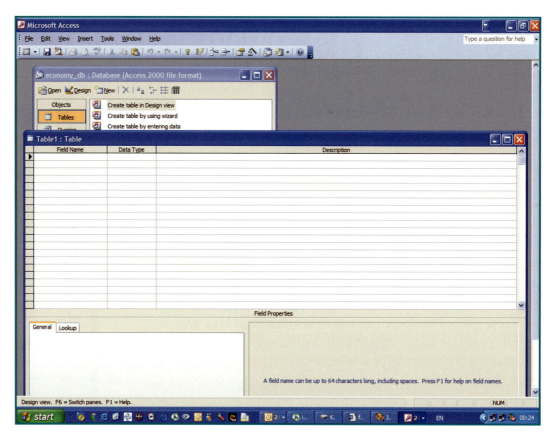

Figure 2.40

- Select AutoNumber as the Data Type for this field, as shown in Figure 2.41.

We need to index this field and specify that there should be no duplicates for the CustID.

- Go to the Indexed box on the General tab.

- Use the drop-down arrow to select: Yes (No duplicates).

We also want to add a description to our database fields so that anyone who works on our design in our absence can see exactly what each field is for. Figure 2.42

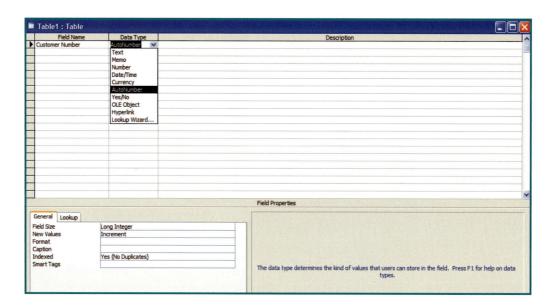

Figure 2.41

shows the completed field names for the Customer database. Some fields are self explanatory so we don't have to provide a description for all of them.

● Click File/Save As in order to save the table structure.

● The Save As dialogue box will appear with the default 'table 1' filename.

● Give the table the name Customer.

● Then click OK to save the file.

A message will display informing you that there is no primary key defined, as shown in Figure 2.43.

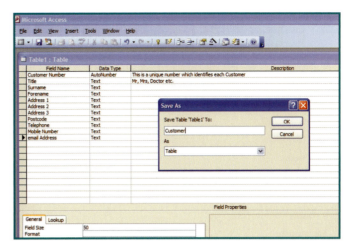

Figure 2.42

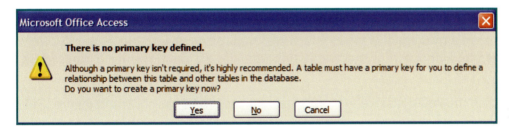

Figure 2.43

The primary key is used to identify a single field name that is guaranteed to be unique in our database. The CustID field is ideal for this, as the AutoNumber data type chosen will generate a new number for each customer. None of the other fields would be suitable for this – for example, the Surname field is likely to include duplicate names as there are many people with the same surnames.

● Click Yes and Access will automatically assign the CustID field as the primary key.

You will notice in Figure 2.44 that Access has attached a small key icon to the left of the CustID, indicating that this is now the key field.

As we've been setting up our table structure we haven't made much reference to the bottom half of the screen: Field Properties. As we develop our database structure we will return to the properties to build in additional functionality for our system.

● Click the red cross in the top right hand corner of the Customer table to close this file and commence the next.

Field Name	Data Type	Description
Customer Number	AutoNumber	This is a unique number which identifies each Customer
Title	Text	Mr, Mrs, Doctor etc.
Surname	Text	
Forename	Text	
Address 1	Text	
Address 2	Text	
Address 3	Text	

Customer : Table

Figure 2.44

Figure 2.45

Figure 2.45 shows that Customer table now appears in the Tables list for our 'economy_db' database.

Now we'll start on the next table in the database, the Orders table.

● Select 'Create table in Design view'.

● Click Open to commence your next table structure.

● Create your table using the list of fields your made in your plan.

We continue with this process until we have built the table structures for our four tables: Customer; Orders, Goods and OrderLine.

Setting up the relationships

There are a number of ways in which we could proceed with our database. We've chosen to continue with the overall view and get the relationships organised. To do this:

● Click the Relationships button on the Access toolbar as shown in Figure 2.46.

Figure 2.46

The Show Table dialogue box will be displayed.

● Highlight the Customer table.

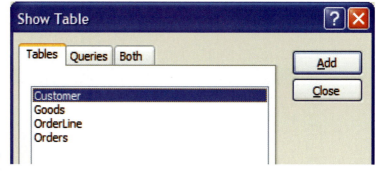

Figure 2.47

- Click Add to add the table to the Relationships window.

- Repeat this with the rest of your tables.

- Click Close.

Your four tables will now all be visible in the Relationships window, as shown in Figure 2.48.

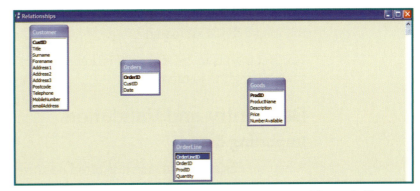

Figure 2.48

Note: In tables with many fields you may not be able to see all the fields. You can increase the size of a table by left-clicking and dragging the bottom of the table so that all of the fields become visible.

The Relationships window shows us the four tables as well as all the field names within each table. It is in the Relationships window that we add the links between the tables. To make these links we simply select a field and drag it to its associated field in another table. As an example, following our ERD, we need to build a relationship between the Customer table and the OrderLine table. We do this by linking a common field in both tables. In this case, we link the primary key CustID in the Customer table to the foreign key CustID in the OrderLine table.

- Click on CustID in the Customer table.

- Drag it to CustID in the OrderLine table.

The Edit Relationships dialogue box will display.

- Tick the Enforce Referential Integrity checkbox.

By enforcing referential integrity, Access will not allow the user to enter an order for a customer who does not exist.

- Click the Join Type button to open the Join Properties dialogue box, as shown in Figure 2.49.

Figure 2.49

We have selected option 3: 'Include ALL records from 'Orders' and only those records from 'Customer' where the joined fields are equal'. Join Properties is one of the most difficult aspects of related tables to grasp. During your test routines, you must check that the results you output are actually the results you expect. If they are not, it is highly likely the join type is incorrect.

Now we need to create the link between Orders and OrderLine. For this relationship we need join type 2:

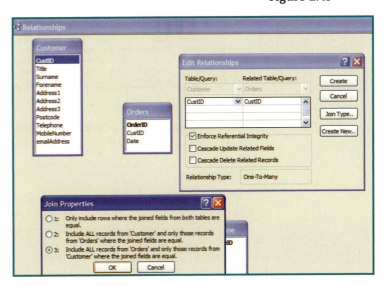

'Include ALL records from 'Orders' and only those records from 'OrderLine' where the joined fields are equal'.

The last step is to create the final relationship between OrderLine and Goods, this time setting the join type to 3.

Data Entry and Validation

Importing data

When we design a database it is often because our existing systems have become outdated or because the company is growing and more efficient processes are required in order to keep up-to-date. In our case, we have a list of customer details that has been kept in an Excel spreadsheet. A spreadsheet is fine to use as a starting point for managing customer lists and other data tables but at some stage a company will need to use some of the advanced features that only a database can provide. Because our Excel customer list is established and current it would be a waste of time and energy to re-enter all the data into our database. Access has a feature allowing us to import files from other external data sources. We will use this feature to capture our Excel data.

Portfolio Builder: **As part of your e-portfolio you will need to import external data into your database. Use Microsoft Excel and create a customer details spreadsheet (or a spreadsheet that your teacher or lecturer has specified). Your teacher or lecturer will be able to give you guidance about the column headings you should use. The column headings will translate into fields when you import the file into your database. You will need to enter about 20 customer records in your spreadsheet.**

Our customer spreadsheet is shown in Figure 2.50.

Figure 2.50

Now we need to import our spreadsheet into Access. As part of the importing process, Access will convert the Excel data into a form that it understands.

Note: The column headings in your spreadsheet must be the same as the field names in the target database. In addition the cell contents must be of the same data type as those used in the target database.

- Open your Access database but don't open the Customer table.

- Select File/Get External Data/Import (see Figure 2.51).

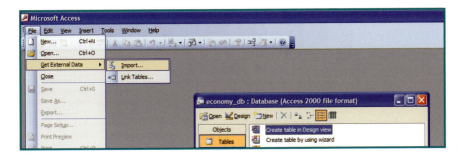

Figure 2.51

The Import dialogue box will open (see Figure 2.52).

- Navigate to the directory where your Excel file is stored.

- At the bottom of the dialogue box, use the 'Files of type' option to select Microsoft Excel Files. You need to do this because the default is set to Microsoft Access files and you won't see your Excel file.

- Click the Import button.

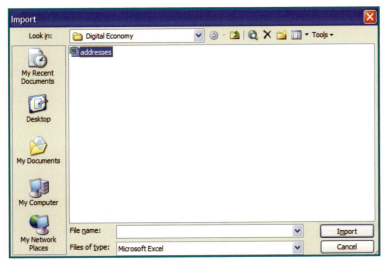

Figure 2.52

> **Tip:**
>
> As with all automated processes, you must check that the data is imported exactly as you expected. Your teacher or lecturer will be looking for evidence of your test procedures, so make sure you record your steps and support your documentation with appropriate screenshots.

Figure 2.53 shows the Import Spreadsheet Wizard which will now display. This wizard makes easy work of placing the data from your customer details spreadsheet into your Access database.

The Import Spreadsheet Wizard has already started the process of capturing data from our Excel spreadsheet. It has found our column headings, which it will now translate into the field names within our database. Access assumes that Sheet1 holds the data, so it places this on-screen for our approval. If you want data from another worksheet you must select that from the list displayed. We do want Sheet1, so we leave this option selected.

● Click Next to go to the next step in the import process.

● Click the checkbox 'First Row Contains Column Headings'.

If we don't do this Access will automatically assume our spreadsheet contains data only and will consider each of our column headings as data. Checking the box tells Access to effectively ignore the first row of the spreadsheet.)

● Click Next.

Figure 2.53

The next stage in the process asks us if we would like to store our data in a new table or an existing table. We've already got our Customer Table in place, so we need to select the existing table option.

● Click the 'In an Existing Table' radio button

● Choose Customer from the drop-down list.

As you can see in Figure 2.54, all of our the tables in our database appear in this list.

● Click Next and then Finish.

Now we can check that things are in order following the import.

● Double-click the Customer table.

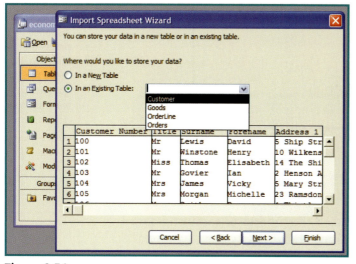

Figure 2.54

Figure 2.55 shows the Access Customer table populated with the data from our spreadsheet.

Manual data entry using forms

The data for our Goods table is also available in an Excel spreadsheet and can be imported in the same way as described above. But the data for our Orders table will have to be entered manually. We will set up a form to be used for the data entry.

We will also have to think about the data for our OrderLine table at the same time. Entering the data necessary for our four table database is a little complicated because of our OrderLine table. (Remember that we needed this to show individual lines in each order. If we hadn't used this as part of our solution, and just used three tables, we would have only had the opportunity to enter one product per order.)

We will use a **form** to enter our data with a sub-form within it. The main form will capture the data for the customer and will feed into the Orders table. The sub-form will capture the data for each individual product the customer orders and will feed into the OrderLine table.

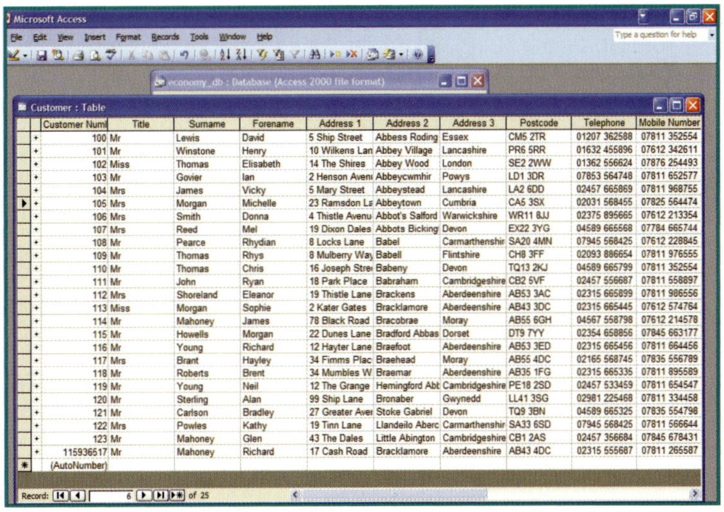

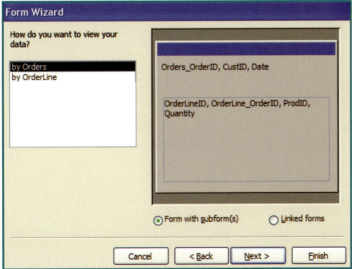

Figure 2.55

To start this process:

- Click Forms in the Objects pane.
- Select 'Create form by using wizard'.
- Click the Design button to display the Form Wizard dialogue box.
- From the drop-down list, choose Table: Orders.
- Select the fields you want and use the arrow button to add them to Selected Fields. (We want the Order ID, CustID and Date fields.)
- From the drop-down list, choose Table: OrderLine.
- Add the OrderLineID, OrderID, ProdID and Quantity fields to the Selected Fields.
- Click Next.
- We want to view our data by Order, so select 'by Orders'.
- Select the 'Form with subform(s)'.

Figure 2.56

Tip:

Please consult your teacher or lecturer about the type of database you should use. They may well advise you to stick to a two table, one-to-many database. If that's the case, you won't need the detail of the following explanation, but you can use it to gain an insight into the power of an Access database when used in a real situation.

- Click Next.

- Choose Tabular, then an appropriate style.

- Go to the end of the wizard and click Finish.

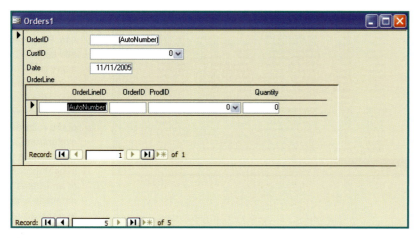

Figure 2.57

Figure 2.57 shows our finished sub-form with a form.

The top part of the form allows you to enter multiple purchases on the order (showing records 1 of 1 at the moment). The bottom part is where you would move on to the next customer order (showing record 5 of 5 at the moment).

We're now going to add a feature that will ensure that at least one item of the data entered is error free. We will use a **combo box** to allow the data entry clerk to select the customer who is placing an order from a list. This gets around the difficulty of the clerk having to enter either a customer ID number or an actual name, which is prone to error.

- Open the form.

- Click the Design icon.

- Right-click on the CustID data field

- Select 'Change To', then 'Combo Box'.

This will open the Combo Box dialogue box, as shown in Figure 2.58.

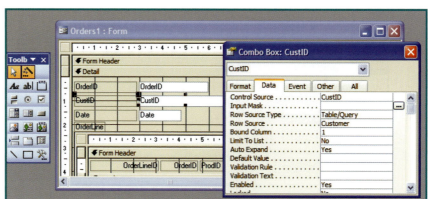

Figure 2.58

- Click the Data tab.

- Choose Control Source: CustID.

- Then choose Row Source: Customer.

You may also need to go to the Format tab to adjust the format to make the form appear as you would like (see Figure 2.59).

In Figure 2.59, you can also see that we have also changed the ProdID field to a combo box and set the attributes to pick data from the appropriate field in the Goods table. In this way we don't have to remember what all the goods are – we simply choose from the drop-down list. This method of data entry is a very effective way of preventing data being entered that isn't in the database. By implementing these changes, you are reducing potential data entry errors.

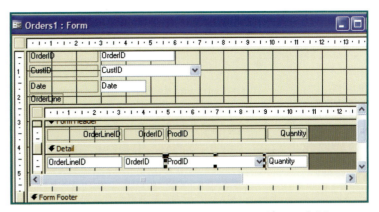

Figure 2.59

Data validation

We took a brief look at validation in chapter 2.8, and you may like to review this before we look at the practical application of validating data. Validation isn't about eradicating errors altogether, which is virtually impossible – it's more about minimising the likelihood of errors occurring during data entry. In our database we set up the tables at the start just to get the structure in place. Now we need to revisit the record structures and insert some validation controls to reduce the possibility of error.

Examples of validation include using **input masks** and **validation rules** to assist in increasing data entry accuracy.

Validation rules

In our imaginary company all the goods are priced at £9.99 or more. Therefore, we do not want our data entry clerk to accidentally enter any amount that is less that £9.99 into our Goods table. We can ensure this takes place by using a validation rule. Here's how to do it.

- Select Tables in the Objects pane.

- Select the Goods table.

- Click the Design button.

- Select the Price field.

- Enter the Validation Rule using mathematical symbols.

As you can see in Figure 2.60, our validation rule is **>=9.99**. The rule means that the value entered must be greater than or equal to 9.99.

- Enter the Validation Text, which will appear on screen as an error message if the user breaks the rule.

Let's see what happens as we enter data into the Goods table.

- Double-click to open the Goods table.

The Goods table will open ready for data entry. To enter data just treat the table in much the same way as you would enter data into a Word table. Please note that you do not have to enter the product number (ProdID) as this field is set up to be an AutoNumber.

Tip:

To test your validation rules, always enter some examples of invalid data. Take screen shots of the resulting screen shots as evidence for your e-portfolio.

- Place the cursor in the appropriate field and enter your data.
- Use the tab key to get to the next field.

To test our validation rule we are going to deliberately break the rule by entering the value 7.00 into the Price field. Access immediately spots the data entry mistake and displays a warning dialogue box for the data entry clerk (as shown in Figure 2.61).

Although our validation rule has brought the mistake to the attention of the data entry clerk, it can't actually correct the error or give any indication of what the actual value should be. It's still up to the clerk to check what the true value should be and enter that figure instead.

Figure 2.60

Figure 2.61

Exercise

In your database, enter a validation rule for a fields with the data type Number or Currency, using one of these symbols: >, <, >=, <= or <>

(You will find more information about using these symbols on page XX.)

Carry out some testing to prove that your validation rule works and save all screenshots for inclusion in your e-portfolio.

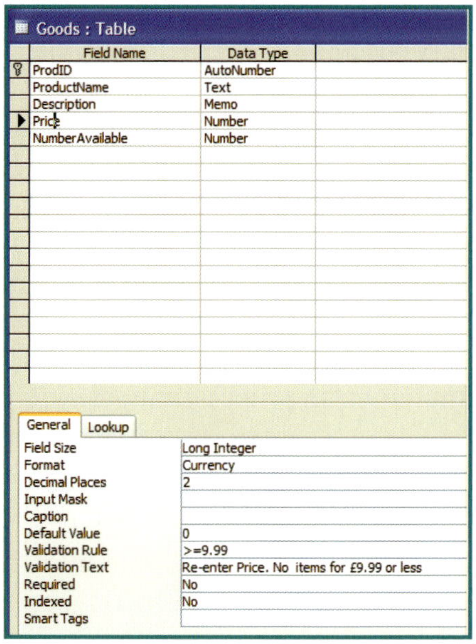

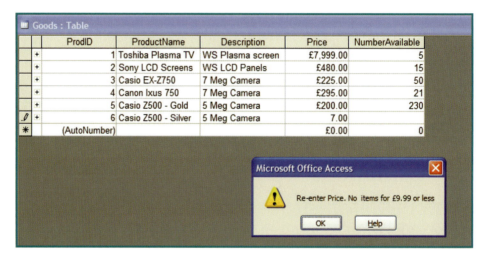

Input masks

Now we are going to concentrate on the Postcode field in the Customer table. As this is a required field, we will put in place a **presence check** to ensure that all records contain a postcode. Then we will apply an **input mask** that will require that postcodes are entered in the correct format.

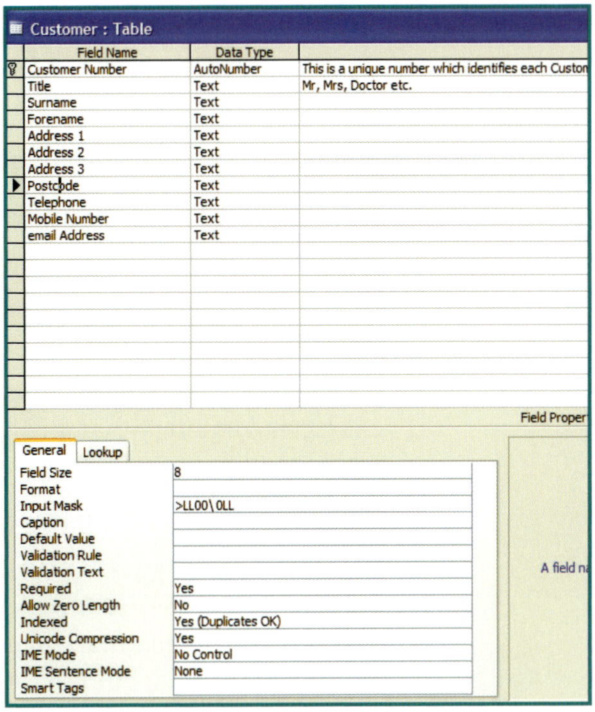

To put the presence check in place:

- Open the Customer table.

- Select Design view.

- Highlight the Postcode field (in Figure 2.62 you can see the black triangle indicating that it is selected).

- Look at the Field Properties area at the bottom of the dialogue box.

- Click in the Required box and use the drop-down list to select Yes – this means that data entry personnel will be required to enter a postcode in every customer record. If they don't they will be prompted to enter one. Try this out for yourself.

Figure 2.62

We now want to apply an input mask that will require the postcode to be in the format: two capital letters, two numbers, a space, a number, two capital letters.

- Click in the Input Mask box in the Field Properties area.

- Type in the required mask.

- The expression needed here is **>LL00\ 0LL** (you can see this in place in Figure 2.62).

The elements of the mask expression can be explained as follows:

> – specifies that all the letters that follow will be converted to upper case

LL – specifies that the user must enter two alpha characters (the case doesn't matter because the mask > will force them to upper case)

00 – specifies any two digits between 0 and 9

**** – specifies that the character that follows will be represented exactly (in this case we've inserted a space to make a gap in the middle of the postcode)

0 – specifies one further digit

LL – specifies two alpha characters.

This may seem a little long-winded, but remember, you only have to set the mask once in your record structure. After that all postcodes will have to be entered in that format, improving overall data accuracy.

We also want our data entry personnel always to use an upper case first letter and lower case for the rest of the letters in the Surname and Forename fields.

- First select the Surname field.

- Then input the expression
  >L<????????????????? (see Figure 2.63)

- Do the same for the Forename field.

The expression **>L<?????????????????** works as follows:

> – specifies that all letters that follow will be converted to upper case

L – specifies that the user must enter one alpha character (required) that will automatically be forced to upper case.

< – all letters that follow will be converted to lower case

? – letter (A to Z) entry is optional. This means that the 17 question mark placeholders do not all have to be used, but are there if required. Note also that the maximum number of letters allowed for surnames here is 18 (the upper case first letter, plus up to 17 lower case letters).

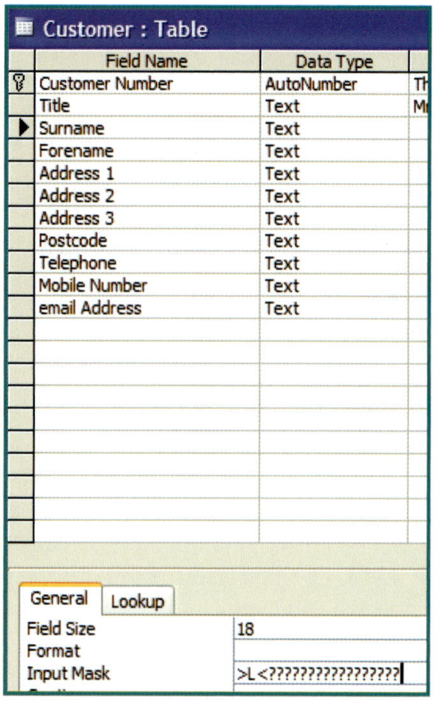

Figure 2.63

Exercise

Create a similar set-up in your own database for the Forename, Surname, Address2 and Address3 fields, so that the first letter of the first word will be set to upper case. Why do you think you shouldn't use this mask for Address1 also? (Think about the data that this field contains.)

Exercise

Try using the same principles to create an input mask for your telephone number fields. You can find definitions of all the valid input mask characters on the Microsoft website. Go to www.office.microsoft.com, select Access from the Products menu and run a search for input masks. click on the link Input mask syntax and examples, and then on Valid input mask characters.

Sorting

There are two ways of sorting data in Microsoft Access. The first way is to use the **sort** option – this is a very quick method, but it permanently changes the table, which you may not want. The second way is to run a **query** – the benefit of running a query is that the original table remains unaltered.

Sorting using the Access sort facility

Let's try the quick method first. We want to sort out Customer table so that the surnames are in alphabetical order.

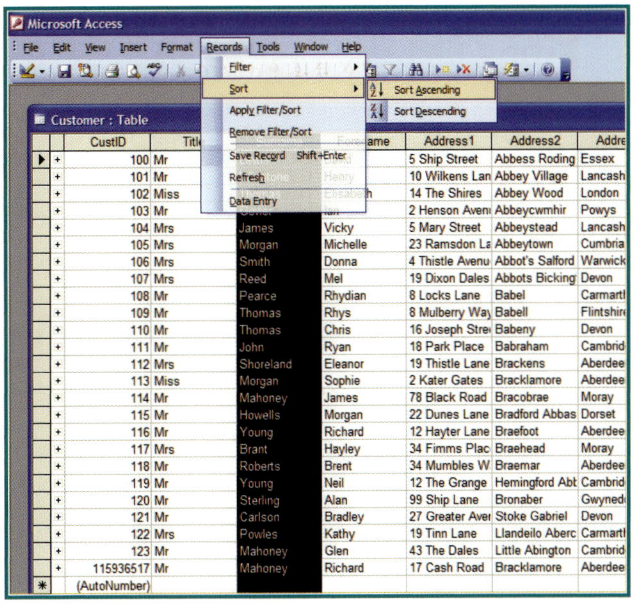

- Highlight the Surname field by clicking on the field name at the top of the page.

- Then select Records on the toolbar menu.

- Click Sort, then Sort Ascending (to sort from A to Z).

Figure 2.64

This sorts the entire table into alphabetical order of surnames, as requested. The problem with this method is that it means the table is no longer in order of CustID, which is our primary key. Depending on the skill of the database user, this could lead to problems in the future management of the database.

Another quick way of sorting is to use the Filter/Sort option in the Records menu. This method has the disadvantage that it can't be saved and can only be applied to the table that is currently open.

Sorting with queries

Queries have the advantage that they can be saved and they don't affect the original table. They are the usual way of sorting data for experienced database users. Let's set up a query to sort our Customer table into alphabetical order of surnames.

- Open the database.

- On the opening screen, click Queries in the Objects pane.

- Select 'Create query in Design view'.

Figure 2.65

Tip:

It might seem a bit confusing that you need to select the Tables tab rather than the Queries tab. But just remember that you are running a query on one of the tables, so you need the Tables option.

● Click the Design button.

At this point the Select Query dialogue box will open, together with the Show Table box.

Select the Tables tab in the Show Table box.

● We will be sorting the customer records so select Customer.

● Then click Add.

Figure 2.66

This will place the Customer table into the Select Query workspace.

● Click Close.

● With your cursor in the Field box, select Surname from the drop-down list.

● Leave the Show box checked to indicate that you want the query to show this field.

● With your cursor in the next box to the right, select Forename from the drop-down list (as shown in Figure 2.67).

● Leave the Show box checked as before.

● In the next Field box to the right, add the Telephone field in the same way.

● Check that the Show boxes are checked for all the fields selected.

● In the first column, under Surname, click in the Sort box.

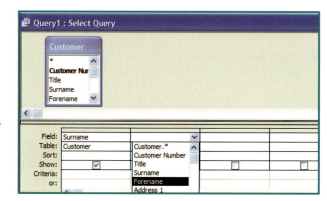

Figure 2.67

● Select Ascending from the drop-down list (as shown in Figure 2.68).

● Repeat this process for the Forename field.

We have set up two sorts within our query – to sort first by Surname (as this is in the first column) and then by Forename. We are now ready to save our query.

- Click File/Save As…

- Type over the default file name (Query 1) to give the query a more meaningful name. We have chosen 'Ascending Sort – Surname' for our query, as shown in Figure 2.69.

- Click OK and the query will be ready for use.

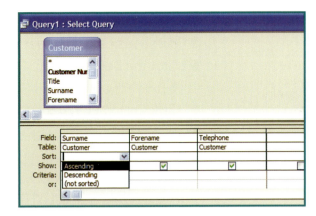

Figure 2.68

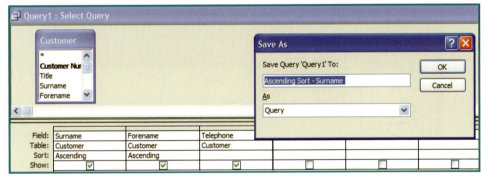

Figure 2.69

The next step, as in all software design, is to test our query by running it. After all, we're only human and might have made a mistake as we set it up.

- Click the Run button on the toolbar (it has a red exclamation mark icon).

As soon as we click the button, the sorted table appears in a new window, as shown in Figure 2.71. Notice that only the fields we specified in our query appear. You see why it was important for us to sort both the Surname and Forename fields. By doing this, we have ensured that the three Mahoneys in the table appear in the correct order of forenames: Glen, James and Richard.

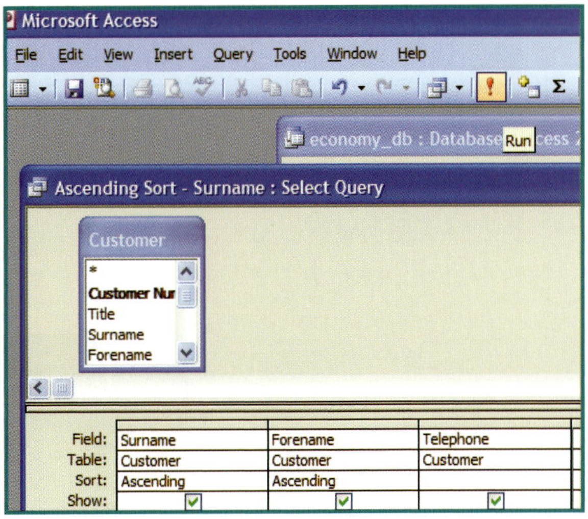

Searches

Queries are also useful for performing searches on your data, especially if you would like to be able to save the search for use on another occasion.

Running a query on two tables

We are going to query our database for the surname and forename of all customers who have ordered goods since the 7th November 2005. To do this we will have to interrogate two tables, the Customer and the Orders tables.

Figure 2.70

Ascending Sort - Surname : Select Query

Surname	Forename	Telephone
Brant	Hayley	02165 568745
Carlson	Bradley	04589 665325
Govier	Ian	07853 564748
Howells	Morgan	02354 658856
James	Vicky	02457 665869
John	Ryan	02457 556687
Lewis	David	01207 362588
Mahoney	Glen	02457 356684
Mahoney	James	04567 558798
Mahoney	Richard	02315 555687
Morgan	Michelle	02031 568455
Morgan	Sophie	02315 665445
Pearce	Rhydian	07945 568425
Powles	Kathy	07945 568425

Record: 1 of 25

Figure 2.

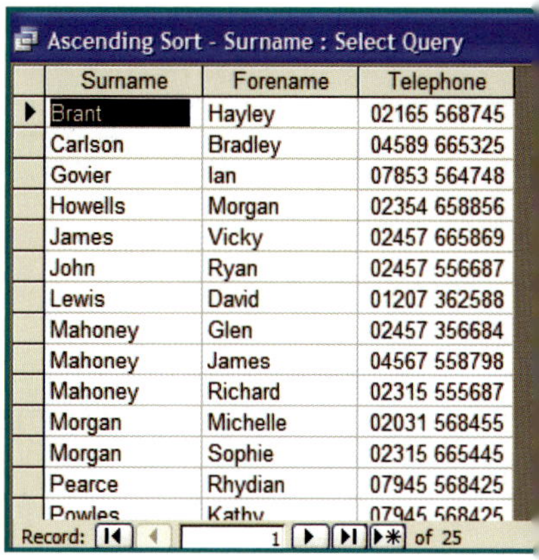

- Click the Queries icon in the Objects pane.
- Select 'Create query in Design view'.
- Click the Design button. The Show Table dialogue box will appear.
- Click Customer and then the Add button.
- Click Orders and then the Add button.

As you can see in Figure 2.72, the two tables are displayed in the Select Query pane with the relationship between them also visible. The next step is to select the fields we would like to display.

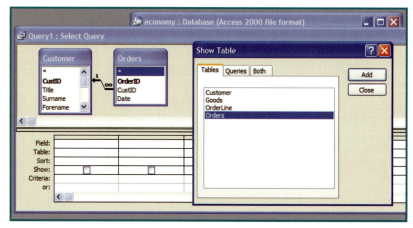

Figure 2.72

- Close the Show Table dialogue box.
- Select the fields you require for the Field boxes of your query.
- You can do this by selecting them from the drop-down lists or by dragging each of the required fields from the table lists into the Field boxes.
- You will need Surname and Forename from the Customer table and Date from the Orders table.

The Table box automatically displays which table each field is from, as shown in Figure 2.73.

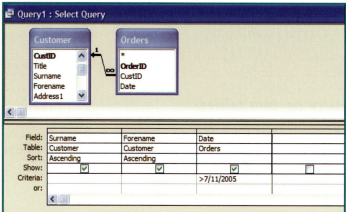

Figure 2.73

- In the Sort box under Surname select Ascending.

- Do the same for Forename.

This will sort the query results into first surname and then forename order.

- Click in the Criteria box under Date.

- Enter the expression: **>7/11/2005**

This will find all records with a date greater than (i.e. after) the 7th November.

- Save your query with an appropriate name.

- Run the query by clicking the Run button on the toolbar.

Figure 2.74 shows the results of the query – the forenames and surnames of all customers who have placed an order after 7th November 2005, as well as the date of their order. You'll notice that the output doesn't look too good; we will tackle this issue when we look at reports.

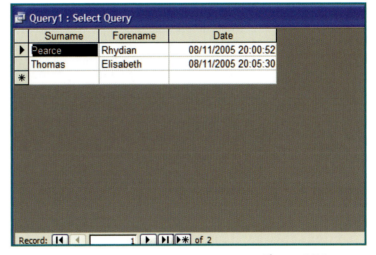

Figure 2.74

Using logical and relational operators

There are a number of logical and relational operators available to us within Access. These include:

> greater than

< less than

<> not equal to

>= greater than or equal to

<= less than or equal to

If two or more criteria need to be met we also use the **AND** or the **OR** operators.

We would like to know if one of our best customers, Elisabeth Thomas, has made a purchase for more than £500 and, if so, on what date. To do this we need to interrogate all of the tables in our database.

- Select Queries in the Objects pane.

- Click New.

The New Query dialogue box will open (see Figure 2.75).

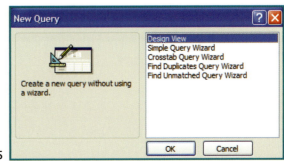

Figure 2.75

- Select Design View and click OK.

The Show Table dialogue box will open. We need to select all the tables:

- Customer for the required surname

- Orders for the date

- OrderLine for the quantity

- Goods for the product name and price.

- Select each of the four tables in turn and click Add.

- Then click Close.

- Drag the appropriate fields from the table boxes in the Select Query workspace into the Field boxes below, as shown in Figure 2.76.

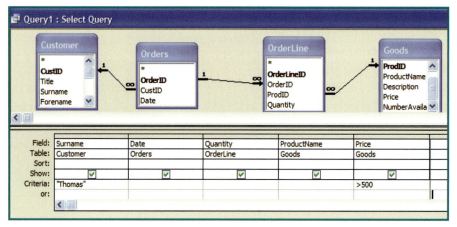

Figure 2.76

- In the Criteria box for Surname type **Thomas**.

- In the Criteria box for Price type **>500**.

- Click the Run button on the toolbar.

Figure 2.77 shows the results of our query, indicating that Mrs Thomas has purchased one item that meets our criteria.

Surname	Date	Quantity	ProductName	Price
Thomas	I/2005 20:05:30	1	Toshiba Plasma TV	£7,999.00

Figure 2.77

Producing reports

Let's take a look at the Access facility for creating reports. We've already noticed that the output from our queries looks a bit basic and undesigned. That's fine if we just want the data for our own information, but if we need to present it in any way, it would be nice to make it more visually appealing and professional looking. Reports allow us to do just that. We're going to create a report that will list all our customers who have made a purchase. We will use the report wizard to do this.

● Select Reports in the Objects pane.

● Select 'Create report by using wizard' (see Figure 2.78).

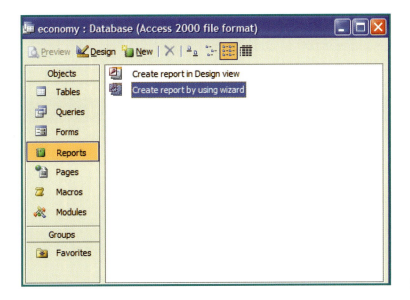

Figure 2.78

● Click the Design button.

This will open the Report Wizard window. We need to select the table or query we would like to use for our report. As we're creating a report on customers who have made purchases, we need to select the Customer table.

● Click in the Tables/Queries box.

● Select Table: Customer from the drop-down list (see Figure 2.79).

Figure 2.79

All of the fields in this table will be displayed in the Available Fields box. We need to select the fields that we want to appear in our report. In this case we want the title, forename, surname and telephone number to appear.

- Select the first field that you want in your report.

- Click on the single arrow to add it to the Selected Fields box.

- Repeat for all the other fields that you want.

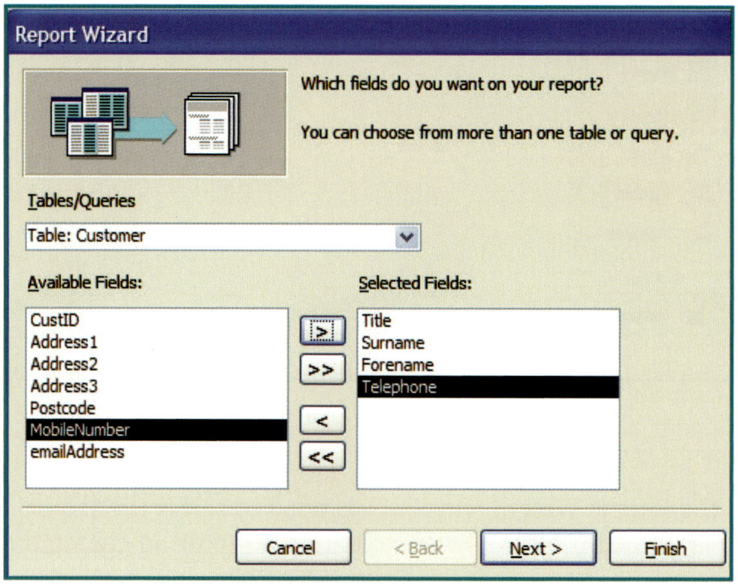

Figure 2.80

Note: If you needed all the fields, you would click on the double arrow. And if you make a mistake, you can remove unwanted fields from the Selected Fields box using the reverse arrow.

We now want to select fields from our OrderLine and Goods tables so that we can add the quantity of items ordered, the product name and price to our report.

- Go back to the Tables/Queries box.
- Select OrderLine from the drop-down list.

Figure 2.81

- Select Quantity and use the arrow to move it into the Selected Fields box.
- Select the Goods table in the same way.
- Move ProductName and Price to the Selected Fields box.

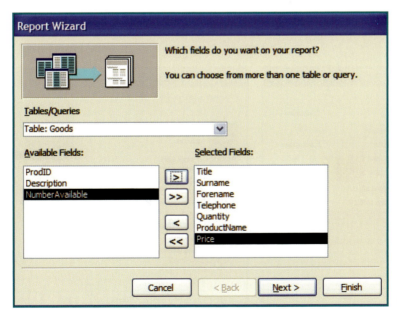

Figure 2.82

- Click Next.

Now that we've selected all the fields that we need, the next step is to select an appropriate way of presenting our data. We already know that we need to be able to print a report giving us information primarily about customers, so we are going to select to view our data by customer.

- Answer the question 'How do you want to view your data' by selecting 'by Customer' (shown in Figure 2.83).

- Click Next.

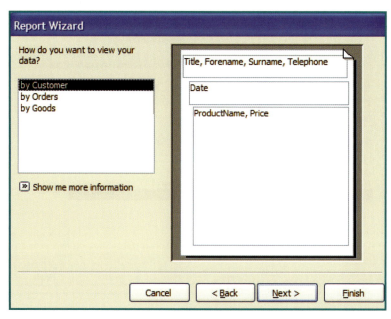

Figure 2.83

The next two dialogue boxes in the wizard (not shown) ask us about grouping levels and sorts. In this particular instance we don't need these so we will ignore them and go to the next step. The next two stages in the wizard allow you to select the layout and style you would like for your report (see Figure 2.84). You will probably want to experiment with the options given here and choose a format that you feel will be appropriate for your e-portfolio.

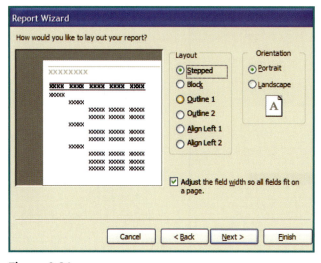

Figure 2.84

- Once you are happy with your report, click Finish.

Figure 2.85 shows our finished report. As you can see, it looks a lot better than the basic table layout.

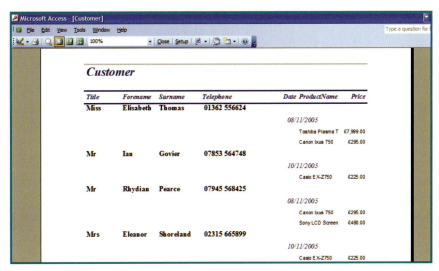

Figure 2.85

Testing

Often students are so relieved to have completed their assignment that they forget one of the most crucial aspects of application development: testing. Your database will need to be totally reliable; users will need to have confidence that it works and that the queries they generate will produce accurate results. Your testing must be rigorous so that you can prove the validity of your application.

Here is one way of tackling the testing of your queries.

- Print out each of your tables containing all of the data that you have been working with.

- Look at each of your queries and ask the question 'What should the results of this query look like?'

- Write down the results that each query should be returning.

- Then run each query and match the output against your expected results.

- If they are the same, then great. If not, you will need to go back and sort out the errors in your queries.

You also need to document your processes and produce evidence of exactly how you carried out your testing. A good way of checking that your database works is to ask your parents or other family members to try using it. You can be assured that if there are any problems with it, another person will help you find the weaknesses.

Exercise

In small groups, design a table that you can use for testing elements of your database (see Figure 2.86 for an example). Choose the element that you are going to test, for example, your validation routines. Compile a series of test data to try out on your validation routine: include a piece of correct data that you would expect to succeed, some incorrect data that you would expect to fail and null strings, i.e. no data input at all. For example, to test a validation rule that the Surname field must only contain alpha characters, your incorrect data input might be to enter the surname J0hnson (where a zero has been 'mistakenly' entered instead of the o).

Example of a testing log

Test Date	Test No.	Field tested	Data Entered	Expected Result	Actual Result	Error Message	Comments

Figure 2.86

As you test your database, the table will help you to record your testing findings and will provide evidence that you have been thorough and have covered all possibilities. Keep copies of your screen output, showing the data entered and all of the associated error messages.

Tip:

The Mark Band 3 assessment criteria require that your testing is thorough and very well documented. So keep copies of everything and document everything you do.

Combine and present information

You've already done some work in this area. You have used database queries in order to interrogate your data and find information from related tables. In addition you have used output from related tables in order to compile meaningful reports. As you work on your portfolio you must gather sufficient evidence to prove you are competent with these concepts. Your evidence will be in the form of printouts containing screen shots of your step-by-step approach towards a database solution.

Add information from one type of software to information produced using different software

Put simply, this means that you must be able to transfer data between applications. The Microsoft Windows environment makes this process much easier than it was in the past. We can produce data in, for example, a spreadsheet and then copy and paste or import the data straight into a word processing file.

Let's try exporting our Goods table so that our web browser can read it.

● Open the database.

● Select Tables in the Objects pane.

● Highlight the Goods table.

● Select File/Export.

● The dialogue box 'Export Table 'Goods' As' will open, as shown in Figure 2.87.

● Choose an appropriate directory on your disk drive.

● In the 'Save as type' box, select HTML Documents from the drop-down list.

● Click the 'Save formatted' checkbox. (This will ensure the field names will be included.)

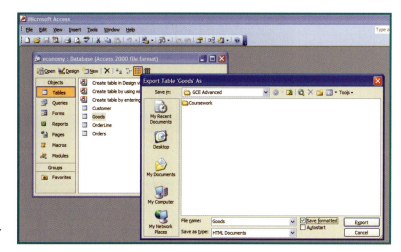

Figure 2.87

● Click Export.

● The HTML Output Options dialogue box will appear.

Figure 2.88

● Select 'Default encoding'.

● Click OK.

Do you remember what we said earlier about the Windows environment facilitating the transfer of data between applications? With this in mind:

● Open your file directory using Windows Explorer.

● Locate the Goods HTML file.

- Open your web browser (as shown in Figure 2.89).

- Select the HTML file 'Goods' and drag it anywhere on the open web browser.

- The browser will load the Goods file into the browser space and display it in Figure 2.90.

Alternatively, you could simply double-click on the Goods file to open it directly into your browser.

Figure 2.89

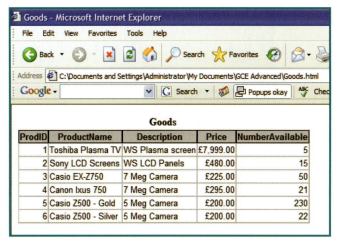

Figure 2.90

Well that's a quick review of databases and hopefully you've come out of this without too many bruises and are still relatively sane! Some of the work we've completed in this chapter is quite complex. Microsoft Access does require commitment in order to master some of its more advanced features. You may not see the benefit now, but if you decide to go on to do a BSc in Computing, you will be glad that you put in the work at this stage. The more you work with it, the more you'll grow to like it.

Problem solving

OBJECTIVES

● To understand the concept of decision-making and how it affects our lives

Decision-making

Whether we like it or not, life is full of decisions. For every decision there is a consequence, which may change the course of our lives. In this unit, The Knowledge Worker, we will be reviewing the whole process of decision making. We will consider ourselves, other people, circumstances and the consequences of decision-making. The assessment of this unit is taken via an external examination. You will be given a spreadsheet and some data from which you will need to recommend an appropriate course of action. This section of the book will help you to succeed in the exam.

As we go through our daily lives we absorb information from a variety of sources. Television, radio, magazines, books, parents and teachers all present us with information which may influence what we do. For example, you might read in the newspaper that an electronics store has an offer on MP3 players and then go out and buy one.

Information can come from multiple sources that combine to help us make one decision. For example, you might see a film you would like to see in a cinema listing in the local paper and then your parents might tell you that you can borrow the car that evening. These two pieces of information will probably influence your decision to see the film.

Using Information Technology to Help Make Decisions

Information gained from IT sources can also be used to help us make decisions more effectively. For example, the database of an e-commerce company can be used to find and isolate products which have not been selling very well. This method is much quicker than a person having to scan all of the orders to see which items should be dropped from the company's product portfolio. In this chapter we will be looking at how technology can be used to help us with decision-making.

Using a spreadsheet model (1)

Let's make a start by going and buying a car! We'll use a spreadsheet to help us with a decision: How much can we afford to spend on the car? The great thing about using a spreadsheet is that once we have built the model, we can input data as many times as we like in order to see how the output (result) changes. As soon as the formula is established we can alter the variables and observe the changes. As we do this we will be able to make an accurate and justifiable decision.

We already have a nice economical diesel for the road, so now we'll find something for the track. We'd like to get a 650 BHP Toyota Supra with a Veilside body kit. There's one advertised on eBay for £7,700 (as shown in Figure 3.1) so hopefully we'll get it for around £10,500.

Figure 3.1

We need to work out how much we will have to pay on a loan for the car. We have come up with a formula for calculating the total cost of the loan (the compound interest plus the initial loan) over a period of time (which is counted in years):

$PV^*(1+R)^N$

Where:

PV = Principal Value (i.e. the amount we'd like to borrow)

R = Interest Rate

N = Number of years we'd like to have the loan for

Now we need to put our formula into a Microsoft Excel spreadsheet.

● Click Start and then Microsoft Excel.

Each cell in a spreadsheet can hold either:

● labels

● numeric data

● formulae.

We are going to put some labels for our data in column A.

- Place your cursor in the required cell.

- Type in the label.

- Use the arrow keys or the enter key to move to a different cell.

Now we'll enter some initial values in cells B1 to B3. We need to enter the value of the loan (£10,500), the interest rate (8%) and the number of years of the loan (3). We want to set the data in cell B2 to display as a percentage. To do this:

- Place your cursor in the cell.

- Select Format/Cells from the menu to open the Format Cells dialogue box (see Figure 3.2).

- On the Number tab, select Percentage in the Category box.

Our spreadsheet now looks like the one shown in Figure 3.3.

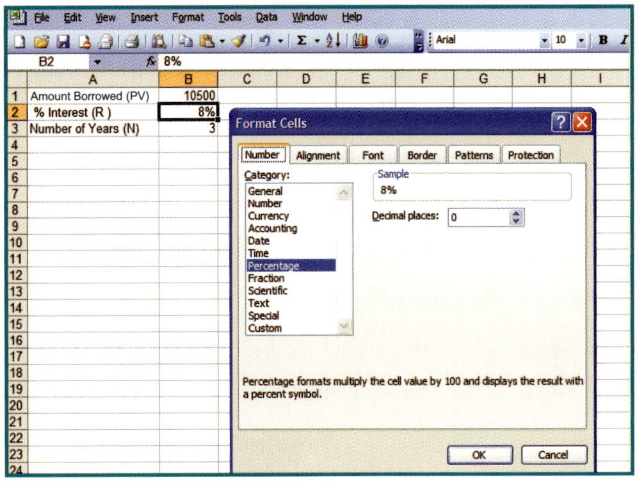

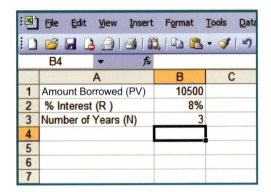

Figure 3.3

Figure 3.2

Now that the raw data is in place, the next step is to enter the formula that will perform the loan calculation for us. We need to convert our formula $PV*(1+R)^N$ into a format that Excel will understand. We will do this using the Excel formula symbols and with cell references in place of our variables.

- Place your cursor in cell B4.
- Enter the formula: =B1*(1+B2)^B3

Notice that you need an equals sign to tell Excel that you are entering a formula, as shown in Figure 3.4.

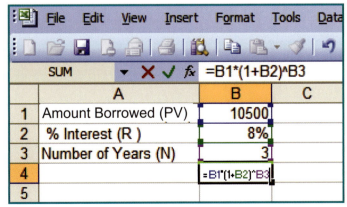

Figure 3.4

● Click Enter and the result is displayed in cell B4.

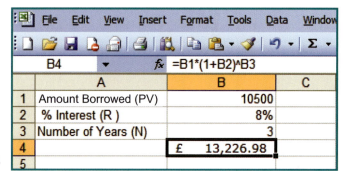

Figure 3.5

Our model is starting to take shape but now we'd like to calculate the monthly payments on the loan.

● Click in cell A5 and type the label 'Monthly Payment'.

● Click in cell B5 and enter the formula for calculating the monthly payments: =B4/(B3*12)

(We need to divide by 12 because that is the number of months in a year.)

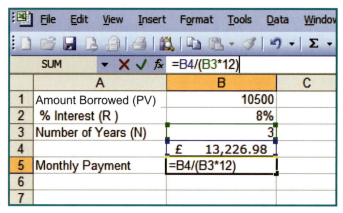

Figure 3.6

Press Enter and the job is done.

We want the values in cells B1, B4 and B5 to display in currency format.

● Place your cursor in the cell.

● Select Format/Cells from the menu to open the Format Cells dialogue box.

● On the Number tab, select Currency in the Category box (see Figure 3.7).

● Make sure that the Symbol is the £ sign and the number of Decimal places is set to 2.

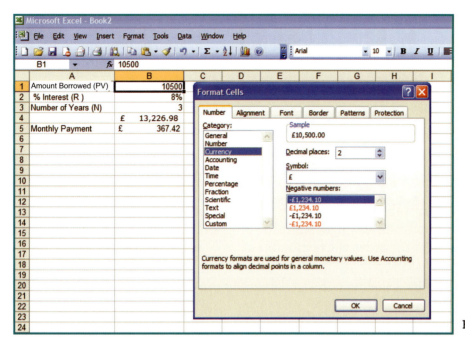

Figure 3.7

Now that our model is complete we are going to test our initial data by checking it against a result that we've calculated manually. Once we've done this, we can then use our spreadsheet to investigate all our 'what if' questions. For example, a monthly payment of £367.42 is a bit more than we can afford. Let's see what happens when we change the purchasing period to 4 years instead of 3 years.

● Place your cursor in B3 and type 4.

This will automatically update the spreadsheet to show the new Total Payable and also the new Monthly Payment, as shown in Figure 3.8. Notice we've also added a new label in cell A4, 'Total Payable'.

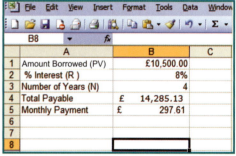

Figure 3.8

We can afford to make monthly payments of £297.61 so we'll stick with this item. All we need to do now is to make our bid on eBay and hope we get the car.

The great advantage of using a spreadsheet is that changing just one data item will automatically update the whole spreadsheet. You couldn't do that with a pencil and a piece and paper!

The steps involved in decision-making

The syllabus makes the point that many decisions we make on a personal basis have little effect on others. It contrasts this with decisions made as an employee in an organisation, when our decision may well impact on individuals, groups and on the organisation as a whole.

There are a number of steps that we follow as we make decisions.

- First we need to define the problem.

- Then, we need information about the problem in order to start coming up with a solution.

- As we gain knowledge about the problem or situation, this will lead to new knowledge.

- We can use the new knowledge to help us progress towards the final solution.

Often the steps follow a programme of events, very much like the steps used within a computer program. A computer program may be defined as a sequence of instructions or steps that the computer can execute in order to reach the desired outcome. This program will usually be required to follow the instructions in an exact sequence. However, we might want the program to respond to outside influences that will alter the order of execution.

Exercise

In a small group, elect one person as the driver (this could be someone who already drives or who is very keen on becoming a driver). Make a list of every step involved in starting a car, from entering the vehicle to driving off. Assume that the car is locked initially and that it has a manual gearbox. Identify the steps that must be followed in a strict order. Also identify those steps where the order is not essential.

When you have completed the exercise answer the following questions:

Were there more or less steps than you originally expected?

Did you omit any crucial steps?

Case Study

A building company is about to carry out a large conversion project on an industrial building. They have already quoted for the job in terms of time and materials. But just as they are about to start they become aware that there may be toxic asbestos in the walls and ceilings. This possibility means that several decisions need to be made before the conversion work can begin. If the project is to be completed it must:

- present a very low risk to people
- incur minimal additional cost
- meet the initial deadline.

They draw up a flow diagram of the decision-making processes that need to take place, as shown in Figure 3.9.

We can use flow diagrams for illustrating decision-making processes in many activities, not just programming. For example, let's take the task of painting the woodwork in a house. There are certain steps that need to be followed in a precise order. This process will require observation, decisions and then action. First we observe the condition of the current level of decoration to inform ourselves of the situation. Based on this information we decide how to proceed. We can represent this task with a flow diagram similar to the one shown in Figure 3.10.

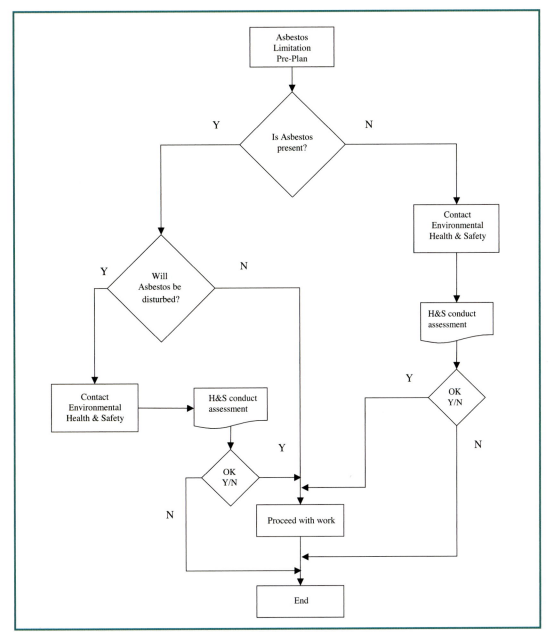

Figure 3.9

Data Processing

Life without computers would be very tiresome. Imagine being presented with a long list of names and addresses on a daily basis and it's your job to record these in alphabetical order by surname, then by forename. As new names and addresses are added you have to reorder the list to bring it up-to-date. How do you think you would feel at the end of each day? Would you make mistakes? If you think you'd make mistakes, why? Although humans can do these tasks quite easily, there are many opportunities for error and dissatisfaction.

You might get bored very quickly doing this job. If your supervisor then asked for the list to be grouped into postal code areas, it might become more interesting for a short time. But boredom would soon set in again.

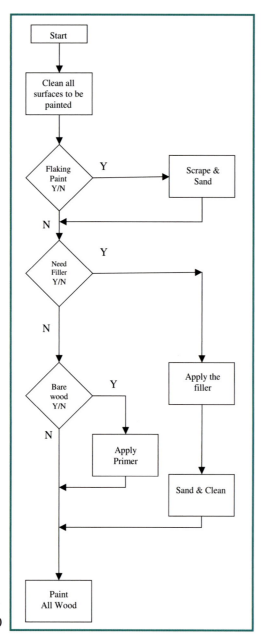

Figure 3.10

Fortunately the computer can come to our rescue with such monotonous tasks. Microsoft Access makes very short work of such data processing tasks and in addition, it will be very accurate. As we saw in chapter 2, computers are able to process large volumes of data. The end result is information that we can use and manipulate for specific purposes.

Some further advantages of using a computer are that they do not take breaks, become ill (although they could pick up a virus), demand a pay rise or go on strike. They do not lose concentration when presented with long and laborious tasks and they never make mistakes – **if they have been programmed correctly.**

As a knowledge worker you would be expected to develop skills in many aspects of data processing, including managing and organising:

● data (unprocessed facts and figures, such as number of hours worked, hourly rate of pay)

● information (the output of processed data, such as the pay slip)

● knowledge (the ability to make decisions based on the information supplied, such as: Can you afford to make a purchase based on how much you earn?)

The case study on the next page highlights a number of don'ts that should be remembered when dealing with data:

● don't lose concentration

● don't underestimate the power of single characters

● don't forget to test

● don't forget to test …

You may think a zero is fairly insignificant, but try omitting one from your £3000 per month salary and see what that results in!

Case Study

This case study contains a lesson for us all with regards to the accuracy of our work. Even the smallest of incorrect details can cause catastrophic results. The following article first appeared in *The New York Times* in 1962 and has been quoted in computer classes the world over ever since.

'For Want of a Hyphen – Venus Rocket Is Lost'
By GLADWIN HILL, Special to The New York Times, LOS ANGELES, July 27, 1962

The omission of a hyphen in some mathematical data caused the $18,500,000 failure of a spacecraft launched toward Venus last Sunday, scientists disclosed today.

The spacecraft, Mariner I, veered off course about four minutes after its launching from Cape Canaveral, Fla., and had to be blown up in the air. The error was discovered here this week in analytical conferences of scientists and engineers of the National Aeronautics and Space Administration, the Air Force and the California Institute of Technology Jet Propulsion
Laboratory, manager of the project for N.A.S.A.

Another launching will be attempted some time in August. Plans had been suspended pending discovery of what went wrong with the first firing. The hyphen, a spokesman for the laboratory explained, was a symbol that should have been fed into a computer, along with a mass of other coded mathematical instructions. The first phase of the rocket's flight was controlled by radio signals based on this computer's calculations. The rocket started out perfectly on course, it was stated. But the inadvertent omission of the hyphen from the computer's instructions caused the computer to transmit incorrect signals to the spacecraft.

Using a spreadsheet model (2)

We would all agree that computers can't help us with all of our decisions. For example, if we left it to a computer to choose a boyfriend or girlfriend, then we could be very disappointed. On the other hand, a computer may well be able to help us decide whether or not we can afford the house we like. Let's look at a spreadsheet that will help us make this decision.

Before we can decide on how much of a mortgage payment we can afford, we need to know a number of details, such as our monthly income, and all our monthly outgoings on food, travel, clothes, etc. We can then set up a spreadsheet to calculate how much we have left at the end of the month. We can then enter different values for the proposed monthly mortgage.

Devise a simple budget, making up the data items and values. Add any additional rows which you feel are missing from the example shown here. You will need to provide your own formulae for Total Outgoings and Balance. For example, to use the SUM function for cells B4 to B10:

Exercise

Look at the spreadsheet shown in Figure 3.11 and use it as a guide for creating your own spreadsheet to calculate how much money is available each month.

- place your cursor in the target cell (in this case B11)
- enter the formula: =SUM(B4:B10)
- press Enter.

Use your spreadsheet to ask some 'what if' type questions about your proposed mortgage payment. Enter some different values for the Proposed Mortgage payment, and your spreadsheet will update itself to present different Balance values (see Figure 3.11). This will enable you to decide the maximum amount you could safely pay back each month.

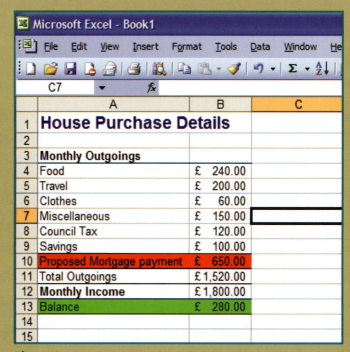

Figure 3.11

The Decision-making Process

OBJECTIVES

- **To review the steps involved in the decision-making process**

As a knowledge worker you will be expected to make informed decisions. You will receive information or data and then make a rational decision based on these facts. There are a number of steps involved in the process of decision-making:

1. Understanding the situation.
2. Identifying knowledge gaps.
3. Researching and selecting reliable information.
4. Analysing the information.
5. Identifying alternatives.
6. Making the decision.
7. Justifying the decision.
8. Explaining your decision to others.

Understanding the situation

The first thing you need to establish is your role in the process. For example, if you are a junior programmer within an organisation, your responsibility and accountability will be very different from that of the project manager. Having establish your role, you must then decide what it is in the given scenario that you are required to decide. This may seem obvious but it is really important to have this clarity of thought right from the start.

Exercise

Imagine that you work as a junior programmer for a company. Your project leader has drawn up a specification for a computer system and asked you to obtain quotes from three different hardware suppliers for implementing the system, and to decide on the best option. Think about what exactly you need to do to carry out this task. Within your role, what are the specific tasks that you need to carry out? Are there any ambiguities in the instructions that you have been given? Would you need to have a meeting with the project leader to clarify any of the points?

It is always a good idea for employees to have written instructions to follow rather than (or as well as) verbal instructions. It is helpful to be able to refer back to the written requirements and there is less likelihood for misinterpretation.

In the ideal world, information that you work with will be:

- clear

- unambiguous

- comprehensive and

- complete.

Some project specifications/proposals may need further clarification. It is important to gain clarification at an early stage in the information gathering process. This is normally achieved by scheduling meetings with all key players. And where information is incomplete, you must identify the gaps and seek help if you are unable to locate the necessary information yourself. In some cases, the information may be clear but our understanding requires further effort. We may need read through the specification a number of times in order to improve clarity.

Case Study

A project manager is working on a system for a small local business. The project brief was fairly comprehensive but lacked vital information about the work of the company. System security was mentioned in the proposal, but in no great depth. It was only once the project was well underway that the project manager discovered that part of the business's portfolio was work on a government defence contract. It became clear at this point that the security needs of the organisation were much greater than the project manager had originally thought.

Identifying knowledge gaps

The next task is to decide what information you need to obtain in order to complete your assignment. When you are searching for information it is very important not to lose sight of the initial target. Take time to review the task and ensure that you are not getting sidetracked by the sheer volume of data that you will encounter. As you identify the gaps in your knowledge, try to categorise them as follows:

- significant – without this knowledge you could not do the task

- trivial – there is a gap, but the information is not relevant to the success of the project.

The category you assign to each information gap will depend to some degree on the time available.

The aim of your research should be to gain additional knowledge about the situation. In the case of our computer system example, you would be interested in finding:

- appropriate suppliers

- hardware that meets the specification.

Once you have identified the significant information gaps, you can start researching the information you need to fill these gaps.

Researching and selecting reliable information

In this information age there is no shortage of sources of information. As an example, we ran a Google search using the keywords **computer**, **hardware** and **suppliers**. Google returned 50,400,000 results, as shown in Figure 3.12.

Figure 3.12

We hadn't planned on looking through quite so many listings, so we are having to be very discerning as we review the results. We may not even need to use an Internet search at all – our project leader may have a list of approved suppliers for us to approach. Alternative sources of information for this type of project could come from other colleagues, catalogues, company representatives, etc. Although we live in an age of electronic technologies, the knowledge worker can still gain information from human and paper-based sources as well.

Exercise

Select two well-known hardware suppliers and find out the different methods they use for presenting information.

As we've seen from our Google search, a few mouse clicks on the Internet will bring millions of related websites. This information overload is of little benefit to us because we would never have the time to review all of the links. Some of our search results may also be misleading and not related to our area of interest. Others will be appropriate but in a different country and therefore not relevant for us. We need to focus our search so that we can review a range of sources and gain a worthwhile picture of what is available. All manufacturers' sites are likely to be biased towards their own product range. What we need is a site that will help us evaluate the systems available, so we need a website that either:

- evaluates systems and provides product reports – for example, PC Pro

- or provides side-by-side reviews of the features of advertised systems – for example Dabs.com

In the first category are companies such as PC Pro (**www.pcpro.co.uk**), which provide unbiased product reviews of all computer-related equipment. This information can be invaluable to an employee who is asked to produce specifications and/or quotations for specific equipment. The reports are detailed and may be used as a starting point for further research.

In the second category are computer equipment suppliers that are not tied in to any one company or brand. Some of these websites (such as **www.dabs.com**) offer a side-by-side comparison service (as shown in Figure 3.13), which gives the user the opportunity to compare product features and be better informed to make their decision.

Figure 3.13

To complete our task, we need to shortlist three hardware systems, so gaining information from both the types of source listed above will help us to achieve this. It is also often useful to gain the opinions of colleagues before coming to our final decision.

Reliability of information

As we seek knowledge, we must establish the validity of sources. Any website we use to gain information should be:

- accurate
- up-to-date
- well written
- true
- authenticated (i.e. including contact details, etc.)

A website with its own dedicated URL (for example, **www.pcpro.co.uk**) is much more likely to present reliable information than a site that has been build in a free, hosted web area where anyone can store their own web pages on any subject they like (for example, http://[domain_name]/my-computer-hardware-site). That's not to say that such pages won't ever contain useful information, but it's worth remembering that we will have the responsibility for any consequences of our choice. So it's much better to go with an obviously reliable source of information.

Analysing the information

One of the most important aspects of your decision-making process is the analysis of the information gathered. This involves assessing and comparing the key factors that will affect your decision. There are various approaches you could adopt for this part of the process. One simple and effective method is to generate a table in Microsoft Word that you can use to record key points as you complete your research. Figure 3.14 shows an example, which can be adapted to suit the particular project you are researching.

Information Reference	Source	Description	Key aspects

Figure 3.14

Identifying alternatives

As you establish alternatives it is important to note any advantages and disadvantages of each possible solution. In some cases the solution that looks the best might be beyond our budget for the project, so we must look for alternatives. In certain situations there may only be one viable solution to the problem. In other situations there may well be a variety of solutions that will achieve the desired outcome – where there seems little difference between solutions, it is up to us to use our judgement or seek the advice of more experienced colleagues.

Making the decision

Making the decision is very often a pressure point! Having gathered the information, analysed and selected viable alternatives, the time has now come to make a choice. It is important to recognise that when certain decisions are made, there may be no going back. In certain situations, the choice may be very straightforward with no potentially damaging after effects. In other cases, the choice may be critical and will need to be justified with documentation of all the steps in the process. If you have completed all the stages in the decision-making process effectively, taking into account all the information available, then your decision should be appropriate and the project should succeed.

It is important to make rational choices based on:

- the available information
- the documented constraints (e.g. time, budget)
- any assumptions that have been made.

You should always bear in mind that the first solution you discover may not be the best or the most appropriate.

Exercise

In a small group, discuss why assumptions sometimes have to be made when considering possible solutions for a new project. What problems might these assumptions present?

Justifying the decision

Knowing at the start of your project that you may have to justify your decision will help to keep you focused on your task. It will encourage you to keep accurate records of the processes that led to your decision (often known as an **audit trail**). It's a good idea to identify the key factors involved in your decision and decide which are the significant ones you are likely to have to justify and which are trivial and probably will not require any justification.

A group of your colleagues would like to take files home in order to complete work to meet their deadlines. In the past they have used floppy disks, but recently file sizes have become too large for this media. It has been decided to purchase pen drives as a solution to this problem. Your task has been to identify a suitable pen drive and order a batch for the employees.

In this case study, there are at least four aspects for consideration: manufacturer, cost, colour and capacity. There may be other aspects, but these are probably the most significant. You have established the order of priority as:

● capacity, cost, manufacturer and colour.

You will need to justify the capacity and cost because the drive must have enough memory to be usable and the cost must be reasonable. The choice of manufacturer may require less justification, although there may be questions about the type of warranty offered by the chosen manufacturer, for example. The colour is probably too trivial to require justification.

Explaining your decision to others

This is the final stage of the whole decision-making process and is a very important part of it. Sometimes you will have to 'sell' your decision to others and get others to 'buy into' your idea. Your solution may have aspects which others find threatening. For example, you may be introducing a computerised solution into a traditionally manual work area. Your presentation must be as equally well thought out and planned as your chosen project solution. If you can't convince the managing director and other key players then your work may well have been in vain.

When you present your decision it is very important to list all of the advantages, areas of concern and all assumptions made. You will need to accept the fact that not everyone will be pleased with your presentation. Some may feel threatened and others may just be disinterested in your well thought out solution. Don't be discouraged by this. Getting your solution in place and seeing it work successfully will bring its own rewards for your hard work.

Understanding the Situation

OBJECTIVES

● **To understand different situations and how to manage them**

Once a decision has been made and the solution has been implemented, it is not always successful. Failures are not always a bad thing, as long as we learn from our mistakes. On this course you will make many decisions regarding your coursework and how you submit it – some will be good decisions but others may not be. There's a saying, 'If you get up one more time then you fall down, then you have succeeded'. As we gain experience, our mishaps should decrease and our project successes will increase.

In this chapter we will look at ways in which we can succeed in decision-making by making sure we thoroughly understand the situation. We will be working through a case study in order to cover the necessary ground and to show how a spreadsheet can be used to solve business problems.

Case Study

A web design company have always priced their website design services using a mixture of gut feeling and what they think the customer might be prepared to pay. A new finance manager has been appointed who wants to implement a more consistent approach to estimating the project cost. She would like to improve the spreadsheet that is used to assist with the estimating process. You have been given the task of coming up with a solution for this problem.

What exactly do you have to decide?

First of all you need to clearly define the solution that you have been asked to develop:

● to develop an improved spreadsheet that will help to standardise the process of estimating project costs.

Next, you need to decide on the information that the spreadsheet should contain and identify the information gaps that you will need to fill. You need to make sure that your spreadsheet includes all the costs involved in the process of web design. So you need to define all the different costs. You could start by drawing up a list of questions help you to find out the information that you need:

● What set-up costs are involved in building a website?

● What are the costs involved in creating each page of the site?

- What are the costs involved in producing and editing graphics?
- How much does it cost to host a website?
- Will a number of updates be built into the costs?
- Are any discounts offered to clients for large websites?

Exercise

This is a basic list of questions and each of them will need further questions in order to answer them. Choose one of the questions from the list and think about what information you would need to answer it. For example, to find out the costs involved in creating each page of the site you will need to find out how long a page takes to design and how much the web designer is paid. You might also think about whether the pages will be templated, and the impact this could have on costs.

Once you have established the information you need to gather, you can go about researching it. Document the process as you go and write up the information you gather in an orderly manner. You could do this in a table in a Word document, with a column for your questions and a column for each of the answers. You must take care to check and validate the information you include.

The different viewpoints

Whenever there is a project that involves people (and that's all projects!), it is highly likely that there will be differing viewpoints. For example, the marketing manager may well have a different view to the finance manager. This is normal – each person's role and their areas of responsibility will determine what their priorities are.

Exercise

Put yourself in the position of each member of staff and highlight one concern for each of them. Why do you think they each may feel differently about the new way of quoting, even though they all work for the same company?

Refining the existing solution

You will need to review the method the company is currently using to price its web design jobs so that you can refine and improve it. The spreadsheet that is already in use is shown in Figure 3.15. We have entered some sample data into the spreadsheet to obtain a price for a four-page website with 15 graphics that is to be hosted for one year, including four updates.

The formulae used in the spreadsheet are shown in Figure 3.16.

Case Study

Let's take another look at the case study and see what the viewpoints of the different employees are regarding the way that quotations are handled.

The **web designers** feel that each site is unique and presents its own set of challenges. Quoting for a job can't be standardised because websites vary enormously in complexity: some sites are simply paper-based brochures that have been turned into an online version, while others are much more complex, such as those that need a database for managing stock.

The **sales and marketing** staff want the sites that they sell to be easily categorised so that their jobs are simpler when it comes to presenting prices to potential clients.

The **finance manager** wants the quoting process for each website to take into account every chargeable aspect. In this way the company should maximise their income potential.

The **graphic designers** know that some companies want straightforward images with minimal work, such as cropping and brightness/contrast control, while other companies require time-consuming animations and detailed graphics. They would like to see the charges reflect the complexity of the images, but they fear that clients will always choose the cheaper option and they won't get to use their animation skills (the more fun aspect of their job).

	A	B	C	D	E
1	The Web Design Company				
2	Pricing System (based on one years cover)				
3					
4			Cost/item	Totals	
5	Standard set-up Costs		£ 200.00	£ 200.00	
6	Number of Pages	10	£ 35.00	£ 350.00	
7	Number of graphics	35	£ 15.00	£ 525.00	
8	Hosting?		£ 90.00	£ 90.00	
9	Updates included		£ 130.00	£ 130.00	
10					
11	Total Price of the Job			£ 1,295.00	
12	Notes:				
13	Updates = four/year max 3hrs work each				
14	Graphics = no extensive manipulation				
15					

Figure 3.15

	A	B	C	D	E
1	The Web Design Company				
2	Pricing System (based on one years cover)				
3					
4			Cost/item	Totals	
5	Standard set-up Costs		£ 200.00	£ 200.00	
6	Number of Pages	4	£ 35.00	£ 140.00	
7	Number of graphics	15	£ 15.00	£ 225.00	
8	Hosting?		£ 90.00	£ 90.00	
9	Updates included		£ 130.00	£ 130.00	
10					
11	Total Price of the Job			£ 785.00	
12	Notes:				
13	Updates = four/year max 3hrs work each				
14	Graphics = no extensive manipulation				
15					

Figure 3.16

This spreadsheet isn't really detailed enough to provide an effective pricing solution. However, it is able to answer some basic 'what if?' questions. For example, if we have changed the specification of the website so that it has 10 pages and 35 graphics then we need to obtain a new estimate for the company, as shown in Figure 3.17.

Exercise

As part of the external assessment you will be given a spreadsheet model to work with. Using the above spreadsheet as a starting point, refine the spreadsheet so that it complies with the requirements of the task specified in the Case Study at the beginning of this chapter. Use all the information given so far in this chapter, as well as the questions you came up with in the exercise on page 181. Take into account the varying viewpoints you have to deal with – you will need to justify your decisions with sound arguments as it will be almost impossible to please everybody. You may like to return to this exercise at a later point as you gain further spreadsheet skills and master new techniques.

	A	B	C	D	E
1	The Web Design Company				
2	Pricing System (based on one years cover)				
3					
4			Cost/item	Totals	
5	Standard set-up Costs		£ 200.00	£ 200.00	
6	Number of Pages	10	£ 35.00	£ 350.00	
7	Number of graphics	35	£ 15.00	£ 525.00	
8	Hosting?		£ 90.00	£ 90.00	
9	Updates included		£ 130.00	£ 130.00	
10					
11	Total Price of the Job			£ 1,295.00	
12	Notes:				
13	Updates = four/year max 3hrs work each				
14	Graphics = no extensive manipulation				
15					

Figure 3.17

So the old system does provide a starting point for the new solution, but it does need quite a bit of refinement.

Comparing current and previous decisions

As you make a decision you should always ask yourself the question:

- How does this decision compare with similar decisions you've made before?

This can be problematic when you have no prior experience of a particular problem area. For example, imagine you have decided a develop a spreadsheet to model different ways in which you could solve a problem within a set budget. You have chosen to use a spreadsheet because you can ask 'what if' questions by entering different variables in order to find a set of costs that work. You need to think of how previous experience helped you come up with this solution. Try to think laterally and find a situation that helped to prepare you for this situation. For example, you may have had a set amount of money available to buy something. This would have involved you researching different options in order to find the keenest price for the same or a similar product.

Are there variations from time to time and place to place?

In the case of this model there will be details that vary depending on the time or the place. For example, some companies who want a website design may want you to go and meet with them to discuss the way their product is presented. The company may have many different offices in other locations and there may be a requirement to visit these. The deadline for delivery may be very tight, which may involve you asking staff to work overtime in the evenings and/or weekends. All of these different scenarios will have additional costs and must be accounted for within your price. If these 'extras' are not considered and charged for, then you could end up working at a loss, which will not be good for the long-term prospects of your company.

Having considered some of the potential extra costs, it would be a good idea to integrate these into the quotation spreadsheet: for example, add rows for overtime hours, differing rates of pay, travel costs, etc. These won't be needed for every project, but if they are already present in the spreadsheet it will make pricing a lot easier when they are needed.

A different example

Case Study

A company operative needs to fill a container with an expensive liquid. The emphasis is on getting the container filled to the mark in the quickest possible time. There are two supply sources of this liquid available. Supply A comes from a tank with a small hose which will fill the operative's container in 45 minutes. Supply B comes from a tank with a large hose which will fill the container in 30 minutes. The operative decides to fill the container with both supply hoses at the same time and needs to calculate exactly how long this will take.

Let's work through this with the aid of a spreadsheet. If you're saying 'It's quicker with a calculator', then you are correct, but let's use this scenario as a trial run for when we get to larger problems.

First we need to establish what we already know. We know that Supply A will fill the container in 45 minutes. Supply B will do the same job in 30 minutes. Using this knowledge we can see that the fastest time possible with just one supply is 30 minutes.

We need to make sure we get the maths right in order to move forward. Often, looking at the task from a different perspective will help. Let's say that Supply A will fill 1/45 of the container in one minute and that Supply B will fill 1/30 of the container in one minute. If we add these together we'll find the combined speed for every minute.

First we enter these values in the spreadsheet.

- In cell B4 enter: **=1/30**

- In cell B5 enter: **=1/45**

We need to use the equals sign to inform Excel that what follows is mathematical. If we were to enter 1/30 with no equals sign, Excel would assume that we were trying to enter a date (as that is how Excel interprets the forward slash). Figure 3.18 shows the formula we entered to get 1/30 (for Supply B) and the decimal value of 1/45 (for Supply A).

Now we'll use the AutoSum feature to add cells B4 and B5 together.

- Place the cursor in cell B6.

- Click the AutoSum icon (found on the Excel toolbar). Excel 'guesses' that we want to add the numbers directly above it and highlights them ready for our confirmation (see Figure 3.19).

- Press the Enter key to confirm and the result appears in cell B6.

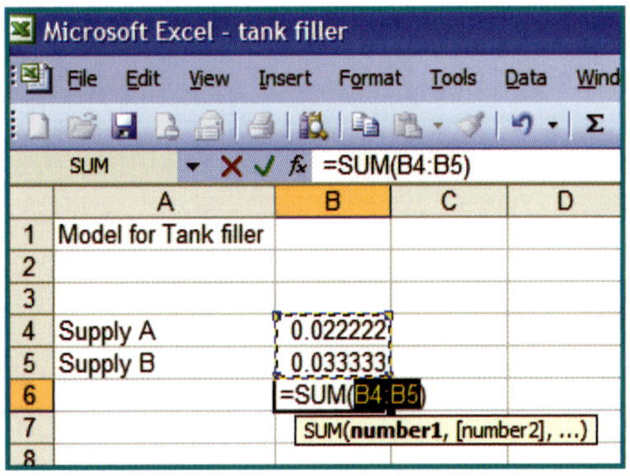

The value in cell B6 shows how much of the container will be filled per minute. If we divide this value into 1, it will give us the length of time in minutes to fill the container.

- In cell C6 enter: **=1/B6**, as shown in Figure 3.20

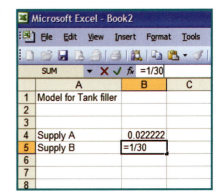

Figure 3.18

Figure 3.19

Tip:

Notice that we haven't attempted to round any of these values at this stage. To do so, with more calculations remaining, would introduce errors into our model. The rule is to round only once, at the conclusion of all processing.

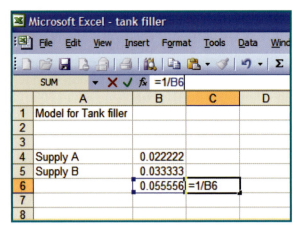

Figure 3.20

● Press Enter to display the final value (in minutes) in cell C6.

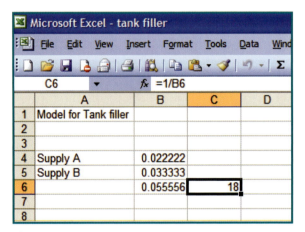

Figure 3.21

It will take 18 minutes to fill the container.

As we have seen from this example, modelling needs to be based on logic so that working formulae can be established. We may initially need to do some pencil and paper work to see exactly what maths formulae we need to use and how to translate these into Excel.

Sources of Information

OBJECTIVES

- To determine existing knowledge
- To define any knowledge gaps
- To review additional information
- To establish the reliability of information

As we go through the process of gaining knowledge it is important for us to establish what we know and what we need to find out. We have various resources available to assist with this, including the Internet. It is important for us to gather the right information. It is easy to become sidetracked in our search for knowledge – surfing the Internet is a typical example of how we may become lost as new links draw us away from our goal.

What do we need to know?

First we need to establish what we need to know. For example, imagine you have been presented with a problem by another team in your company for your comments. You aren't familiar with the project that this team is working on, so in order to make a meaningful comment you need to gain some knowledge of the scenario first. If they are looking to you for a solution to their problem, then you will need to gain an in-depth knowledge of the situation. You will need to understand the problem together with any constraints that are attached to it. And you will need to have other resources available in order to provide the solution.

Case Study

A project manager has been asked to manage the transfer of widgets from Point A to Point B. He identifies the information he needs to find out as follows:

- how many people are available to make the transfer
- how many widgets each person can transfer at once
- any time constraints (i.e. does the job have to be completed in a certain number of hours)
- how fast they can they travel while carrying widgets
- how fast they can they travel on the return journey
- whether they need to stop for breaks
- what happens if someone gets ill and can't carry

This list may extend to include many more considerations.

Some parts of this problem will have to be 'live tested'. Someone will need to carry out a dummy run to gain an idea of the number of widgets that can be carried together with the speed. With this knowledge, the project manager could then use a spreadsheet to estimate the likely completion time for the whole job.

Exercise

Set up a spreadsheet to solve the following problem: 50,000 widgets are to be moved by an industrial robot from Point A to Point B, 1000 m away. The robot is capable of carrying five widgets at a speed of 10 m per minute. The return journey takes eight minutes. Set up your spreadsheet so that, if necessary, a second robot can be brought in to speed up the process. Your spreadsheet should also have the facility for handling heavier widgets, which reduce the carrying capacity of the robot to three widgets with a carrying speed of 7 m per minute.

Utilising relevant knowledge

When you are using modelling to solve problems there will be two main knowledge areas that you will be drawing on:

- your knowledge of the problem
- your knowledge of spreadsheets.

In your assessment you will be presented with a scenario and an existing spreadsheet. The spreadsheet may have formulae present which you will be expected to work with. You may also need to add some formulae of your own in order to establish a solution. As far as the scenario is concerned, you will need to analyse the situation and think of formulae that will help you to gain a solution.

Identifying and filling knowledge gaps

As you review any given scenario you will discover elements of missing knowledge. These missing pieces in the puzzle may not be relevant. If, for example, in a Web design scenario, the company logo was missing we would probably take this as irrelevant. On the other hand, if we didn't know the hourly rate of pay for one of the web designers then we would be in trouble if we proceeded with our quotation system.

There are some points to note here. Sometimes, we may think we have a complete knowledge of the solution. For example, we may have designed a spreadsheet and not realised that, although a solution works, it may have significant deficiencies. These deficiencies may not materialise at the initial stages, but can become apparent later on.

For example, we may design a spreadsheet solution for a company that takes a product and a pre-VAT price, then calculates the total price including VAT. Let's take a quick look at the spreadsheet model, which works yet has a major deficiency. This deficiency reinforces the fact that we may not be familiar with the spreadsheet we have used to create our model.

Here's our poorly planned formula (the contents of cell C3 in Figure 3.22):

=B3*0.175+B3

We will now replicate the formula into cells C4 through to C7. You will notice that Excel is intelligent enough to know that the copied cell (C3) must change its contents slightly as it replicates into each cell. You'll see what we mean shortly.

Right-click on the target cell C3 and Select Copy (see Figure 3.23).

Highlight each cell where the target must be copied to (i.e. highlight C4 down to C7), then right-click on cell C4 and Select Paste.

Now let's look at the pasted cells and scrutinise the contents. Switch on 'show formulae' by clicking Tools/Options (see Figure 3.25).

Then click the Formulas checkbox in 'Windows options'. This displays the formula used in each cell (see Figure 3.26).

Notice how each cell contains an updated version (rather than a direct copy) of C3, which has incremented each reference to cell B3 right the way down to B7.

The problem with this solution is that if the VAT changes we will have to edit each formulae. This is not a big job on a small spreadsheet but can be an onerous task on a large commercial spreadsheet where many references will need to be changed.

We can now see that even though we have produced a fully working solution, it may present users with significant difficulties later on! We will cover solutions to this difficulty later (see 'Absolute and relative referencing!' in Chapter 3.12, page 233).

As we proceed with our scenario it is probably a good idea to have a plan that we can use to help develop a solution. A good starting point would be to write down a list of missing data in tabular form, as the table below demonstrates.

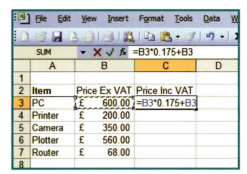

Figure 3.22

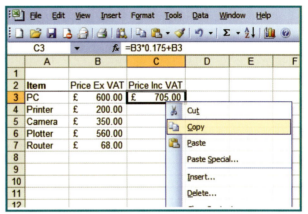

Figure 3.23

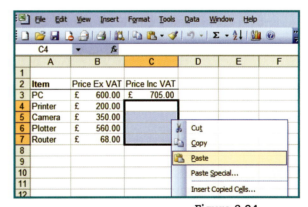

Figure 3.24

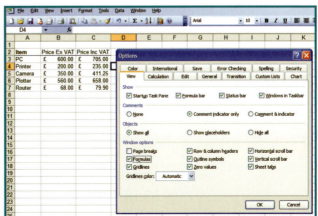

Figure 3.25

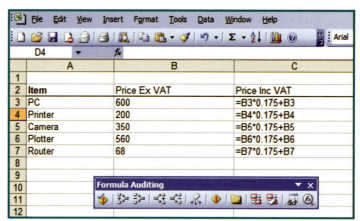

Figure 3.26

Knowledge gap	Relevance	Could it be located easily?

You may find it useful to attach a scale of importance to elements within this table – e.g. relevance could be on a scale of 1 to 5. As with many things in life project work is time-bound, and we will need to manage our time in order to meet any deadlines that have been set. We may find we don't have enough time to find some of the less-important information. In these cases, where the information is still fairly relevant, we may need to make documented assumptions. The process of making assumptions will certainly help us with our time constraints but must be well thought out and used with care.

What information do we already have access to?

Good communication is vital within project work. The initial scenario must be sufficiently clear and detailed in order that the project team may progress towards a realistic solution. Again, a table is a useful way of presenting existing knowledge. It serves as a visual way of presenting what we already know, as the example below demonstrates.

What do we know?	Where is it found?	Of what use is this information?

As we itemise our knowledge base we may find that when we get to the 'uses' column we can leave it empty. In the case of an empty cell the data entry becomes insignificant to the success of our project.

Sources of additional information

Your main source (prime) of information will always come from the scenario. This is the project specification which has been presented in order to gain a working solution. The information may be presented to you in a variety of formats, including:

- textual information
- tables of data
- graphs and/or charts
- mathematical formulae.

As you utilise a spreadsheet other data will be derived from a combination of formulae and the data you use.

Evaluation of sources for reliability

When you read a newspaper article, does it give an accurate account of a situation? When you find an article about nuclear physics on the Internet, is it accurate? As you go through the process of gathering information about the scenario you will need to consider whether the information is:

- accurate
- detailed
- complete
- relevant
- from a trusted source.

Pascal programming was taught to a group of first-year computing students. It was interesting to note that if the student's program displayed a result on the screen without crashing, the student would automatically think the program worked. Of course, this is incorrect and particularly bad practice. Gaining a result is not the same as gaining the *correct* result. Imagine, for example, you have been asked to design a spreadsheet for calculating the area of stainless steel required to manufacture water cylinders. If you inadvertently declare Pi as being 4.312 instead of the correct value of 3.142, then your calculations will be in error. Although this is quite a small inaccuracy, it will magnify the consequences as we build larger tanks.

Even when we have been through the process of reliability checking, simulation and modelling does not always give accurate or sometimes the expected results.

Over the years vast amounts of accurate data using complex measuring systems have been collected with regards to the famous 'British weather'. One would suppose that with all of the data and computer power expended on this activity, the weather forecast would be precise and accurate. As we all know this is not always the case. This shows that computer modelling is not always as accurate as we would like.

Other Factors to Consider

OBJECTIVES

- **Consideration of the 'human' factor**

Most decisions are not made purely on facts, where we take the known, consider the unknown, apply a little assumption, then come up with a decision. The main part of the process will be the gathering together of facts. However, with many decisions there will always be that human touch. It is true to say that some decisions are capable of damaging the organisation. For example, a manager within a company might not appoint the most capable, qualified and experienced staff because he/she may perceive that experienced staff could threaten his/her position. This is clearly an erroneous train of thought, but one that does present itself in some organisations.

In the Edexcel scheme, the following factors are listed as possible contributors to the decision-making process.

Gut feeling

This is difficult to describe, and even more difficult to justify without an accompanying armoury of facts. The following case study demonstrates that gut feeling alone is no justification for a rational decision.

Case Study

An employee was asked to recommend a system for operating a potentially hazardous process. If the new system worked it would enable the process to operate with almost no human intervention. The cost of the system was £250,000 and the employee said: 'In the absence of facts, it is my gut feeling that this system will work'.

It's fairly obvious that this situation is highly unlikely to happen in real life. However, it does illustrate that gut feeling alone has no real place in an industrial or commercial setting.

By way of contrast, some people make a living out of a combination of gut feeling, experience, luck and skill. Football players use these combinations to be in the right place at the right time to score winning goals. Police officers sometimes follow these same feelings as they go about the job of apprehending criminals.

Emotion

Emotion is another difficult factor to quantify. In many ways, the knowledge worker would be correct in leaning towards solutions with a high level of logic. The solutions will be very much rule-based with outcomes that may be mathematically deduced. However, emotion may well present itself and, either consciously or unconsciously, contribute to the final decision.

In real-life decision-making the final choice is often a combination of many of the preceding factors already discussed. We may have 70% hard facts, 20% assumptions and a 10% 'feel' that this would be the correct choice. Take the example of Mr X, who is choosing a new car. Pure, calculated logic indicates that the diesel Ford Mondeo is the correct choice for the family. It is economical on fuel, it has plenty of luggage space, it carries five people and it has a reasonable insurance group. However, if Mr X were making an emotional decision, he would choose the TVR Cerbera, which also has five seats! It's useful to remember that in a work situation members of a team will be striving for balance of emotions in the decision-making process.

In a computer system there's not much room for emotion. Attempts have been, and are being made, to try to make the computer more human-like. Health professionals have been proactive in designing systems to provide initial patient diagnostics, thereby reducing the total of consultant's time expended. Following the computer's initial results, the consultant or doctor then analyses the data and makes the final decision based on the output generated. However, most systems are used largely for processing facts and figures, and then leaving the human to make the final decision.

Even though emotion seems to be non-quantifiable, it is still possible to capture data that can be quantified in some small manner.

Case Study

An employer is keen to employ only the best professionals for the company. In order to do this she has derived a list of criteria by which she will judge prospective candidates. The list includes: relevant experience, attendance, dependability, honesty, team person, motivated, hard-working, communicator, positive, practical and well qualified. Having established the list she then attaches a grade to each attribute as the individuals are interviewed. The grade system is:

Excellent = 4; Good = 3; Average = 2; Poor = 1.

The employer is well aware that this system could be considered quite crude.

However, in the absence of anything else, she is prepared to pilot this system.

As you can see from the case study, we have a model that could be realised by a spreadsheet. As we tackle this particular scenario, we're not saying that the employer's model is correct. We are, however, responding to her request for a system that may help in her interview processes.

Of course, this spreadsheet is only a part of the decision-making process. All the other knowledge-gaining tools must also be used before making the decision.

In certain decisions there is no room for emotion. When a runner of a marathon crosses the line first, the decision is already made: he or she is the winner. Emotion takes a backseat and logical rules take over. There will be plenty of emotion regarding the result, but it will not have contributed to the decision.

Exercise

Design a spreadsheet that will fulfil the scenario as specified in the case study. You will need to have a mechanism that will total all of the grades. You will also need to have represented some sort of average score. Having completed a spreadsheet try it out with some sample data to see how it functions. Then compile a short report for the owner of the company detailing any deficiencies that you have found with her model.

It's also worth remembering that the outcome of all decisions have a consequence. It is often better to review these possible consequences before making a decision than it is to revert back to the situation prior to the decision being made. In certain situations, having made the decision, there is no turning back! For example, if you decide not to be an astronaut somewhere between where the rocket launch countdown reaches 3, 2, 1, ignition and blast-off, then you have probably left things a little late. You will have to live with your decision. If you can't afford a ride on a Space Shuttle to prove this theory, then a bungee jump will give you the same result. Once you decide to step off the platform the consequences of your decision are taken out of your hands and passed over to gravity! In a workplace scenario, you may press the button that instructs a machine to manufacture ten widgets when the specification actually needed one. You may not notice in time to make a correction, resulting in a potentially expensive mistake!

Sentiment

It takes character to make certain decisions. This is especially so if we have to make a decision that we think may cause bad feeling among other people within our group. Take the scenario of a job interview: if there are other colleagues on the interview panel it can sometimes be difficult to air your views without subconsciously worrying what the others will think. There are a number of ways to handle this.

- If we involve people along the way, giving them some ownership of the final outcome, they may well be more supportive of the final conclusion.
- Ignore their feelings and continue with the decision anyway.
- Don't make the decision because it's going to upset someone.

A manager has received a number of requests from staff asking if they can work from home for a proportion of the week. They are all in jobs that require them to use a PC and the Internet to work on files both individually and collaboratively. The manager likes the idea because she feels this flexibility would ultimately help her in reaching her deadlines – i.e. staff may be more likely to work longer hours in order to complete a task. Her big concern is that a small percentage of the team are not very motivated, and she fears the lure of the armchair and TV will spoil the concept.

Ambition

Ambition can be a strong motivator but, if used selfishly, it can also hinder the progress of the company and its employees. A 'go-getting' individual may allow ambition to affect the decision-making process in way that doesn't entirely benefit the company. For example, an individual may feel that a decision to cut costs on a manufacturing process will make him or her look more efficient and cost-effective, and therefore well suited to promotion. The desire for promotion may have skewed the decision from arguably the right solution to a cheaper, less effective alternative.

Lack of knowledge

We may ask ourselves: 'Are the gaps in our knowledge regarding the scenario significant?' If the answer is no, then we may decide to proceed, either by dismissing the gaps as insignificant and agreeing that further time spent researching the gaps is unjustifiable. We could also review the gaps, then make rational assumptions in order to bridge them. If the knowledge gaps are important to the success of the project, then we have more of a problem. It is very difficult to proceed with a project when we know there are significant gaps in our knowledge that may have a detrimental effect on the final outcome.

For example, we may have designed a spreadsheet to model a solution to a problem, with part of the solution requiring an 'if/then' statement. In this situation, if we are unfamiliar with these statements we need to gain knowledge in order to implement our model. Without this knowledge, our model will fail to work.

In the example on page 194 the solution is quite easy. We can either gain the skills ourselves or we could buy in additional expertise to ensure the success of the project. That said, some knowledge gaps may not be quite so easy to reconcile.

Making a Decision

OBJECTIVES

- To consider the role of the spreadsheet in the decision-making process

- To review our knowledge and then decide on a course of action with the aid of a spreadsheet model

By the time you reach this point you will have gained a wide variety of knowledge concerning the given scenario or problem. Before you can actually make a decision you will need to analyse all of the relevant information and also review alternative solutions. Much of the information that can be gained probably has been! We have already reviewed:

- problem solving

- the decision-making process

- understanding situations

- sources of information

- other factors

At this point we may think that making the decision is easy. After all, look at the amount of work and energy we have already expended on the problem. It is important to realise that there is sometimes little or no relationship between the amount of work invested in a problem and the result that is achieved.

There may well be more than one viable alternative. What would you do then? In all of our considerations it is very important to try to see the other person's frame of reference. Something that you see as easy and straightforward may not be so simple for someone else. Perhaps you have heard the story about the chicken who said to his friend the pig: 'Why don't we treat the farmer to bacon and eggs for breakfast?' The pig responded: 'That's fine for you my friend, but in this case you're just making a donation, whereas for me it will be a total sacrifice!' The chicken's idea seemed fine from her point of view, but she had spent little time in thinking through all of the consequences.

The moral of this story is that you have to try to see other points of view and ignore them at your peril. It's much easier to do as much as we can to get everyone on board rather than have one sole individual who is determined to make it fail. Of course, we can't win everyone over to our way of thinking all of the time. But if we do try to see their point of view it will make things easier in the long run.

Perhaps now is the time to look at decision-making tools in more detail. We've already discovered that the spreadsheet can be used to answer 'what if' type questions. Let's look at another example of how the spreadsheet can give us alternatives based on the input data supplied to our model.

Sometimes the volume of data we are faced with is so large that we may easily be confused as to what course of action we should take. We may use a spreadsheet in conjunction with other mathematical tools to come to a conclusive decision when faced with a multiplicity of possible solutions.

Case Study

Eleanor has just completed college and has decided to set up her own beauty salon, 'Elle's Belles'. There are a number of options she could choose from in order to start this new venture.

1 Borrow money from the bank, rent a suitable building and equip it.

2 Purchase a property that already has an existing salon, making some equipment additions.

3 Work from home to minimise on borrowing but still incur equipment costs.

Of course, this is quite a large modelling exercise. We therefore do not have the time for a full data analysis or a discussion on:

● the waste of finance in refurbishing someone else's premises to start a new business

● the significant start-up costs associated with a property purchase

● the possible reduced number of clientele if Eleanor works from home.

These issues are part of a much bigger discussion and beyond the scope of this exercise. Nevertheless, these topics would be vitally important in a real-life scenario.

For the purpose of the exercise, which alternative in the Case Study should Eleanor choose? Number 1, 2, 3, or none of those? The last option has to be there because it may well be that the current level of thinking does not account for a realistic solution. For example, Eleanor may not be able to proceed with any of the options because of lack of finance.

A first attempt at a model could look like the spreadsheet shown in Figure 3.27. (Formatting, which will be covered in Chapter 3.12, has been added for clarity.) We haven't specified the exact equipment list, all of which is covered by the £17,000 bank loan.

Scenario 1: Renting

Although there's a lot of information in the spreadsheet it is very easy to set up. There are no complicated formulae. We've used AutoSum to complete most of the sum functions. This is an easy feature to use: you simply type in your column of data, place the cursor in the cell where you want your result to 'live', and click AutoSum.

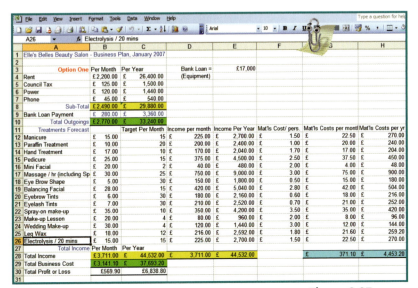

Figure 3.27

AutoSum then looks at the adjacent cells and tries to comprehend which ones need adding. If it sees a column of numbers or currency, it will automatically highlight them for you (see the dotted lines around the whole of the G13 to G27 range in Figure 3.28). All you need to do is confirm the highlighted area is correct by pressing Enter.

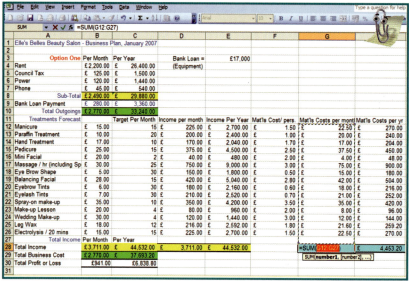

Figure 3.28

Notice that we've placed our cursor in G28, clicked AutoSum on the toolbar, and Excel goes ahead and highlights what it *thinks* we want (i.e. G12 to G27) then adds them all together after we press Enter. Note: we do get a visual check of what Excel thinks we want to add together; it highlights the cells prior to performing the calculation.

Let's take a look at subtraction – B28 minus B29.

Place the cursor in cell B30. Then type =B28-B29. This gives the formula =B28–B29. You will also notice that we've named this spreadsheet 'Renting' (see the bottom tabs on Figure 3.29)

Figure 3.29

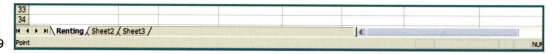

To do this, point the mouse at what was the sheet1 tab, right-click and select 'Rename'. You can then rename this to 'Renting'.

Exercise

Review the 'Elle's Belles' spreadsheet (see Figure 3.28) and try to work out which cells contain data and which contain a formula. On completion of this task, draw a rough sketch of the whole spreadsheet with gaps where the calculations are, then enter the actual formula. Alternatively you can build the model in Excel exactly as shown, completing the formula as you go. Note: the Bank Loan is a data cell; it is not connected to a formula for calculating interest.

After you have completed the previous exercise you should have a functional spreadsheet allowing you to alter input data and achieve different outputs. At this stage you must be careful not to enter data into a cell that holds a formula. If you do you will prevent the spreadsheet from working properly and introduce errors into your model.

The next step is to generate spreadsheets for the other two options – i.e. 'Purchase' and 'Working from home'. Much of the content that we have already worked hard to achieve is present in the Renting spreadsheet. It makes sense then to copy and paste this into the Sheet2 and Sheet3 spreadsheets, then modify these slightly to suit our 'Purchase' and 'Homework' options. Follow the text below for how to do this.

Hold the Ctrl key while clicking and dragging the 'Renting' tab (bottom left of screen) on to the top of the 'sheet2' tab. Then release; this will copy the whole of the Renting spreadsheet into sheet2 while renaming it Renting(2), as can be seen in Figure 3.30.

28	Total Income	£3,711.00	£	44,532.00	£	3,711.00	£	44,532.00
29	Total Business Cost	£3,141.10	£	37,693.20				
30	Total Profit or Loss	£569.90		£6,838.80				
31								
32								
33								
34								

◄ ◄ ► ►► \ **Renting** ╱ Renting (2) ╱ Sheet2 ╱ Sheet3 ╱

Ready

Figure 3.30

Rename Renting(2) to 'Purchase', by right-clicking and selecting 'Rename'.

Follow the same procedure and copy 'Renting' into the Sheet3 spreadsheet, and rename this 'Homework'. Then right-click and delete the blank Sheet2 and Sheet3 spreadsheets. If we leave them in place they will serve no purpose and just complicate the screen view (see Figure 3.31).

Scenario 2: Purchasing

The next step is to select the 'Purchase' tab and make some changes to certain parts of the spreadsheet so that we can see what happens with the finances if Eleanor decides to purchase a property for Elle's Belles. All of

Figure 3.31

the data and formulae regarding the beauty treatments can stay. These will be required in our model in order to see how viable a purchase may be. We will make the assumption that there is a suitable salon available for £170,000 and that it includes all of the equipment Eleanor will require for Elle's Belles, with the exception of a spray tan facility. We will assume that the mortgage payment will be £1100 per month and that the bank loan can be reduced to £65 per month because most of the equipment will already be in place (see Figure 3.32).

We'll need to change the following cell contents (notice the existing cells that need changing are shown on the left column of the table).

Figure 3.32

SUM			=SUM(G12:G27)		
	A	B	C	D	E
1	Elle's Belles Beauty Salon - Business Plan, January 2007				
2					
3	Option One	Per Month	Per Year	Bank Loan =	£17,000
4	Rent	£2,200.00	£ 26,400.00	(Equipment)	
5	Council Tax	£ 125.00	£ 1,500.00		
6	Power	£ 120.00	£ 1,440.00		
7	Phone	£ 45.00	£ 540.00		
8	Sub-Total	£2,490.00	£ 29,880.00		
9	Bank Loan Payment	£ 280.00	£ 3,360.00		
10	Total Outgoings	£2,770.00	£ 33,240.00		
11	Treatments Forecast		Target Per Month	Income per month	Income Per Year

Renting spreadsheet (1)	Purchase spreadsheet (2)
A4: Rent	A4: Mortgage
B4: £2,200	B4: £1,100
E3: 17,000	E3: £4000
B9: £280	B9: £65
	Insert a Spray Tan in the Treatments Forecast @ £25 and completing 30 sessions per month. Materials = £2.50 per treatment.

Scenario 3: Homework

For the last spreadsheet, 'Homework', there is no building to buy or rent. In effect Eleanor will be renting the room she decides to use as a salon from herself. With this in mind we'll charge a nominal sum, which she will then use for tax purposes against her business. Eleanor will need to tread carefully here, because the tax office may decide that her business activity is significant. Then, any relationships between the business and the house may be taxable under capital gains tax if she decides to sell the house at a later stage.

Renting spreadsheet (1)	Homework spreadsheet (3)
A4: Rent	A4: Room Hire
B4: £2,200	B4: £100
E3: 17,000	E3: £16,000
B9: £280	B9: £250
	Insert a Spray Tan in the Treatments Forecast @ £18 and completing 8 sessions per month. Materials = £2.50

The loan will still be required to carry out some minor changes to the room – e.g. addition of hot and cold water, sink, stud partition. There will also be equipment purchases, although not as much because of the limitations of the room being used. It is envisaged that the number of treatments carried out for this option will be at least 40% fewer and the prices will need to be reduced by 30% because of people's perception of the facilities.

Exercise

Complete the two new spreadsheets using the additional information presented in the two tables. Having completed the spreadsheets, write a short report for Eleanor specifying your recommendations for each option and giving reasons for the preferred choice. For example, one of the recommendations for 'Homework' may be minimum disruption and risk while still being able to operate a business. Another reason may be that this will give you time to work out the market trends and consider moving up into a purpose-built premises.

Computer Modelling

OBJECTIVES

● **To determine the accuracy of a computer model.**

As we have seen, spreadsheets are very good at modelling various situations in order that we may make better informed decisions. Depending on the input data, our output will change accordingly. For example, in a sales model we can establish exactly how many items we need to sell before we break even.

As we construct our model, the information we generate will only be as accurate as the data we put in. This presupposes that our model is accurate in the first place. As we've already seen, if one element of a formula is incorrect then the whole model will present inaccurate results. Let's review some of the issues that occur with computer-based models.

Is the logic of the model correct?

Even if all of our data is accurate and it's entered into the computer correctly, it will fail if the model has errors. For example, let's suppose we are given the task of calculating the speed of a vehicle given the time it takes to travel between two markers exactly one mile apart. There are a number of places where this model has the potential for error.

● The distance between markers may be incorrect.

● The timing device used to measure the time taken may be inaccurate.

● The formula used to perform the calculation could be incorrect.

● The data entry may be inaccurate.

Let's talk about known values for a moment. We know that if the car travels between the markers in exactly 60 seconds, then it is travelling at the rate of 1 mile per minute. Therefore, in 60 minutes the car will have travelled 60 miles. To put this in a familiar term, the speed would be 60 mph.

From this we should be able to build a model that centres on an equation calculating the speed in miles per hour. Developing this, we know that if the car travels much more quickly and completes the run in 30 seconds – i.e. twice as fast – then it must double the previous figure of 60 mph to 120 mph. If we juggle the maths a little, we will see that the number of seconds in one hour = 3600. The mathematics for this exercise will look something like the formula: Actual Speed (mph) = 60 × 60 ÷ Time Taken (secs). The spreadsheet used to perform the calculations will look something like the Excel sheet shown in Figure 3.33.

Notice that our formula, which is shown in cell B4, is currently showing a 'divide by zero' error. This is because it has tried to perform a calculation without any data in cell B3. This will function correctly as soon as we enter the time taken in cell B3.

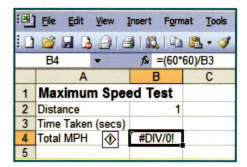

Figure 3.33

With this formula in the spreadsheet we will now complete a top speed test for a road car. For this exercise we've taken the Bugatti Veyron out of the garage and driven it down to a local aircraft runway. With a flat-out running start it hits the first marker at somewhere near its top speed; 15 seconds later it reaches the second marker. Now assuming that all of our previous four criteria are in place (and accurate), we should be able to place some data into our spreadsheet and confirm the average speed of the Bugatti between the markers.

From the values in the spreadsheet it looks like our model is behaving itself. We know that if the ground between the markers is covered in 60 seconds, then the vehicle is travelling at 60 mph. In this case the vehicle completes this in 15 seconds, which is four times as fast. This means that the vehicle must have been travelling at 240 mph, which is confirmed in Figure 3.34. It's important to see that once we've determined the accuracy of our spreadsheet, we can then rely on it for all future calculations. For the sake of completeness let's see what happens if our model is set up *incorrectly*.

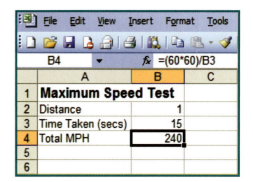

Figure 3.34

Exercise

Change the formula in cell B4 on your spreadsheet to: (60 × 60) × B3
What happens to your result? How fast is the Bugatti now?

Obviously, as powerful as the Bugatti is and even downhill with the wind behind it, it's never going to make 54,000 mph! Do you see how one small error can make a very significant difference to your results? That's why it's so important to get the formula correct right from the start. In the previous example, the mistake in the result was so large that it was very easy to spot. Unfortunately, not all errors are that easy to spot so we have to be particularly diligent in our checks and testing routines.

Are data formats appropriate?

Each cell within the spreadsheet may be set as a 'container' for specific data types. This is much the same as we saw in Chapter 2 with field properties in our Access database. In our spreadsheet, we could set a series of cells to the currency format. Thereafter, all data entered into the cells will be automatically switched to currency. The advantage of this is that Excel can then worry about how the data will look on the page. In this case it will ensure that:

- a '£' sign is displayed
- only two digits will be displayed after the decimal point (representing pence)
- commas will separate the values into thousands – e.g. £5,000,550.00.

To do this select Format/Cells and the Format Cells Dialogue box will open.

Figure 3.35 shows the Excel Format Cells dialogue box. You will notice that Excel allows a variety of different cell types depending on the data you use.

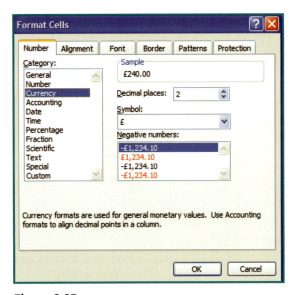

Figure 3.35

Syntax problems

As we go through life we build a massive database of experiences that help us in our daily communication. A rushed note to the milkman saying 'won extra pint please' would still result in us getting '*one*' additional bottle of milk delivered.

Our communication skills are often very refined and don't always need to be written or spoken. In the world of computing there are no such luxuries. Computers require exactness and even though the Windows environment has simplified things 'up-front' on the user interface there is still a hive of activity behind the scenes that requires everything to be very precise!

'Syntax error' sounds very technical yet it simply means you've entered a keyword the computer didn't understand.

Groucho Marx once said: 'Fruit flies like a banana.'

Does this mean fruit can fly? Or does it mean there is a type of fly that eats bananas?

Even though we may know nothing about insects, our life's experience and knowledge will allow us to deduce that statement number two is correct – our logic being: 'Well fruit can't fly, so it must be the other choice.' We gained the correct answer through our own life's experience, not via our knowledge of *Drosophila melanogaster* (fruit flies). Computers are unable to use their life's experience to do this. They have no intelligence and are therefore very much command driven.

Let's do some more work with this spreadsheet to see how the syntax is critical to our accuracy. The data in Figure 3.36 has been taken from:

www.natives.co.uk/news/2001/0501/03highestlifts.htm to show the highest ski lifts in the world.

Here, we want to establish the average height of ski lifts for the top ten highest lifts in the world. We've typed in 'avg' (short for 'average') as a guess in cell B12, together with the B2:B11 range of cells. As soon as we press Enter, Excel displays an error message, but is intelligent enough to provide us with what it thinks we are trying to achieve. Even though it knows our syntax is incorrect, in this instance it has some in-built tools to help us get to our destination (see Figure 3.37).

Figure 3.36

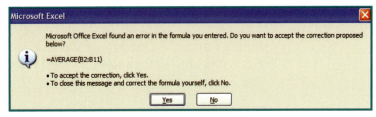

Figure 3.37

Figure 3.38

Windows was correct in its assumption about establishing the average, so click 'yes' and the job is done!

That's one example of incorrect syntax in a spreadsheet. On this occasion the spreadsheet came to our rescue with some 'in-built intelligence'. In actual fact, though, the software engineers at Microsoft thought someone may use 'avg' as a shortened form of the word average and built this into their system.

Importance of correct cell references

One way of avoiding referencing the wrong cell is to 'point to it'. In other words instead of typing =B1*C1 as the required formula, try the following:

Press the '=' key.

Left-click cell B1 with the mouse pointer.

Press the multiply key '*'.

Left-click cell C1 with the mouse pointer.

You'll notice that as you click, the cell reference is automatically entered into your formula. This process gives you a much better visual clue as to which cells are being selected.

One of the most common areas for cell contents 'misbehaving' is when we copy cells. For example, whenever you have a single, 'relatively non-permanent' data item that will be used in many formulae, it is common to represent this value in one position on the spreadsheet and not include it many times in each formula. VAT is an example of 'relatively non-permanent' data – i.e. if the government decided the current value of 17.5% was not enough it could enforce a new value of, say, 20%! Let's see what happens when we include VAT in a model and then try to copy cells.

In Chapter 3.4 we've seen how Excel uses the Copy command to replicate cells *and* increment the target contents correctly. Now we're going to repeat this, but this time we will watch it all go wrong! We've already decided that including VAT in the body of our formula is a bad idea, so we'll try setting up our spreadsheet with the VAT value in one cell.

In the spreadsheet in Figure 3.39, we have not used VAT in the formula but rather 'pointed' to it in a single cell (D1), which we have kept for holding the value of VAT. The formula in cell C3 is shown in the formula bar and calculates the value of VAT then adds it to the £600.

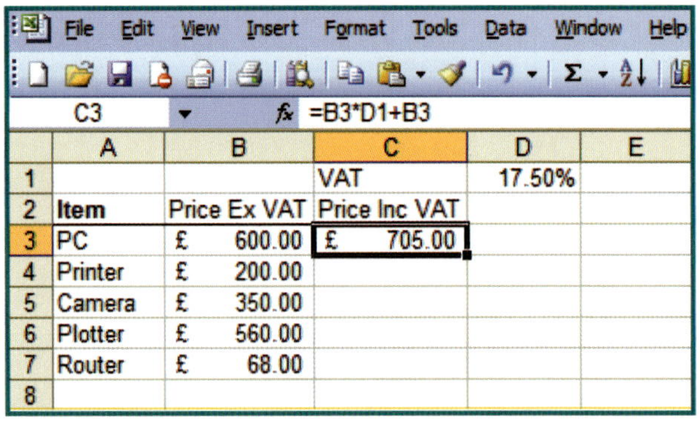

Figure 3.39

Notice the formula entered in cell C3 works. The formula bar shows the correct formula, so we now have a high level of confidence regarding our model! The next step is to replicate this formula held in cell C3, into cells C4 to C7. We simply follow the procedure previously outlined in Chapter 3.4 for copying cell contents (see page 189).

Figure 3.40 shows our completed spreadsheet with all the cells copied and *no error messages*. Great, we've succeeded. We already know that our original formula in C3 is correct, but what about cell C4? This is incorrect. The price of the £200 printer is the same in cells B4 and C4 (even after the VAT has been added)! The other cells below are also incorrect; interestingly there was no error message to indicate that we were doing something wrong!

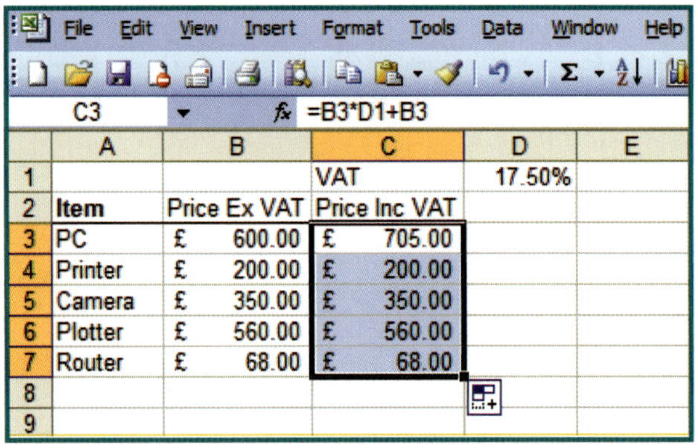

Figure 3.40

Tip:

If you want to perform the copy a quick way, with the cursor in C3 just place it over the cell until the bottom right corner changes to a small black cross. Left-click the cross and drag it down to cell C7. This gives the same result as the Copy process previously demonstrated in Chapter 3.4 (pages 187–191), only much quicker.

Exercise

Take a close look at the values of the formula in each of the target cells C4 to C7. You need to look at the values of cell D in particular to establish what is going wrong with this Copy process. Hopefully you can see what has gone wrong here. The workaround for this type of scenario can be found in the section entitled 'Absolute and relative referencing!' in Chapter 3.12, page 233.

A Model to Consider Alternatives and Justifying the Decision

OBJECTIVES

- **To use a spreadsheet to help clarify a decision between a number of alternatives**
- **To consider the results of the model and other factors in order to make a decision**

As we've already seen, the accuracy of the model is crucial to the success of all future decisions. Computer modelling is very good with facts but does have some drawbacks with certain aspects of decision-making. The example of weather forecasting was one such area. As long as we're aware of the limitations, computer-based modelling can still be very useful in the decision-making process.

Decisions that produce the best results

For every decision made within an organisation there should be a result that will add benefit or value. But not all decisions will bring a benefit; in certain cases a change of process or product may be detrimental. A simple system known as 'Cost Benefit Analysis' attempts to ascertain the equivalent monetary value of a project in order to determine whether the scheme is worthwhile or not. As you review a problem you may have imparted a high level of creativity and resource in order to get the best possible result. It may be that after all this work and expense the project may not be worth implementing because of the total costs involved. Let's take the simple case of an enthusiastic manager and his departmental telephone bill.

Case Study

An eager new manager decided his employees should complete a form giving details of their personal phone calls made in company time – the idea being that the employees pay the finance department the private call charges at the end of every month. The manager thought this was a great idea for saving company resources.

At first glance this seems to be a good money-saving idea. However, before embarking on strategies such as this it is worth reviewing aspects of the implementation. For example, the time taken to complete the forms needs to be considered (the employees are highly likely to tackle this task in work time).

Consider also the finance department's time to administer the process. There may also be a loss of goodwill from employees. With these and other considerations in mind, if the staff usage is actually a moderate amount per month, it may well be best to dismiss this idea. The costs and inconvenience of administration may well outweigh any benefits. With Cost Benefit Analysis we have a relatively simple technique for deciding whether or not to make a change and implement a new system. The basic principle is to add all the benefits together, then subtract the associated costs.

Sometimes the costs are a little more complex to work out because they may be fixed or ongoing, but this is still a worthwhile system for establishing a cost-effective solution.

Case Study

Mendon's Music Store is investigating a plan to develop its business. The owner has seen a noticeable decrease in Internet sales in the last few months, including Christmas sales which are normally much higher. At the moment the store is selling most of its CDs over the Internet but feels there is potential to rapidly expand sales at its premises, which happens to be on the corner of a busy high street. To do this will require additional resources and will be a drain on staff as further training is implemented. The following tables give approximate details of the costs envisaged.

Number units	Equipment	Cost per unit	Total
5	Display counters	£789.00	
10	Storage units	£330.00	
2	Computers	£780.00	
2	Printers	£350.00	
3	Electronic cash registers	£445.00	
Total			
Training Costs			

Training need	No. staff	Cost per person	Total
Cash till	3	£90.00	
Keyboard skills	3	£110.00	
Sales training	3	£220.00	
Total			
Other factors			

Losses	Days	Cost	Total
Sales time	22	£150 per day	
Total			
Total costs:			

All expenses	Costs	
Costs		
Training		
Other factors		

Company benefits/projections

	Income
Extra CD sales on premises	£12000
Estimated increase in sales because of improved face-to-face communications	£5500
Estimated increase in sales because of better feedback ref. products	£2500
Increased Internet Sales with new customers	£2000
Total	

The data in the previous tables is shown in Figure 3.41. This spreadsheet lays out all of the known expenses and estimates in order that we may predict the benefits (if any) of expanding the business. This is a business model based on the data Mrs Mendon supplied. It is a first step and it may necessitate meeting in order to clarify certain aspects and gather more data.

The bottom line, based on all of our data, looks pretty good and does indicate that this venture seems to have some possibilities (at least based on the supplied data).

Notice that we've renamed the Sheet1 tab at the bottom left-hand side of the spreadsheet. To do this right click it, Select 'Rename' and enter 'Cost Benefit Analysis'.

The alternatives

There are alternative options that could be built into the model. For example, we could decide to make the expansion without the need for all of the staff accounted for. This would reduce costs but it would also increase pressure and could potentially lose customers as a result of reduced levels of service. The great thing about the

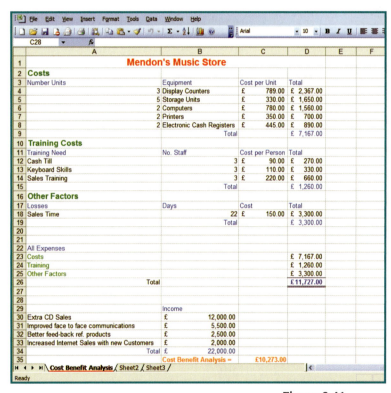

Figure 3.41

Tip:

If you want to generate a slick solution to this, you'll need to refer to the information from the section entitled 'Absolute and relative referencing!' in Chapter 3.12 (see page 233. This makes multiple 'What ifs' (when you change each percentage value) a lot easier – i.e. storing the percentage reduction in one cell only. Choosing the decision that gives the best result will really be down to the company and its longer-term goals. For now, this spreadsheet will enable it to adjust the figures in order to make a final choice.

spreadsheet is that we can enter many different scenarios, then see exactly the differences the changes will make to the company profit margins. It may be that Mendon's is prepared to work with the expansion and perhaps take a loss over a given period while the company increases its turnover. We could look at further cost-cutting exercises – e.g. we could recommend two refurbished computers and one printer with an electronic switch that could receive data from both computers, all at reduced costs.

It may be that we could add features to the model that could make a difference to the overall profit. As we continue reviewing the model it is clear that it is assisting with a possible decision regarding expansion. However, the more we think about it the more it seems that additional information may be required in order to make an informed decision.

Exercise

Try entering different data into the spreadsheet and see what sort of differences it makes to the overall profitability of the store. Write a short report for the attention of Mrs Mendon, giving her a breakdown of some of the possible alternatives, including those that don't return an immediate profit.

Factors that differentiate between them

As we look at this very simple scenario we can see that it starts to get more complex the more we think about the possibilities. How important is an initial profit to Mrs Mendon? Perhaps she is willing to place resources into the expansion, beyond her initial means, in order to ensure a more successful outcome. For example, she may consider a bank loan that would provide a buffer in the initial stages of the project. She might also consider one of her staff as a partner, who could then share some of the expansion costs.

All of these alternatives add to the complexity of the scenario and are very important in the project's development. These models are generally dynamic with new features added as the situation evolves. That's why effective communication through meetings is imperative if the project is going to succeed.

Things the model does not take into account

This is a very basic business planning model and there are many aspects that could be refined. The model only looks at 'additional' resources for the Music Store. The assumption is that the existing Internet sales revenue and the staff costs do not need to be included because this side of the business is already functioning. This, of course, would need to be made more robust in the real world, especially as Internet sales are decreasing. Staff wages, CD wholesale costs, existing stock costs, delivery charges, power, interest rates, bank charges, transport, fuel costs, rent and so on would all need to be built into the model. Even with all of this additional data there would still be assumptions regarding projected new sales and such things as increased customer loyalty as a result of face-to-face sales and so on. The model does not account for different options in the store hardware being purchased. Are there different counter specifications or electronic cash registers that are more economical for example?

What the impact of these might be

In every decision there will always be an element of the unknown that could surprise us as we see the outcome of the whole process. It may be, for example, that if we did include the whole of the existing Internet company data, we may find it is in itself profitable even though sales seem to be reducing. This profit may then be used to substantiate the new venture to a greater degree than was first expected. This reminds us of the need for accuracy in gaining precise data so as to provide precise information for our decisions!

Case Study

As we have seen, the Mendon's Music Store gave us some very sparse information on which to inform the decision-making process for company expansion. The owner mistakenly decided that the Internet side of the business did not need to be included as part of the resources in the new business model. This was, of course, an error; as we delved more deeply into the new model it became apparent that (possibly) additional funds would be required to ensure the success of the high street venture. Even if this extra finance wasn't required, it was still a naïve step *not* to include the whole company profile in the original data sheets from which the model was produced.

The moral of this scenario is 'include everything initially'. It is far easier to ignore existing data than it is to find data that hasn't been presented in the first place.

Exercise

Make a list of all the things you can think of that you would like to know about the Mendon's Music Store in a document entitled: 'Information required for the business model'. On completion, compare notes with your friends, then update your own findings.

Up until this point you have considered the results of the model and asked 'what if' type questions to establish the limitations. As a knowledge worker you will reach the point where you can make a valid decision from all of the considered alternatives. This decision should be one that is the best available given the constraints you have worked with.

Throughout the processes it is vital to record all aspects of your progress. This action will enable you to present your results and answer questions regarding why some steps were taken, but not others. You must consider others who may be affected by the decision. It is important to recognise that the decision may help the company and its employees to become more profitable and to raise its profile. On the other hand, a poor decision could have the inverse effect and may make the company's position weaker as a result.

We are at a point where the decision is made; now we have to justify it! This will be a fairly easy process if we recorded the steps that preceded the decision. This is commonly called an audit trail in other aspects of business. The audit trail enables you to justify your final decision by providing a reasonable argument for all of the previous steps. One way of keeping the audit trail is by recording key steps in a spreadsheet. The following example may be appropriate for your needs.

Date	Description	Evidence location	Main action
5/4/07	Reviewed last year's Internet sales noting steady decline.	Accounts file 2005–2006	Arrange emergency meeting with MD.
7/4/07	Meeting with Mrs Mendon ref. decline	Minutes of meeting 7/4/07	Mrs Mendon to consider high street possibilities

In the case of Mendon's Music Store the decision is about whether or not it should keep a discrete online business or whether it should also expand this into a high street facility. As we review the cost benefit analysis we will see that the company, with its existing projections, will benefit. This benefit is not large, so the music store will need to present some convincing arguments in order to gain approval.

As we've already seen, the existing model does have a fundamental weakness in that it hasn't considered the level of profitability of the online store. In addition, the costs represented in the model are dynamic because all the initial start-up costs are mainly one-offs – i.e. they will be purchased once and so will not come out of the budget as the months progress. This being the case, this proposal is in a stronger position. If we take Mendon's as the example we should mention the start-up costs and training costs.

It is always important to own up to the weaknesses or shortcomings in a project to prove that you have given consideration to some of the negative aspects as well. Very rarely would you expect to present a project proposal that had no downsides. In our scenario some of the key points we are likely to be quizzed on will be such things as the income 'guesses'.

- How do you know you have extra CD sales?
- How do you know how many?
- How do you know there will be improved face-to-face communication with customers?

These are the issues that may well arise when you have to justify your decision. The great thing about the model is that you can supply a number of different scenarios, which illustrates how the income is likely to be affected. For example, you could enter revised costs for the equipment based on the idea of buying refurbished computers and perhaps one less printer. This type of thinking can be incorporated into the model in order to review the associated decreases in costs (see Figure 3.42).

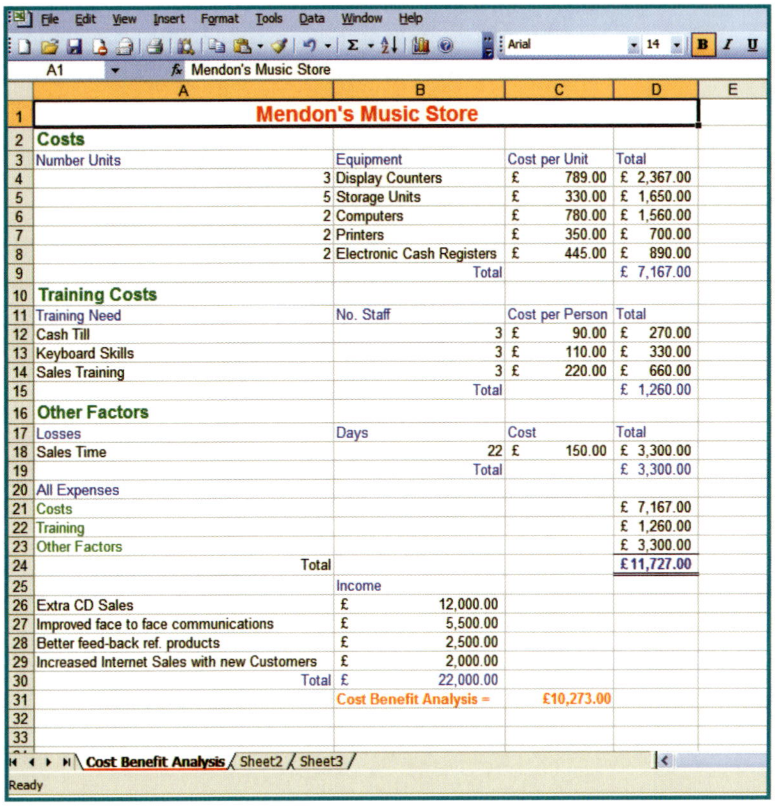

	A	B	C	D	E
1	Mendon's Music Store				
2	Costs				
3	Number Units	Equipment	Cost per Unit	Total	
4	3	Display Counters	£ 789.00	£ 2,367.00	
5	5	Storage Units	£ 330.00	£ 1,650.00	
6	2	Computers	£ 780.00	£ 1,560.00	
7	2	Printers	£ 350.00	£ 700.00	
8	2	Electronic Cash Registers	£ 445.00	£ 890.00	
9		Total		£ 7,167.00	
10	Training Costs				
11	Training Need	No. Staff	Cost per Person	Total	
12	Cash Till	3	£ 90.00	£ 270.00	
13	Keyboard Skills	3	£ 110.00	£ 330.00	
14	Sales Training	3	£ 220.00	£ 660.00	
15		Total		£ 1,260.00	
16	Other Factors				
17	Losses	Days	Cost	Total	
18	Sales Time	22	£ 150.00	£ 3,300.00	
19		Total		£ 3,300.00	
20	All Expenses				
21	Costs			£ 7,167.00	
22	Training			£ 1,260.00	
23	Other Factors			£ 3,300.00	
24	Total			£11,727.00	
25		Income			
26	Extra CD Sales	£ 12,000.00			
27	Improved face to face communications	£ 5,500.00			
28	Better feed-back ref. products	£ 2,500.00			
29	Increased Internet Sales with new Customers	£ 2,000.00			
30	Total	£ 22,000.00			
31		Cost Benefit Analysis =	£10,273.00		
32					
33					

Figure 3.42

You should have a number of these spreadsheets summarised in your proposal but also attached as full documents as additional evidence.

Even though your proposal may be the best thing since the invention of the wheel, it's down to you to sell it to the audience. With this 'sales' theme in mind we are about to enter Chapter 3.10, in which we will discuss further issues relating to this task.

Portfolio Builder: ***Using the spreadsheet skills and techniques that you have gained, think about a business model for a small company of your choice. For example, you could set up a small business that sells second-hand CDs or computer games, a surf or skateboard shop, beauty or health products. Having selected a business idea, go ahead and organise a business plan taking into account the cost of premises, rent, rates, supplies, staff and other aspects that you can think of. It may be helpful in the initial stages to organise a small discussion group to make sure that you have covered all aspects. You will need to use the Internet to establish premises costs and to see what typical rents and rates you will have to pay. You will need to source a supplier to price the stock and also to think about profit margins. Once you have a good idea of what all the costs are likely to be you can build a spreadsheet model to forecast the growth of your new enterprise.***

Reporting to Others and Evaluation

OBJECTIVES

- To use effective presentation techniques to present your recommendations
- To see how the model may have helped in the decision-making process
- To consider whether the model needs extending

The decision is made; we have spent time thinking through the consequences and justified our processes in every way. The next step is reporting back and presenting our thoughts to others. We may feel that our presentation skills are lacking. Indeed we may even feel that we can't do it! If this is the case we will need to get the 'big guns' out and find ourselves some additional support! If we are going to sell this idea and we're not very confident, then we'd better get something on our side to level the pitch.

PowerPoint is the ideal tool for this. It can assist us in the task of presenting our ideas in a logical and professional way. Further information on the use of PowerPoint can be found in Chapter 1 and also in Chapter 3.12 ICT Skills (see pages 224–247).

Summary of the current situation

It is important to give your audience a 'where are we now' picture in order to remind them of the base reference point. This helps to clarify the current situation and also to ensure that everyone is 'reading from the same page' as you consider the company situation. The summary need not be a long document and can even be as simple as a number of short bullet points that establish the situation as it stands.

If we take Mendon's Music Store as an example, our 'first draft' PowerPoint slides may look something like those shown in Figures 3.43 and 3.44 .

Sources of information and alternatives

As with any report, sources of information are crucial to the success of our proposal. If our sources are legitimate and have a feeling of quality, then it will add credibility to our proposal (see Figure 3.45). If, on the other hand, our sources are limited and contain elements of hearsay, then their validity may well be questioned by those to whom we look for approval.

Other factors taken into consideration

Your audience will be very interested in other factors that have been considered as you've progressed with this project. It's worth remembering that some of the

Figure 3.43

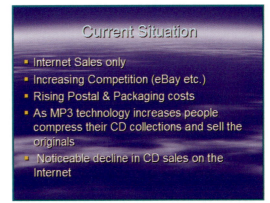

Figure 3.44

audience may well be shareholders in the company and as such have an investment to consider. There may be employees who could be anxious at the thought of change within the organisation. In addition to this, people are generally very inquisitive and would like to know exactly how much research you will have applied to this problem. The more of this type of consideration they can observe, the more their confidence in you is likely to rise (see Figure 3.46).

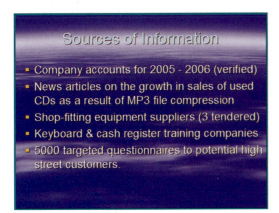

Figure 3.45

Figure 3.46

Method used to reach your decision

Much of the work for this scenario would have been collected and then analysed in our model. The basic model was a starting point, but that would need additional refinement to include the current position of Internet sales, staffing levels, wages and so on. As with everything else already discussed it's important to be able to present this information to the target audience.

Your decision

As you are recommending a change based on your research you will need to send a clear message that your proposal has merit. A slide showing a pictorial representation of the company's current sales position may well have the type of influential weight that is required. Again, PowerPoint is a powerful supporter to have on your side at this point in the proceedings (see Figures 3.47 and 3.48).

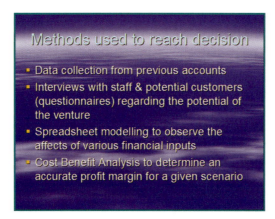

Figure 3.47

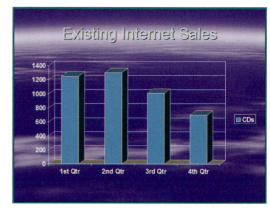

Figure 3.48

Tip:

PowerPoint is only an aid to a good presentation. It must be supplemented by other recognised aspects of a skilled delivery. Proper use of spelling, grammar and other presentation techniques are all essential aspects of this final production, and they should not be underestimated. People in your audience will make up their minds about you in the opening minutes, so ensure you dress appropriately, speak clearly and maintain suitable eye contact.

Justification, and evidence for it

This is a crucial element in the process because you have to be able to justify what may be a critical path for the company to commit to. Evidence of your efforts must be available together with a logical audit trail that 'proves' and supports your decision (see Figures 3.49 and 3.50).

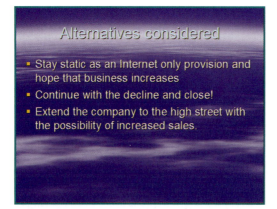

Figure 3.49

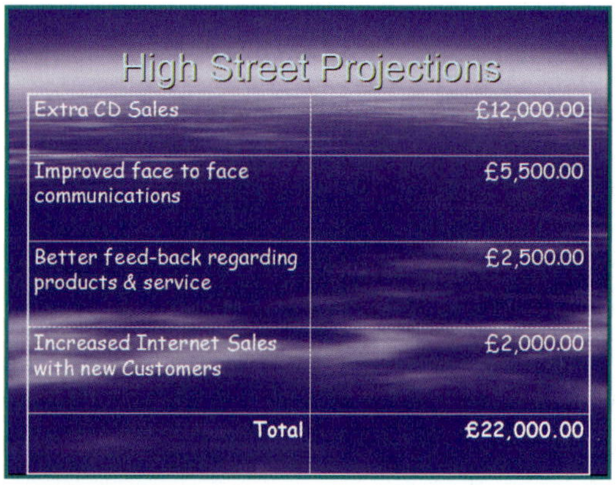

Figure 3.50

This justification will commonly be implemented by a question-and-answer session. Even though you may feel you have covered all aspects within your presentation, it is highly likely that you have omitted certain aspects that should be clarified.

PowerPoint has a notes facility that may help you to deliver your presentation. Even if you are using an interactive whiteboard or overhead projector, it's a good idea to have a paper-based copy of your slides in front of you. This will assist you in two situations.

1 Even with all the technical equipment working faultlessly, the printed sheets will provide helpful prompts to assist you with your presentation.

2 If the equipment fails then you will still be able to continue with the delivery.

Figure 3.51 shows how PowerPoint's features enable us to provide 'polish' to our presentation by allowing us to enter 'Notes' that may be printed for our benefit and will not be viewed by our audience.

Figure 3.51

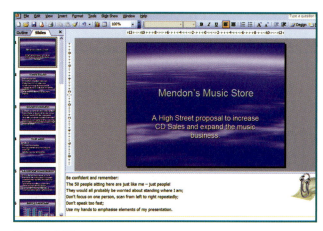

Figure 3.52

To do this place the cursor in the 'Click to Add Notes' box just below and to the left of the current slide. This will allow you to add a few important prompts to help with the presentation (see Figure 3.52).

Obviously, the notes against the slide in Figure 3.51 be comprehensive because you will have time to reflect on these before you are invited to speak. All subsequent slides may need just short phrases that you can scan quickly.

The whole purpose of a model is that it's used as an aid to inform the final decision. An important aspect of this is an evaluation to see if it did what it was supposed to.

Evaluation of the model

It's worth pointing out that there are various organisations that are set up to research the area of spreadsheet risk. See for example EuSpRIG **http://www.eusprig.org/**

EuSpRIG 'is an interest group of academia and industry promoting research regarding the extent and nature of spreadsheet risks, methods of prevention and detection of errors and methods of limiting damage. We bring together researchers and professionals in the areas of business, software engineering and audit to actively seek useful solutions.'

We may ask did the spreadsheet model succeed in helping you to make the vital decision? Was it able to fill in all of the gaps when we asked the 'what if' questions of it?

In order to study this element of the course we will re-visit the Web Design Company. You may recall this was the company that had used a very simple model to enable it to decide on an appropriate price for individuals who required its services.

How well has the model performed?

If we take the original model it was quite effective as a system that enabled the sales team to generate quotations. However, it didn't account for such things as complexity of graphics, cost of stock photography, other photographic costs, Flash content and other animation, travel, overtime, VAT charges and discounts (see Figure 3.53).

If you return to your own version of this spreadsheet solution you can confirm the calculations are accurate and the performance is very responsive as you enter variable data.

	A	B	C	D	E
1	The Web Design Company				
2	Pricing System (based on one years cover)				
3					
4			Cost/item	Totals	
5	Standard set-up Costs		£ 200.00	£ 200.00	
6	Number of Pages	4	£ 35.00	£ 140.00	
7	Number of graphics	15	£ 15.00	£ 225.00	
8	Hosting?		£ 90.00	£ 90.00	
9	Updates included		£ 130.00	£ 130.00	
10					
11	Total Price of the Job			£ 785.00	
12	Notes:				
13	Updates = four/year max 3hrs work each				
14	Graphics = no extensive manipulation				
15					

Figure 3.53

To what extent has the model helped you to make the decision?

In this case the model was built in order that we could make a decision about how much the company should charge for a website. It was able to take in variable data and from that determine a total price for designing and hosting a website. In this way it was effective in its role of helping us to decide on a quotation, which could then be presented to the prospective customer. Of course, we have documented a number of limitations that would need to be addressed, especially following the appointment of the new finance manager.

What else would you like to do?

We know the managing director would have liked some graphical output from the model. Perhaps a bar chart indicating the cost of labour, overtime and gross income could be generated. This may be used for reports and other documents within the Web Design Company. We would also like the model to take on more data in order to provide a more robust system of quote generation. Have a look at a second draft of the spreadsheet (Figure 3.54) which can be seen together with data for a job in progress.

This is for a customer who had the following requirements, along with certain things already in place.

- A Flash intro.

- 20 pages. (No database requirement at the moment.)

- A photographer for around four shots of the workforce and the premises (no stock photographs because they had their own from a previous marketing job).

- The salesperson thought that two on-site visits would be required.

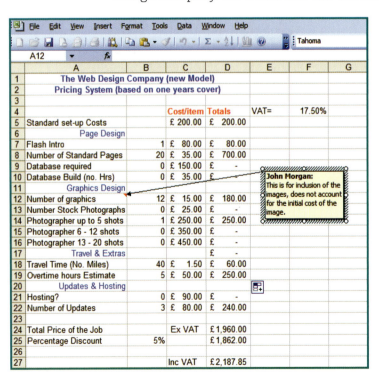

Figure 3.54

- The job was likely to have a fairly tight deadline, so the salesperson was including five hours of overtime just in case.

- The company already has a site and a domain name, which will be used for the new version of the website.

- Three updates will be built in to the price, but they may need more. These will be priced as additional work when the time comes.

- The company negotiated a 5% discount as a result of recommending another customer to the Web Design Company.

Does the model need extending and, if so, how?

Our first model was clearly in need of some serious tweaking. It did the job, but not to the liking of the new finance manager. As part of previous exercises you have probably made some changes to the spreadsheet already.

Exercise

Take the best parts of the above model and the one that you completed on page 000 to produce something that's close to being able to properly satisfy this business need for the Web Design Company. We'll take a look at the next case study and then price an actual job for Ryan's Surf Shop.

Case Study

Ryan has just completed an Art and Design course at his local college. Throughout the course he has always been keen to do something practical with his designs and to combine this with his passion for surfing.

Both Ryan's tutors, Richard and Andy, are keen to see him succeed and think he will be successful if he teams up with Will, another student keen to be involved in surfboard design and production. They've completed a number of prototype boards and Dave the photographer has taken some excellent digital images for marketing purposes. They've all met with the Head of the Innovation Centre, who has agreed to rent them workshop space for a nominal rate. They all think that a website will be one of the first steps in getting them noticed and have approached you with a list of requirements.

Ryan's Surf Shop website requirements:

- one Flash opening page
- 12 pages
- 25 images (supplied), plus 5 stock photographs
- total travel 35 miles
- anticipated 15 hours of overtime
- hosting for one year
- three updates
- database with stock items (approximately 8 hours of work)
- 5% discount applied to before VAT price
- VAT to be charged @ 17.5%.

In addition to the surf company Ryan, Will and Jane also volunteer for the local Lifeboat Service. They have access to three jetskis which are used to provide regular beach patrols and are also used for certain emergencies involving towing.

As this is a new initiative the Lifeboat Service is leasing the jet skis under a pilot scheme from three companies at the following rates:

- Just Jets at £70 per month and £12 per hour with the first 75 hours free of charge

- Fast Ski at £83 per month and £15 per hour with the first 25 hours free of charge

- Jet Ski World at £92 per month and £20 per hour with the first 55 hours free of charge.

The three jet skis are fitted with tamper-proof digital data loggers, which are checked quarterly by each company for billing purposes.

The current annual usage for each user needs to be calculated. Throughout the year Ryan used Just Jets, Will used Jet Ski World and Jane was with Fast Ski.

The task is to see which company represents best value based on the available data. To complicate things a little more all three companies have agreed to provide a discount, *if* the Lifeboat Service is prepared to offer them a sole leasing arrangement. This means that the discount would apply only if they decided to lease the three jet skis from the one company. The discounts being offered are as follows:

- Just Jets   10%
- Fast Ski   30%
- Jet Ski World   35%

In the exam you are likely to receive pre-release materials which may include the spreadsheet model (incomplete) and an overview of the problem.

In this case you are supplied with some base data, which is the current usage that Ryan, Will and Jane make of the Jet Skis. This is a comma delimited file which you will need to import into Excel. You won't import this directly into the model because it may not be in the exact format required. You will probably import it and then Copy and Paste the relevant elements into your model.

In this case the file looks like this:

"Names", "Number of Hours", "Quarter"
"Ryan",88,1
"Ryan",74,2
"Ryan",126,3
"Ryan",105,4
"Will",107,1
"Will",67,2
"Will",89,3
"Will",135,4
"Jane",125,1
"Jane",105,2

"Jane",156,3
"Jane",88,4

Set up this file in Microsoft Notepad, using commas as the delimiters (these tell the Import function in Excel where each cell ends). Then using Excel:

- open a new spreadsheet
- Data/Import External Data.

For a full explanation of this import method, see Chapter 3.12 (pages 224–247).

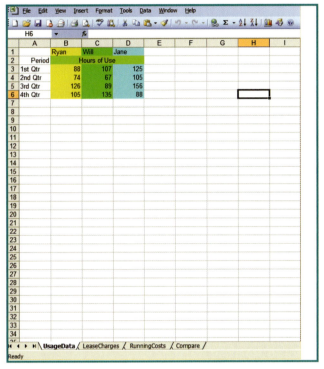

Figure 3.55

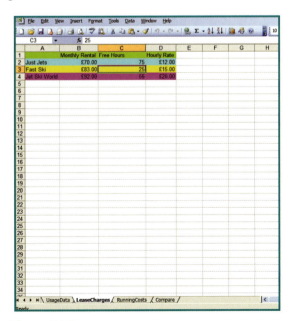

Figure 3.56

Let's take a look at some screenshots of the spreadsheet supplied with this case study. The completed spreadsheet is shown (see Figure 3.55). In the examination you will have to supply some of the formulae yourselves.

The first tab 'Usage Data' shows the number of hours that the jet skis have been in use by the three team members. This may be given as shown as part of the spreadsheet, but it is more likely to be given to you as a text file which you have to import (you'll see how to do this in Chapter 12, in the section entitled 'Importing data from other applications'.

Figure 3.56 shows the Lease Charge arrangements that the Lifeboat Service is using.

Notice that you are now in the area of the second spreadsheet in the same workbook, called 'LeaseCharges' (the tab on the bottom of the screen). There are no formulae in the cells just data.

In Figure 3.57 the formula is shown in cell B2. It looks very complicated but is fairly simple to understand. The more complex formulae are likely already to be in the model for the examination; all you will have to do is have an understanding of how they work!

Basically, the formula is an IF statement that is asking the following.

If the data item in the Usage Data sheet (B3) *minus* the Lease Charges found in C2 (the number of free hours) are greater than zero, *then* take the value in the Usage Data (B3) minus the Lease Charge in C2 and multiply this by the Lease Charges in D2.

It should be noted that all we are calculating here is the cost of the hours over and above the free hours we already get with each jet ski. The very last character in the IF statement, '0', is what goes in the cell if we didn't use all our free hours that quarter – which is, as you'd expect, equal to zero. We don't actually calculate the total cost of the jet ski – i.e. the hourly charge and the monthly charge – until we get to the comparison stage in the last spreadsheet tab.

Figures 3.58, 3.59 and 3.60 show how this formula changes from cell to cell.

Notice how the 'UsageData' enables you to collect data from the other spreadsheet and insert it into the current sheet – e.g. UsageData!B4 is the data item found in

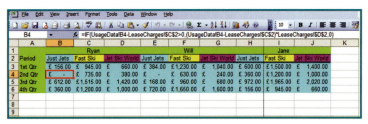

Figure 3.57

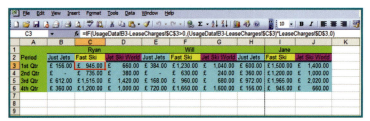

Figure 3.58

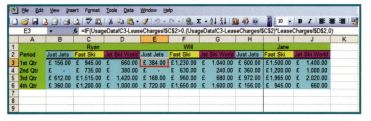

Figure 3.59

Figure 3.60

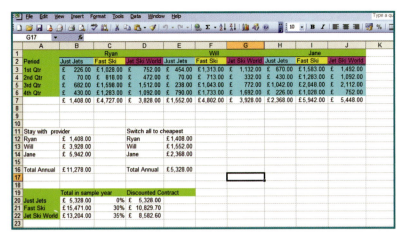

Figure 3.61

cell B4 of the UsageData spreadsheet. You'll also notice some dollar signs. These will be fully explained in Chapter 3.12 in the section entitled 'Absolute and relative referencing!' (page 233).

Probably the easiest way to work through the logic of this is by sketching out the sheets on paper. Make sure you also do a manual calculation so that you can compare your results.

Our last sheet (Figure 3.61) completes a final total for all of the costs for each Jet Ski Company and each team member who has used the jet ski throughout the year.

We've completed this sheet by using some common functions (see Chapter 3.12 for further information) in order to automate certain tasks. For example, we are required to find the cheapest provider. We can do this by using the Min function over a range of cells for each individual (see Figure 3.62). We've then used the SUM function to provide the required additions, together with Copy to adjacent cells (see Figure 3.63).

This completes a quick overview of a model that will allow you to make comparisons and find answers to problems.

Figure 3.62

E14 = =MIN(H7:J7)

Period	Just Jets	Fast Ski	Jet Ski World	Just Jets
	Ryan			
1st Qtr	£ 226.00	£1,028.00	£ 752.00	£ 454.00
2nd Qtr	£ 70.00	£ 818.00	£ 472.00	£ 70.00
3rd Qtr	£ 682.00	£1,598.00	£ 1,512.00	£ 238.00
4th Qtr	£ 430.00	£1,283.00	£ 1,092.00	£ 790.00
	£ 1,408.00	£4,727.00	£ 3,828.00	£1,552.00

Stay with provider / Switch all to cheapest

Ryan	£ 1,408.00	Ryan	£1,408.00
Will	£ 3,928.00	Will	£1,552.00
Jane	£ 5,942.00	Jane	£2,368.00
Total Annual	£11,278.00	Total Annual	£5,328.00

Figure 3.63

B7 = =SUM(B3:B6)

Period	Just Jets	Fast Ski
	Ryan	
1st Qtr	£ 226.00	£1,028.00
2nd Qtr	£ 70.00	£ 818.00
3rd Qtr	£ 682.00	£1,598.00
4th Qtr	£ 430.00	£1,283.00
	£ 1,408.00	£4,727.00

3.12 ICT Skills (a)

OBJECTIVES

- To use a range of ICT applications

Entering and editing data

Let's take a look at a model to gain a picture of exactly how Excel can assist with the day-to-day modelling of scenarios. As an example, we will consider a new company and the need to project future revenue for inclusion in a business plan. To do this we will use a spreadsheet to try to predict the financial status of the company after one year of trading. Please note that this will be a fairly basic model, which we'll use to illustrate the features of Excel. A real-life business model would of course be much more comprehensive.

Start Excel. Enter the labels as shown in Figure 3.64.

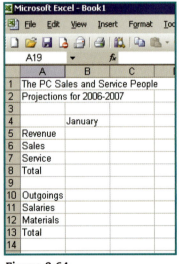

Figure 3.64

We've started to enter the months and, as always, there are quick ways of doing things within Excel. In this case we want to extend January from cell B4 through to cell M4 incrementing the months as we go. To do this place the cursor over 'January' until you see a small black cross in the bottom right-hand corner of cell B4. Left-click and drag the cursor to the right until you get to cell M4. As you do this you will see a yellow box indicating the months as they are replicated (see Figure 3.65).

You'll notice in Figure 3.66 how Excel has tried to enter the data in the default cell size which has cropped September.

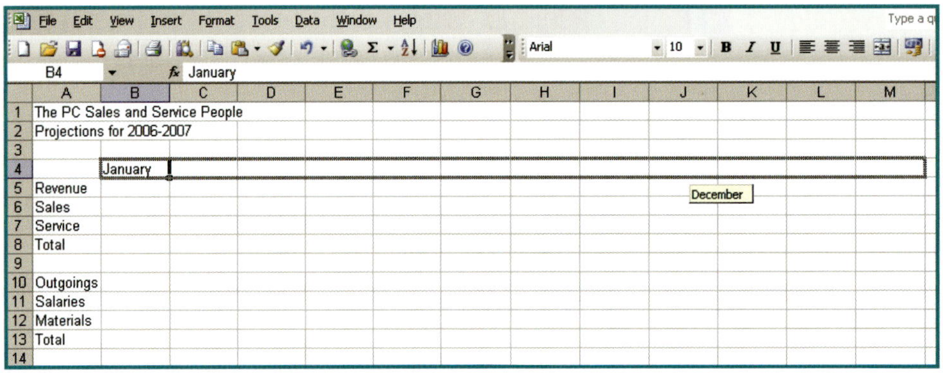

Figure 3.65

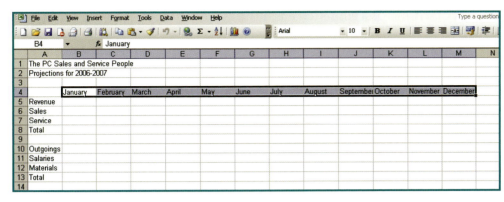

Figure 3.66

With the months still highlighted, Select Format/Column/Width (see Figure 3.67).

Then Overtype the Default 8.43 with 10.00. This will give you additional space for all of your months. Note: we may have to refine these widths further, depending on how large our numbers are when we enter the financial values.

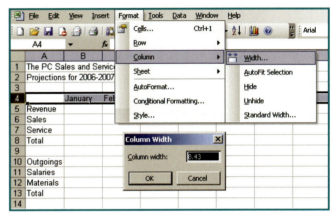

Figure 3.67

The next step is to format the cells so that the spreadsheet looks a little more user friendly. We'll Centre the Title 'The PC Sales and Service People' over all of the columns up to and including December. To do this highlight the cells from A1 through to M1. Then select Format/Cells, select the Alignment tab, and click the 'Merge cells' Text control box (see Figure 3.68).

If you click OK at this point, the cells will merge into one, extending from A1 through to M1. Because this is now treated as one cell, if we click the 'Centre' icon, the title will be centred across the whole of the merged range (see Figure 3.69).

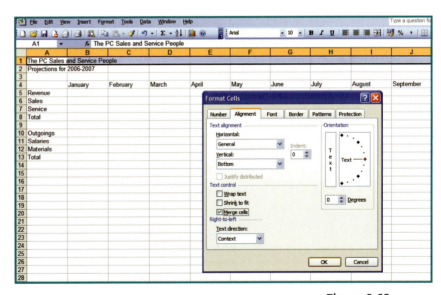

Figure 3.68

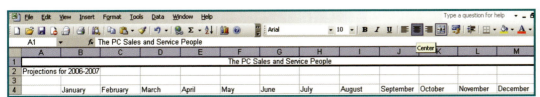

Figure 3.69

We now follow the same procedure to centre the 'Projections for 2006–2007 title (see Figure 3.70). Then highlight both cells (effectively A1 and B1), increase the Font Size to 16, click the Font Colour icon and switch the colour to Dark Blue.

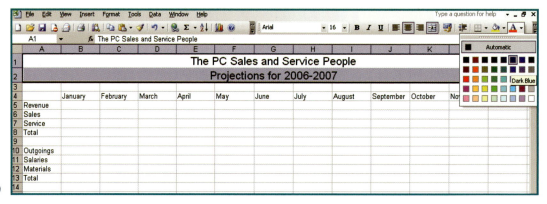

Figure 3.70

Tip:

If you try to drag and select here you will always finish with *all* labels highlighted from Revenue down to Outgoings.

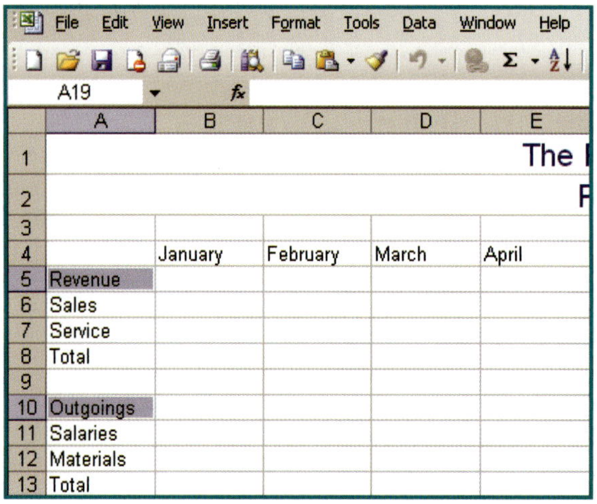

Figure 3.71

Next, we take our main Row Headings, 'Revenue' and 'Outgoings', switch on Bold and change the font colour to blue. To isolate these cells we need to select each heading by pointing at each cell whilst holding down the CTRL key. Notice only the required cells have been selected (see Figure 3.71).

With the cells selected we can complete our formatting by switching the Font Size to 12 and Selecting 'Bold' (see Figure 3.72).

Notice how, with Bold selected, our labels have become too big for their cells!

At this stage, let's highlight the actual data labels Sales, Service and so on, and Right Justify the cells to set them apart from the main title (Revenue, Outgoings – see Figure 3.73).

Next we'll place a border around our Months row (as shown in Figure 3.74). To do this highlight the months by left-clicking cell B4 and dragging across the page to Cell M4. Then click Format/Cell, the Format Cells Dialogue Box will open.

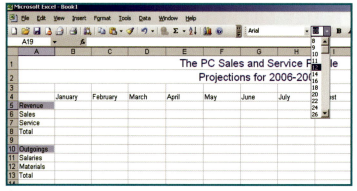

Figure 3.72

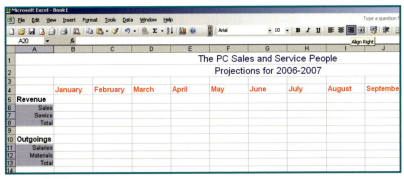

Figure 3.73

Exercise

Change the column width on your spreadsheet to accommodate the new label sizes by using the Format menu as shown in one of the previous procedures. See if you can alter the column width by using another method that doesn't involve Menus or Icons. Highlight Row4 and switch all of the month labels to Red, Bold and Font 12. Re-adjust the Column widths to suit the extended label sizes.

In this case we are going to select 'Outline' which will switch an outline border around the months from January through to December. Before we leave this process we can also select the Patterns Tab (see Figure 3.75). Do this and select an appropriate background colour for your months row.

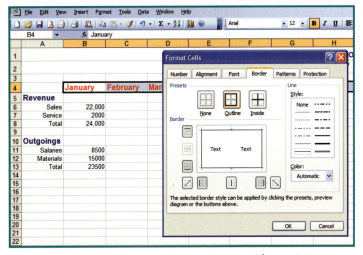

Figure 3.74

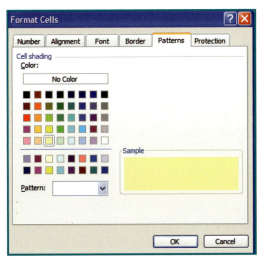

Figure 3.75

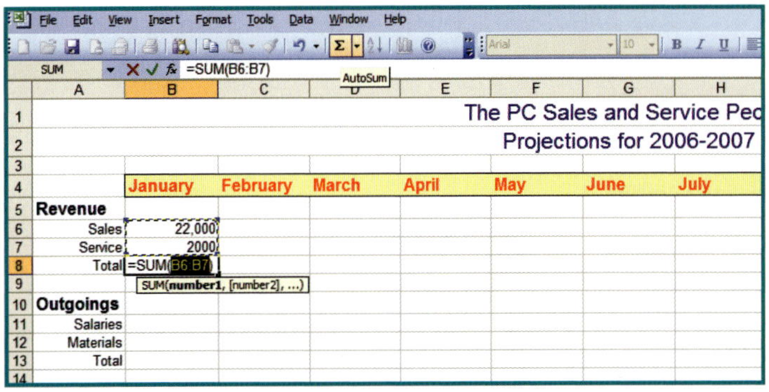

Figure 3.76

At this point you may click OK, which will take us back to our full spreadsheet view with all of the applied formatting in place.

Figure 3.77

The next step is to enter some data. In this case we'll be entering data as estimates – i.e. values we hope to achieve but can never really be sure of. We've made a start with this and also entered a formula for adding the Sales and Servicing Revenue together using the Autosum feature. Notice that we haven't applied any cell formatting as yet so the data is presented as the Default General number rather than as Currency (see Figure 3.76).

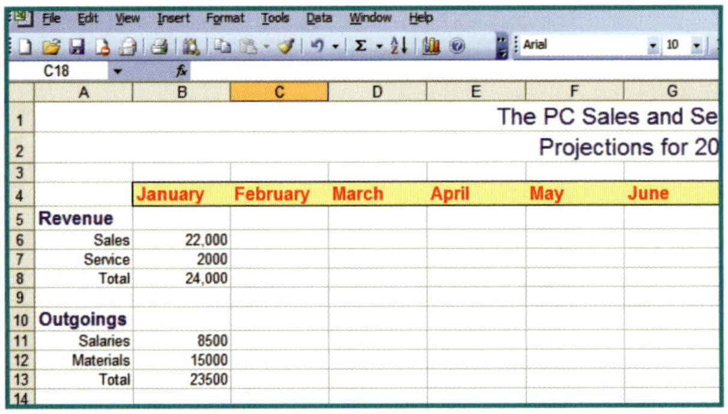

You will see that in the first month of trading we are actually making a small profit (Figure 3.77). This is quite unusual for a new company. Generally you would have to run the business for several months before showing an increase. In many ways this is already highlighting deficiencies within our model because we may not have considered any start-up finances, bank loans and so on. This illustrates the point that a model may evolve over a period of time and become more refined along the way.

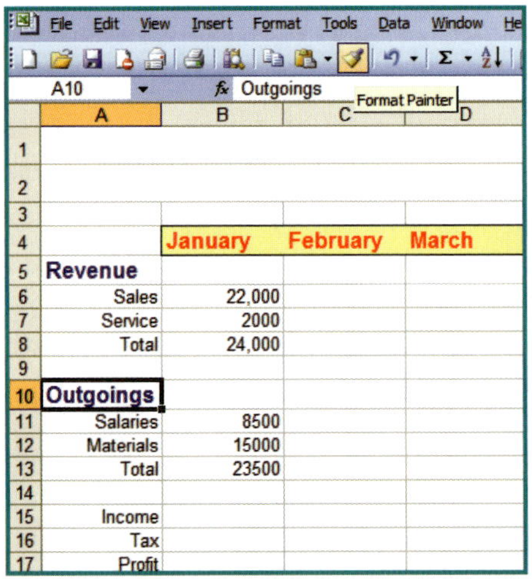

Figure 3.78

The first column is now complete, but the model doesn't really tell us anything about the business in terms of profit or loss. Let's add some further features to help us with this aspect (see Figure 3.78).

Notice the three additional labels: Income, Tax and Profit. Apply the same formatting to the Income label as to the Revenue and Outgoings. To do this highlight Outgoings, click the Format Painter icon on the toolbar and then 'paint' the target cell (in this case Income) with the cursor. The result is that Excel now transfers a copy of all the cell A10 properties – i.e. Left Justified, Bold and Point 12 – to cell A15.

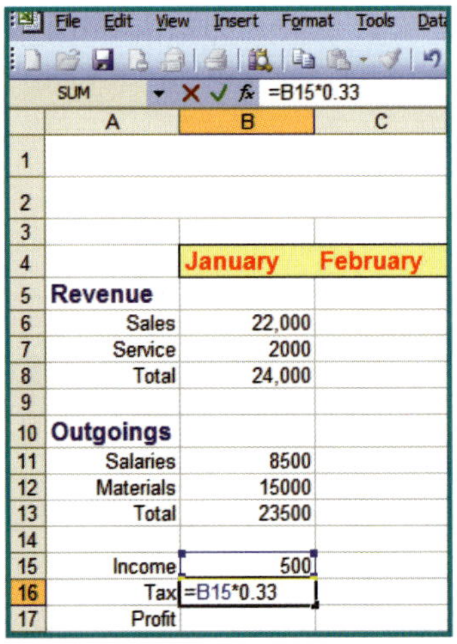

Figure 3.79

Típ:

If you ever enter data into a cell and get '######', this is Excel indicating that the cell is too narrow and you will need to widen it in order to view your data. Note that the data is there; it's just that it won't be displayed properly until you intervene!

Exercise

The spreadsheet needs more formatting in order to clarify some of the cell contents. Switch the appropriate cells to currency, widening the cells as necessary.

Our income will be the difference between Total Revenue and Total Outgoings – i.e. B8–B13. We'll set the tax paid as 33% (this will also include other contributions – in this case B16 x 33/100 (see Figure 3.79). Note that we'll calculate the tax monthly; even if there were a tax change part way through the year, the months prior to the change would still be at the old rate. The Profit will simply be B15–B16 (see Figure 3.80). Let's implement this in our spreadsheet.

So far, the model is taking shape and the figures seem to be fine. The next step is to take a calculator, pen and paper, and work through our spreadsheet, manually checking that it's working.

Another useful feature within Excel is the Comment (see Figure 3.81). This allows us to add notes that are not visible on the spreadsheet until we pass the cursor over the cell with the comment attached. To add a comment, select the appropriate cell – in this case B17 – then Select Insert/Comment. At this point we can add appropriate text that may be used to highlight aspects of the spreadsheet for individual users. All cells with comments have a tiny red dot in the upper right-hand corner.

In this case we would like some visual indication if any currency item ever falls below zero. Select **-1,234.10** in the 'Negative Numbers' box to switch this feature on. This will display values in red if they fall below zero (see Figure 3.83).

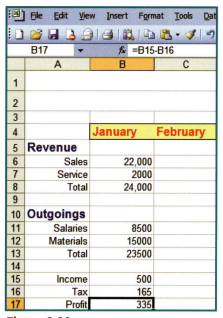

Figure 3.80

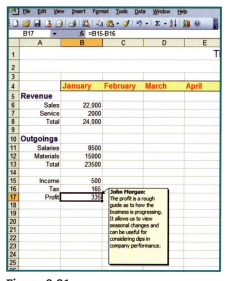

Figure 3.81

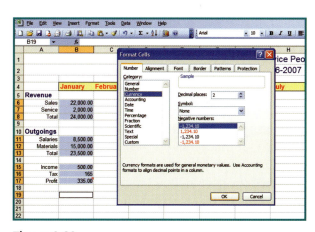

Figure 3.82

Tip:

Don't forget to use the CTRL key to select 'non-adjacent' cells. Where there are many cells to highlight, select all of them by 'pointing' at the first, then hold down the Shift key, then click the last cell (all cells will now be highlighted in the set). Next, hold CTRL and highlight the cells you do not want selected. This will switch the highlight off for each cell selected in this way. Select all labels except for the gaps (see the tip for using the CTRL key). Next, select Format/Cells from the menu bar. Finally, select Currency (see Figure 3.82).

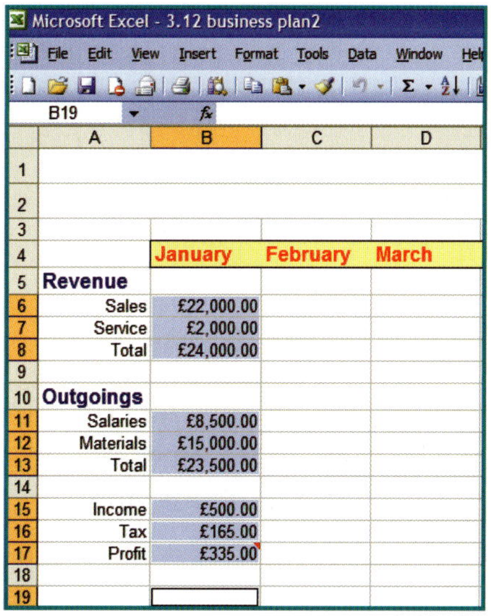

Figure 3.83

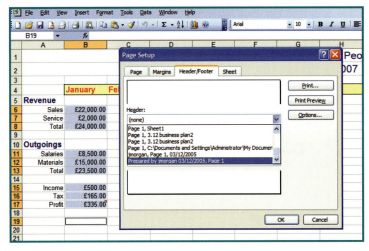

Figure 3.84

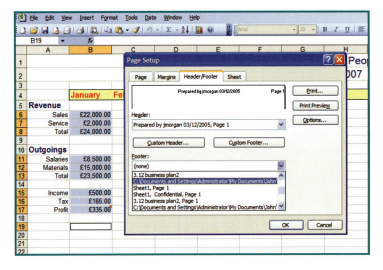

Figure 3.85

Figure 3.86

We'll add some documentation to our spreadsheet by utilising the Header/Footer option (as Figure 3.84 shows). Select View/ Header/Footer from the menu bar. The Page Setup Dialogue Box will open which enables us to select a pre-defined Header and Footer. We have selected the 'Prepared by...' for the Header.

It also gives details of the file location for the Footer (see Figure 3.85).

This will enable others who may be involved with the maintenance of the spreadsheet to know who originated the file and its exact location on the network drive. The next step should be to alter the page layout (see Figure 3.86). (Portrait mode won't be suitable because we have a wide spreadsheet including all of the months in the year.) This will (hopefully) enable printing onto one A4 sheet in landscape mode. If we don't do this our printout will appear on more than one sheet, which makes viewing cumbersome.

To do this, select File/Page Setup. Click the 'Landscape' radio button and click OK. (You will notice that we could have set the Header/Footer from this Menu as well as on the Header/Footer Tab.) Select File/ Print Preview to view the results. Notice the header, footer and also the change to landscape format, as Figure 3.87 shows.

Just a few 'extras' to note: the Headers and Footers only appear on your printouts, not on screen (unless you're in Print Preview mode). By default there are no Gridlines shown, which can make your spreadsheet difficult to read, so it's a good idea to switch these on. Also you may like to see the Row and Column headings, particularly in the early stages of your design model where you may be working from paper-based sheets to fine tune your model's design. Both of these features are activated by selecting File/Page Setup, clicking the 'Sheet' tab, then clicking the 'Gridlines' and 'Row and Column Headings' checkboxes (see Figure 3.88).

Examples of IF Statements

Spreadsheets are very good at comparing data and then displaying an output message or new value, depending on the result. In the examples that follow (see page 000) we have suggested a question that may be asked of the system. We have also provided the Excel syntax for achieving the desired result. We'll clarify how this works by looking at the first example in detail and by showing a sample spreadsheet.

Roughly translated, the formula

=IF(B3>=50,"Well Done, you've Passed","Sorry, you'll need to re-sit this paper")

means if the contents of cell B3 are 'greater than OR equal to' 50, then the target cell (in this case the one with the formula, C3) will contain the text 'Well Done, you've passed' (see Figure 3.89).

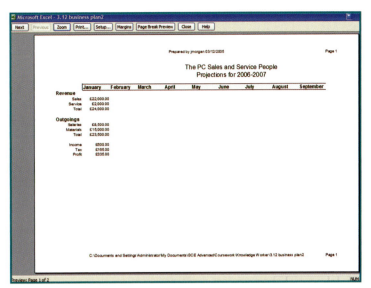

Figure 3.87

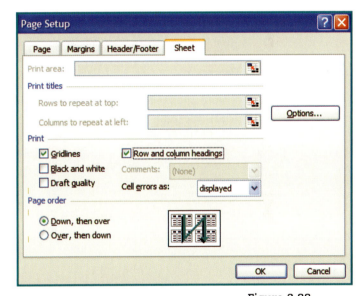

Figure 3.88

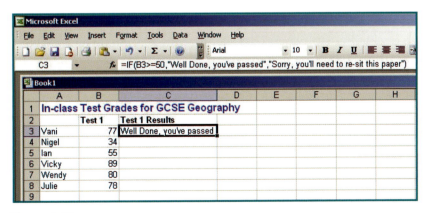

Figure 3.89

Tip:

As with all types of mathematical work, you never really learn by reading about it! Make sure you're working through the following with an Excel spreadsheet so that you can try out the statements.

If the grade is less than 50, then the target cell will contain the text 'Sorry, you'll need to re-sit this paper' (see Figure 3.90).

We'll copy the contents of cell C3 down to cell C8 (see Figure 3.90), then compare the results to see if our model works.

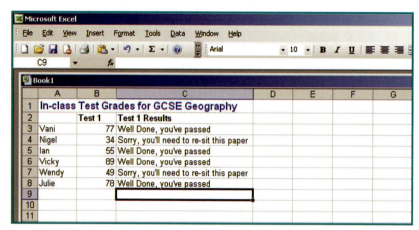

Figure 3.90

Question	Excel Syntax	Comments
If your grade is greater than or equal to 50% you Pass, otherwise it's a Fail	=IF(B3>=50,'Well Done, you've passed', 'Sorry, you'll need to re-sit this paper')	Read the first comma as 'Then' and the second comma as 'Else'.
If you have more than £2000 in your building society account, you will gain 4.8% interest; otherwise it will be 3.8%.	=IF(B3>=2000,4.8%, 3.8%)	If the balance is greater than £2000, then apply 4.8% interest for that month. If it's below £2000, then apply 3.8% interest.

Figure 3.91

Exercise

Using the formula in the second example shown in the table above (Figure 3.91), design a spreadsheet to prove that the formula actually works. Your evidence should show results for all the people named in the sample spreadsheet.

Note: this example shows actual values in the target cell which you will use for *further processing* to establish the new balance for the account in January, cells D2 to D9 (see Figure 3.59).

Exercise

Using appropriate labels in Column A and additional formulae in Column B, calculate the Total opening balance in the building society accounts and the Average balance for the month of January for all customers listed.

Absolute and relative referencing

It's best to see how this works by continuing with the example we began in section 3.4 (see pages 187–191 and Figure 3.92).

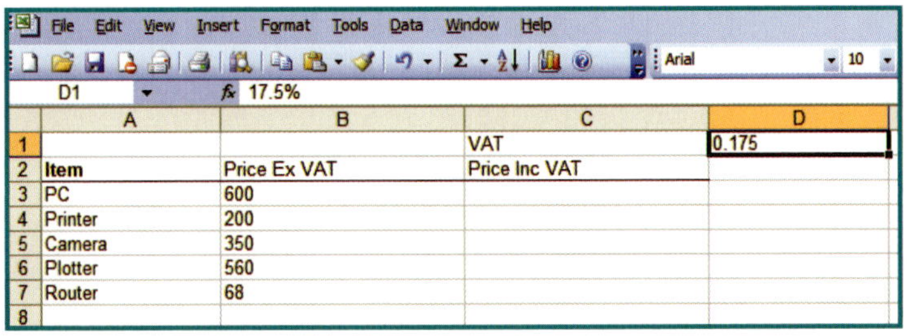

Figure 3.92

We'll leave the Show Formula switched on and enter the label for VAT in Cell C1. Then enter the amount for VAT in D1. Notice that we enter the VAT amount as a decimal value, which is then displayed as the actual percentage in Excel. D1 will also show this as Show Formula is switched off. (See Figure 3.93.) Note: the cell must be switched to Percentages for this to work.

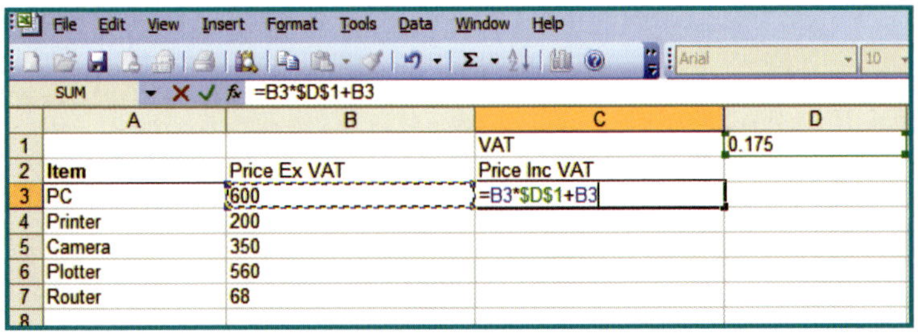

Figure 3.93

Enter the formula, but this time instead of including the actual amount for VAT, use the cell D1 separated with two '$' signs. This signifies that D1 is to be treated as an Absolute address which must not be incremented if any Copy commands are executed on all cells that contain references to it. Let's see what happens when we replicate C3 into C4 to C7. 'Show Formula' is switched off so that you can see what's happening (see Figure 3.94).

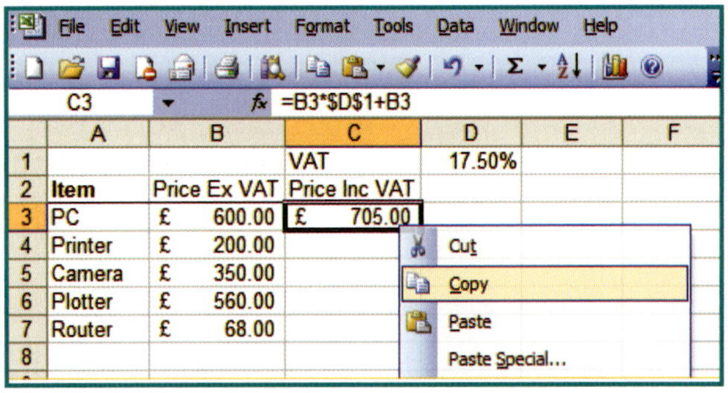

Figure 3.94

Right-click on the target cell C3 and select Copy. Then highlight each cell where the target must be copied to – i.e. highlight C4 down to C7 – then right-click and select Paste (see Figure 3.95).

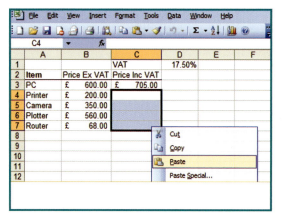

Figure 3.95

This time we still get all the items listed, including VAT, but none of the cells have 17.5% in the formula. This is the result we wanted. All formula are now 'pointing' at cell D1, which is the only cell that would have to be edited if the value for VAT ever changed. You'll notice from Figure 3.96 how all of the values are now correct because we have used the Absolute reference for cell D1 within each of our formulae.

What other features could help us in our business plan? It would be useful if the spreadsheet could give the user a visual warning of how the business was progressing. We could use an IF statement to achieve this and display appropriate messages depending how our Profits were progressing – or not, as the case may be). Let's take a look at IF statements in more detail.

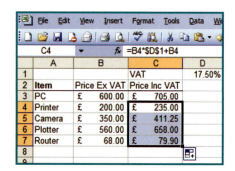

Figure 3.96

Nested IF statements

Let's say that at our next meeting we decide on some broad parameters for success (see the Target Value column in the table below, Figure 3.97). Pick out figures that give some indication as to how the business is performing. We could include all sorts of measures on how much we've sold and how low the staff costs are, but really the only thing that matters here is the profit. In our meeting we've decided on the following alert system that will give us an indication of how the company is progressing, or not!

Exercise

Reproduce the previous spreadsheet with your own data. Enter an initial value for VAT of 17.5%, then change the VAT to 15% and record your results. Complete a manual calculation on at least two cells in order to confirm that your model works.

Target value (in B17)	On-screen display	Action
Less than £300, we will need to monitor this carefully.	Display a warning 'Alert'.	Possibly increase marketing and try to reduce costs.
£300 to £1500, everything's OK, no need for concern.	'Fine'.	Continue to monitor.
Plus £1500, comfortable position.	'Excellent'.	Monitor and perhaps think about expansion and further investment if this continues to rise.

Figure 3.97

In order to achieve this level of alert, we will need to implement a 'nested IF statement', which sounds complicated, but isn't.

We've generated the statement below:

=IF(B17<300,"Alert",IF(B17<=1500,"Fine","Excellent"))

Remember, the first two ',' (commas) are another way of saying 'Then'. The final ',' (comma) replaces the word 'Else'. Everything in " " (quotes) is displayed on the screen, but only *if* the statement is true for that particular part! In a nested IF statement, you must have as many left brackets '(' as there are right brackets ')'. OK, let's try this out in our spreadsheet (see Figure 3.98).

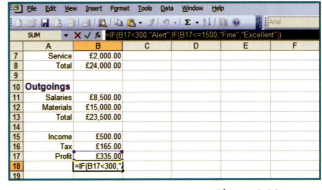

Figures 3.99, 3.100 and 3.101 illustrate some results for this statement.

Figure 3.98

The IF statements seem to be working, but we should be more thorough with our test data and target the boundaries. For example, what happens to the message if we have a Profit of exactly £1500?

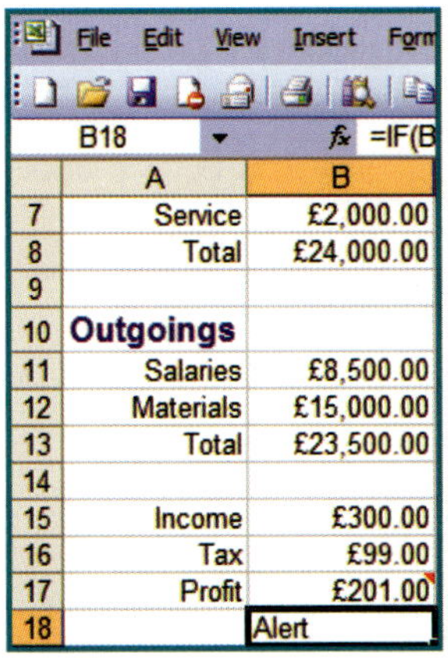

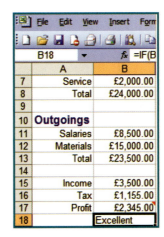

Figure 3.99

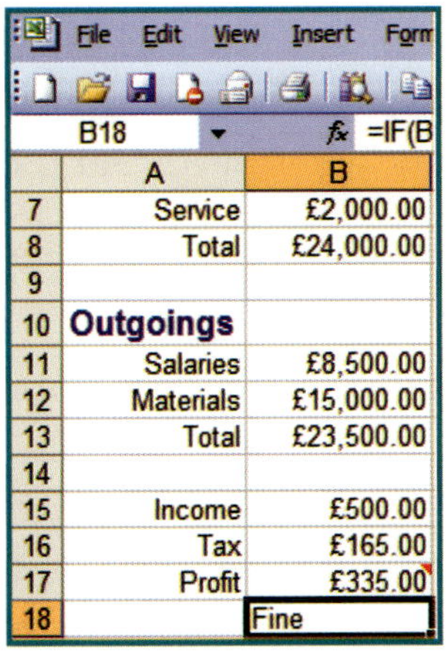

Fig 3.100

Fig 3.101

Using formulae and functions

We've already used some of these throughout this section of the book (see, for example, page 233). A formula comprises cell references, values and mathematical operators. One thing you'll need in the examination is the ability to print your documents showing the formulae, and not the results. To do this you must Select Tools/Options. The Options Dialogue Box will open (see Figure 3.102). In Windows Options, Click the 'Formulas' checkbox.

Exercise

Devise test data that will thoroughly test our Business Plan Spreadsheet. Be mindful of zero, negative, equal and key boundary values for each of the three possible outcomes.

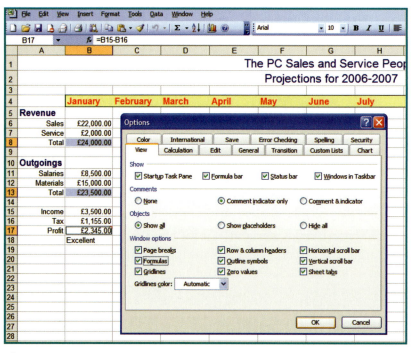

Fig 3.102

> ### Tip:
>
> After you've switched to formula view, it's a good idea to check through the columns and widen them as necessary. The formula that exists behind the data item may contain many more characters than the actual result displayed – e.g. the data item 'Alert' takes up just five characters, but the formula 'behind' it – = IF(B17<300,"Alert",IF (B17<=1500,"Fine"," Excellent")) – is much wider with 53 characters. In almost all cases you will need to widen the columns in order to show the full formula for your evidence.

This will ensure that formulae are now shown on your spreadsheet and not the actual data (see Figure 3.103).

Let's see how we would use some Excel functions on a spreadsheet for Mendon's Music Store (refer back to page 211 to refresh your memory of this example) and examine what else we can do to improve the business accounting.

You have been monitoring the sale of the following selected albums in the Mendon's Music Store over the last few months, and the table below shows the results.

B17 | =B15-B16

	A	B
1		
2		
3		
4		January
5	Revenue	
6	Sales	22000
7	Service	2000
8	Total	=SUM(B6:B7)
9		
10	Outgoings	
11	Salaries	8500
12	Materials	15000
13	Total	=SUM(B11:B12)
14		
15	Income	3500
16	Tax	=B15*0.33
17	Profit	=B15-B16
18		=IF(B17<300,"Alert",IF(B17<=1500,"Fine","Excellent"))
19		
20		

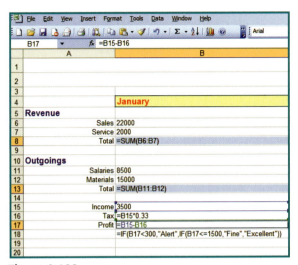

Figure 3.103

Artist	No. US albums released	No. sold
Velvet Revolver	1	250
Kasabian	1	223
Foo Fighters	7	832
White Stripes	6	764
Gorillaz	4	435
Franz Ferdinand	2	270
Kings of Leon	3	300
Linkin Park	4	458
Gwen Stefani	1	185

Design a spreadsheet and calculate the total of all albums sold, the average number of albums the artists have released and the number of artists on your shelves. Create the spreadsheet and enter all of the raw data from the table. Your sheet will look something like the example given in Figure 3.104.

Now we can enter the formulae in the appropriate places, Cell C14 first. Select C14, and press =SUM(C3:C11). See Figure 3.105 for what this will give us.

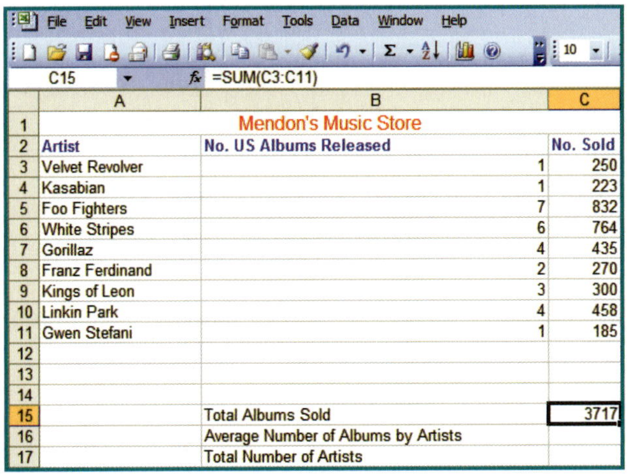

Next, enter the formula for Average (this is one of Excel's Statistical Functions). Notice we're averaging the artists' albums in stock here so it's the data in the B Column (see Figure 3.106).

B17 | Total Number of Artists

	A	B	C
1		Mendon's Music Store	
2	Artist	No. US Albums Released	No. Sold
3	Velvet Revolver	1	250
4	Kasabian	1	223
5	Foo Fighters	7	832
6	White Stripes	6	764
7	Gorillaz	4	435
8	Franz Ferdinand	2	270
9	Kings of Leon	3	300
10	Linkin Park	4	458
11	Gwen Stefani	1	185
12			
13			
14			
15		Total Albums Sold	
16		Average Number of Albums by Artists	
17		Total Number of Artists	

Figure 3.104

C15 | =SUM(C3:C11)

	A	B	C
1		Mendon's Music Store	
2	Artist	No. US Albums Released	No. Sold
3	Velvet Revolver	1	250
4	Kasabian	1	223
5	Foo Fighters	7	832
6	White Stripes	6	764
7	Gorillaz	4	435
8	Franz Ferdinand	2	270
9	Kings of Leon	3	300
10	Linkin Park	4	458
11	Gwen Stefani	1	185
12			
13			
14			
15		Total Albums Sold	3717
16		Average Number of Albums by Artists	
17		Total Number of Artists	

Figure 3.105

C16 | =AVERAGE(B3:B11)

	A	B	C
1		Mendon's Music Store	
2	Artist	No. US Albums Released	No. Sold
3	Velvet Revolver	1	250
4	Kasabian	1	223
5	Foo Fighters	7	832
6	White Stripes	6	764
7	Gorillaz	4	435
8	Franz Ferdinand	2	270
9	Kings of Leon	3	300
10	Linkin Park	4	458
11	Gwen Stefani	1	185
12			
13			
14			
15		Total Albums Sold	3717
16		Average Number of Albums by Artists	3.22222222
17		Total Number of Artists	
18			

Figure 3.106

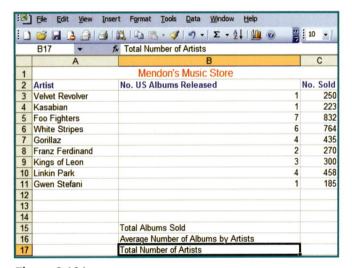

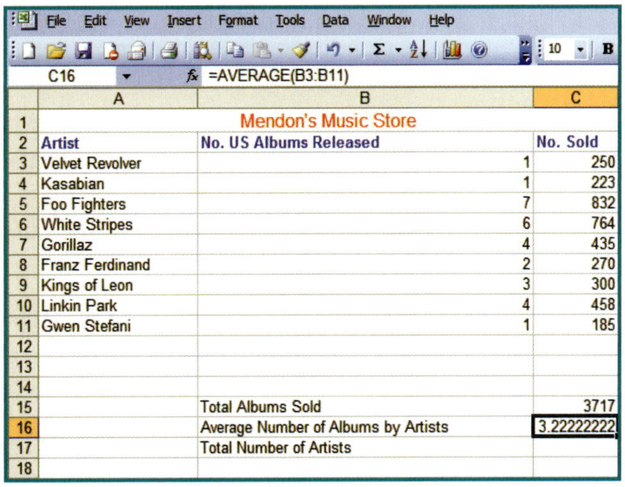

Trim the decimal places down for the average number of albums sold to 1dp. Select Format/Cells/Number, then 1 decimal place (as shown in Figure 3.107).

As Figure 3.108 shows, the total number of Artists in the store is gained by using 'Count'.

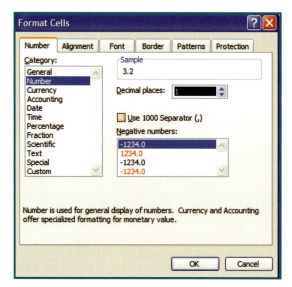

Figure 3.107

Figure 3.108

So that's a review of SUM, Average and Count. Notice they all work in similar ways in terms of the expected format – i.e. Function Name (Cell Range).

You are working with relatively small amounts of data in these exercises, and in some of the tasks it is ridiculous to use a spreadsheet. For example, you could tell at a glance the number of artists held in stock without the use of the Count feature. The reason for this is that you learn to use the tools on easily manageable items that can be checked quickly, before you tackle real problems.

In a commercial environment we may be dealing with massive numbers and it's in these situations that the spreadsheet really excels and makes life a lot easier!

Exercise

Every album at Mendon's Music Store is sold for £9.99 + VAT. Add the following to your spreadsheet: Total Sales (including VAT), a *single cell* identifying the VAT amount, and the CD price. Don't forget to copy D3 down to D11, taking note of the Absolute & Relative referencing notes (see Figure 3.109).

Next, we'll use COUNTIF to establish the number of artists with only one album released. To do this we'll add another label in B18 and also the function in C18. Before we run the Function COUNTIF we'll scan the table and see what the result should be. At the moment Velvet Revolver, Kasabian and Gwen Stefani each have one album on release, therefore COUNTIF should return the value of 3 (see Figure 3.110).

As we can see, the spreadsheet returns 3 so it seems to be working.

To establish the greatest number of albums sold by Mendon's for this period, use the MAX function in the form =MAX(C3:C11). Again the format is the same: Function Name (Range of Cells which it applies to) – see Figure 3.111.

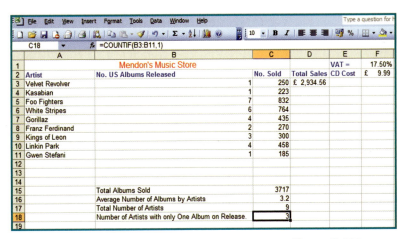

Figure 3.109

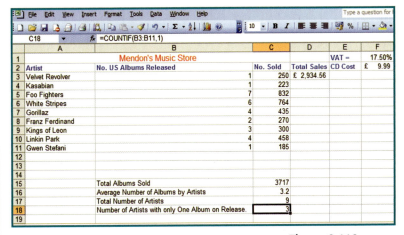

Figure 3.110

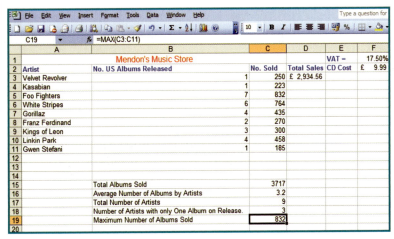

Figure 3.111

Exercise

Use some other known data with COUNTIF and check that it returns what you expect. Edit some of the album sales and see what happens in cell C18 for MAX. Is it working correctly? Use an appropriate function to find the minimum number of albums sold.

Validating and checking data

In Chapter 2 ('The Digital Economy') we have talked a lot about data validation and its importance. Spreadsheets have the same requirements for high standards when it comes to valid data. The data entering a model must be reasonable – i.e. if a cell's properties are set to type 'date' then it makes sense to show a warning message if the user tries to enter something like '3.142', which clearly is not a date.

Data validation in Excel checks to see if the data entered matches pre-set criteria. Let's try this out on Mendon's Music Store. We'll insist that only whole numbers can be entered into the '*Number of US Albums Released'* column.

As shown in Figure 3.112, highlight the range of cells from B3 to B11. Select Data/ Validation from the Menu Bar. Click Whole Number from the Validation Criteria (allow).

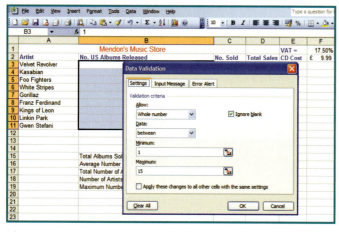

Figure 3.112

We'd like to restrict the data entry to whole number items (we don't stock parts of an album), and make the Minimum value 1 and the Maximum value 15.

Click the Input Message tab in the Data Validation Dialogue Box. In Title: Enter 'No. Albums Released'. In Input Message: Enter 'Please enter a number between 1 and 15 (see Figure 3.113).

Next, select the Error Alert Tab. In Title: Enter 'Albums Released Error'. In Input Message: Enter 'Please enter a whole number between 1 and 15. Thank You' (see Figure 3.114). Then click OK to finish.

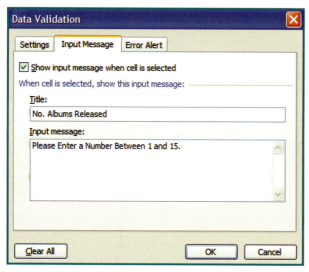

Figure 3.113

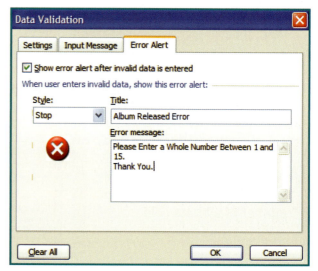

Figure 3.114

Let's try out our validation routine (see Figure 3.115). We already have a column full of data that we've entered. This doesn't matter; we will just overwrite with new data items. In Cell B3 try to enter zero albums for Velvet Revolver. As soon as you hit Enter or the down arrow, you get an Error Message with the opportunity to Retry, this time with valid data.

Enter 1 and try again. This time 1 is accepted and the cursor is moved down to B4 (Kasabian). Try to get 17 entered and see what happens (see Figure 3.116).

Once again, the validation rule halts the process and requests that a valid number is entered. Even with the validation tools there is, of course, the obligation on users to try as far as possible to enter correct data in the first place.

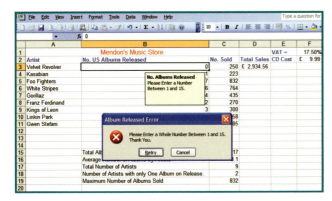

Figure 3.115

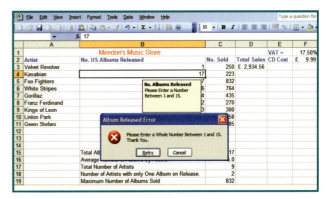

Figure 3.116

Analysing and interpreting data

Before we begin with data analysis, the VAT and CD price cells are moved down to the bottom of the sheet. Notice this move has not affected any cells that were referencing this cell; they have all been automatically updated (see Figure 3.117).

Filter facility

This tool allows the user to quickly bypass the use of sometimes extensive formulae to display the required data. Many of the functions you may like to perform can be managed using the AutoFilter command. With your cursor anywhere in the labels row – i.e. Row 2 – Select Data/Filter/AutoFilter from the Menu Toolbar. The features shown on Figure 3.118 will now appear on the labels row of the spreadsheet.

Notice the 'Down Arrows' in each of the Column Labels. Click the one above Artists. A drop-down box appears displaying some options and also a list of all data stored in this particular column (see Figure 3.119).

Select 'Sort Descending'. Notice the whole sheet has been sorted with White Stripes at the top and Foo Fighters at the bottom of the list (see Figure 3.120).

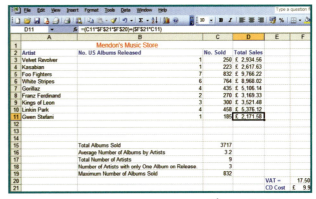

Figure 3.117

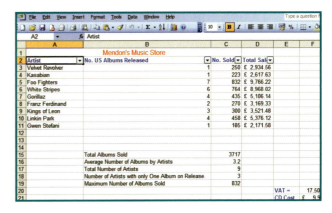

Figure 3.118

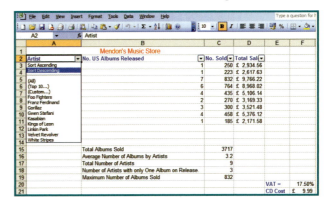

Figure 3.119

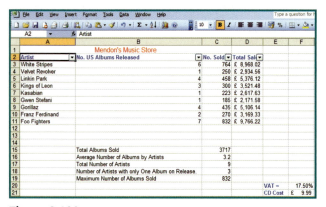

Figure 3.120

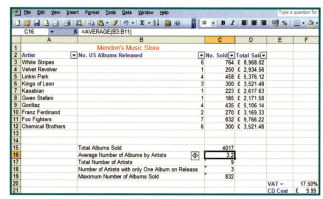

Figure 3.121

The Chemical Brothers, who've sold 300 albums in this timeframe, have been added. You'll notice from Figure 3.121 that they've been added into Row 12, and that some of the formulae previously entered have not recognised this new data! You'll see very small green triangles appear in the top left corners of each cell containing a formula, which indicates there may be a problem with some of the cell contents. It is crucial that you learn to watch for these instances.

If you look at the Formula Bar for cell C16 (the one for Average – see Figure 3.122) you'll notice that it does not take account of B12, which needs to be added for the Chemical Brothers data to be included with the rest.

To fix this problem simply click the yellow Exclamation box to view the Formula Omits Adjacent Cells box and Select 'Update Formula to Include Cells' (see Figure 3.123).

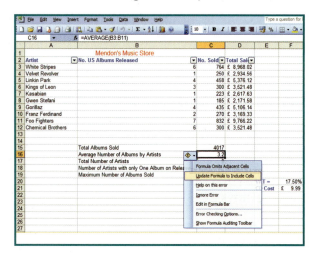

Figure 3.122

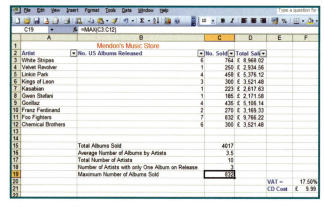

Figure 3.123

Complete this process for each cell with a green triangle to reconcile the inserted data.

Let's return to the Filter facility (see Figure 3.124). Choose 'Custom' on the 'No. Sold' column. With this selected the following Custom AutoFilter dialogue box will be displayed.

Figure 3.125 displays the results for artists with 300 albums sold.

To return to your full spreadsheet, select Data/Filter and Click AutoFilter (to switch it off) and restore the full data screen.

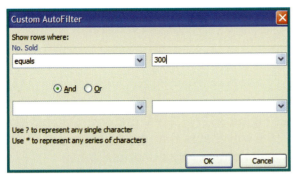

Figure 3.124

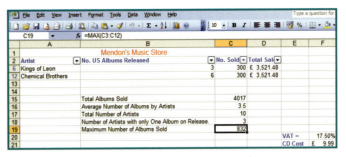

Figure 3.125

Presenting information

Being able to produce something highly visual from data is probably one of the most powerful aspects of Excel. A large table of data expressed as a chart is easier to understand than looking at the same data within a table. The built-in chart Wizard makes the production of graphs and charts a simple and intuitive process.

Let's use the concept of a spreadsheet and its chart facility to produce a Pareto chart to analyse a problem. By doing so it will allow us to use a Pareto chart to:

- break down a large problem into smaller parts
- identify the most major elements of the problem.

Note: Vilfredo Pareto was an Italian economist who observed that 20% of the Italian population owned 80% of the country's wealth. He later found this model applied to other things he observed – e.g. 80% of his garden peas were produced by 20% of the pods. This principle has come to be known as the Pareto Principle, or the 80–20 rule.

Focusing in this way enables us to centre our efforts on maximising improvement. The Pareto Principle confirms that a small number of causes account for most of the problems in any given situation. You can use this tool when the problem can be split into categories and counting can be employed to gain the magnitude of each group. This process can be used early in the project to establish which elements need to be investigated and, later on, to establish which areas of the problem should be addressed first.

Let's take a very simple problem that requires a decision in terms of a priority list of actions in order to progress a struggling company. Here are the steps in the process that must be completed before we can make the decision.

1 Capture the raw data. List each category and its associated data items.

2 Order the data. Do this by placing the categories in order, with the largest data count first.

3 Label the 'y' axis. This will contain the number of instances in the count.

4 Label the 'x' axis. This will contain the groups or categories.

5 Plot the bars for each category.

6 Add a title and legend.

7 Analyse and then prioritise.

Tip:

A shortcut to this would be to click the down arrow key in the 'No. Albums' column and select 300 from the data list.

Tip:

You must be aware that while a bar chart and pie chart *may* be used to display the same data, they do different jobs. The bar chart acts more like a table of data and allows the 'viewer' to quickly judge, for example, the maximum, minimum and the numbers in each category. By contrast, the pie chart represents the 'proportion' of numbers in each category and allows adjacent categories to be easily combined for comparative purposes. For this reason, you must think about why you are presenting your data in this way, and then choose an appropriate format to suit.

Típ:

Don't be afraid to experiment with the Chart Wizard. As you complete each step, a preview of your chart will be displayed within the wizard. If you try a feature and it doesn't work in the way you expected, just click the 'Back' button and give it another try.

Of course, some of these actions will be taken care of by the Chart Wizard on the spreadsheet.

The first step with this problem is to enter the data into a spreadsheet, as shown in Figure 3.126.

Place the cursor on cell B4 (see Figure 3.127). Select the Data/Sort command from the menu. Select Sort By 'Descending' (see Figure 3.127). Check that the radio button for 'My data range' has Header selected. This will ensure that the first row containing the labels 'Complaint and No.' will not be counted as data items.

Figure 3.126   **Figure 3.127**

Típ:

In almost all cases, where 'time' is a part of the data, it will be attached to the 'X' (the horizontal) axis of any graph that you produce.

Click OK. This will sort the data into descending order by number (number of occurrences in the study), as Figure 3.128 shows.

That's sorted the data into order with the complaint with the highest number of occurrences in the top position. Ordinarily this would probably be enough in terms of finding a solution. In this case, however, the owner would like to display this as a chart because she is going to use it as part of a staff development morning later in the week. She is really worried about the situation and wants to shock the employees into action.

Figure 3.128

Case Study

A Chinese take-away has added a delivery service to its list of options for customers. This service has been running quite successfully for about a year, but there has been a high turnover of staff in the last six months. The owner has noticed a steady decline in delivery orders and, three months ago, started giving questionnaires to gain customer feedback. The following data were collected regarding the number of occurrences recorded for areas of service which customers felt was between Poor and Average.

Quality of food	56
Order was wrong	125
Attitude of staff	250
Order was late	564
Bounced cheques	3
Other	34

Let's generate a Pareto chart from this data to see if we can represent the figures in a more powerful, visual format. Highlight the data cells including the two labels on the top row (row 3 – see Figure 3.129).

Click the Chart Wizard icon (see Figure 3.130).

Step 1: Choose Bar from the 'Chart type:', then 'Clustered bar with 3D effect' from the 'Chart Sub-type'. There's a 'Press and Hold to View Sample' button, if you'd like to see a preview. Click 'Next'.

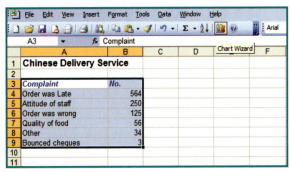

Figure 3.129

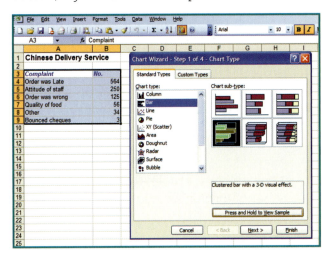

Figure 3.130

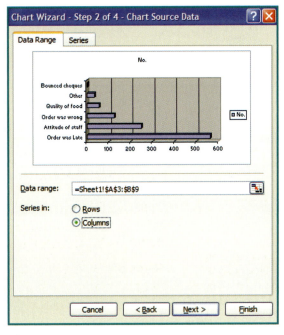

Figure 3.131

Step 2: Select Column for the 'Series in'.

Figure 3.131 demonstrates this process.

Step 3: This allows us to edit the 'look' of our Pareto chart (see Figure 3.132). Add a title in the 'Chart Title' box and also a label for the number of occurrences on the Z axis (this seems the wrong axis, but if you try 'X' and preview you'll see that this is correct).

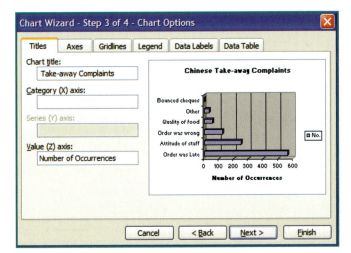

Figure 3.132

Click the 'Gridlines' tab and make sure that the Value (Z) Axis, Major Gridlines are checked. Select 'Legend' and deselect the 'Show legend' checkbox. Select the Data Labels tab. On the 'Label Contains' tick the Value checkbox, click Next.

Step 4: Select the 'As object in: Sheet 1 (see Figure 3.133). Click Finish. Notice the chart is placed in sheet1 next to the table of data (see Figure 3.134).

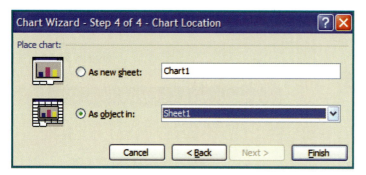

Figure 3.133

Figure 3.134

In this case the chart is enlarged by dragging the corner handle. The data quantity labels are highlighted and the font colour switched to (Yellow) to make them more visible on the page.

It is obvious from this Pareto chart where problems occur within the business. The owner can deduce from this that the 'delivery service' is most at fault, with the 'attitude of staff' in second place. If we think about this for a moment, the attitude of the staff may well be linked to the late orders. If the customer does start shouting at the delivery people, they may well not be handling this stressful situation that well.

This situation just discussed is one for which the chart helps to highlight a problem, which in turn may help to provide a solution. The next scenario is a little different and illustrates why we need to think about the problem in some detail before jumping to a conclusion. Generally, the higher the bar, the bigger the problem and therefore these are the issues that should be addressed first. However, this is not always the case as we shall see.

In this new example it is fairly obvious where our concentration should be focused. There are 1200 surface scratches that need to be looked at. Start the Chart Wizard as before (see page 245). However, when you come to the last step (Step 4), instead of

Case Study

A manufacturing company has a problem and wants to use a spreadsheet to model its data in order to establish a solution to save money. The spreadsheet shown in Figure 3.135 shows some of the collected data regarding the process. This spreadsheet has also been sorted into descending order by No.

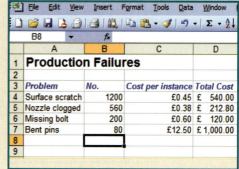

Figure 3.135

creating the chart in Sheet1, this time select Sheet2 from the drop-down menu. (This will give more room to view and compare the charts later.) The Pareto chart is based on the problem and the number of occurrences, as you can see from Figure 3.136. But careful scrutiny of this chart reveals that we shouldn't be quite so quick to judge the situation.

Let's revisit the chart but this time we'll select the Problem and the Total Cost of Failure as our data sets (see Figure 3.137). To do this, select the first column of data together with its label. Hold down the CTRL key, then select the Total Cost column with its label. Start the Chart Wizard again and create the Pareto chart shown in the figure, but this time with a more interesting set of results. Notice that the sheets within the workbook are labelled. Sheet1 has now become Production Failures and Sheet2 is now Pareto charts.

This time we can see that data selection for a chart is all-important, because now it is clear that the biggest problem we have is Bent Pins (not Surface Scratches), which account for £1000 of losses. Look at how low on the scale Bent Pins are on the first Pareto chart. The lesson here is to scrutinise your findings to ensure that you focus on the main problem (usually the one that costs you the most money).

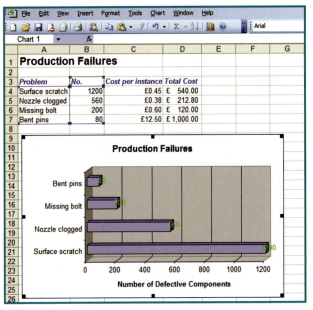

Figure 3.136

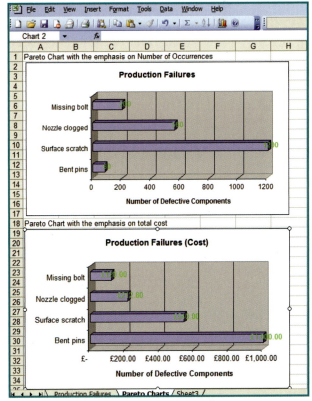

Figure 3.137

ICT Skills (b)

3.12

- **Communicate effectively and impart information to an audience**

Producing word-processed documents that communicate effectively

You have probably gained quite reasonable word-processing skills by this point in the course. You will need to be able to use a word processor within the assessment to present your report on the spreadsheet model you've investigated.

Section 2.4 of the ICE (Instructions for the Conduct of the Examination) states: 'Candidates work will mainly take the form of printouts… Each printout must bear the candidate's name, number and centre number. This information MUST be entered before printing… This being the case you should be familiar with the Headers/Footers facility within Word, Star Office or other suitable word processing application.'

A header and footer enable the user to store information on the printouts that is outside the normal document area. In addition, the header or footer information can be replicated across all pages. If a page number is included, this will not only be replicated but also incremented to reflect the current page.

To add information into a Header or Footer, Click View/Header and Footer (see Figure 3.138).

Notice that as you do this, the Header/Footer Tool bar will open and default to Header information. We've entered a Student Name, Number and Centre Number.

To switch to the Footer, click the 'Switch Between Header and Footer' on the Header and Footer Toolbar (see Figure 3.139).

> **Tip:**
>
> While you are working in a Header or Footer area, the main text will be grey. When you are in your main document *and* Page Layout View, your Header and Footer will be grey. The active part of the document will always be black text.

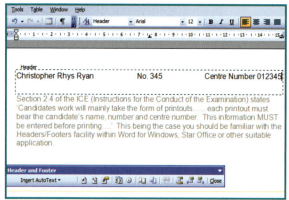

Figure 3.138

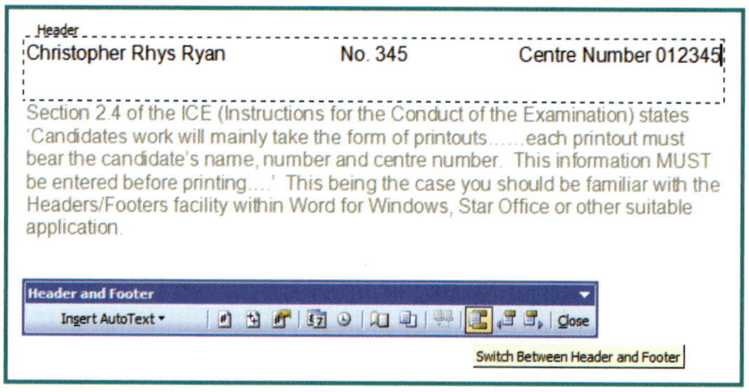

Figure 3.139

Doing so will open the footer area at the 'foot' of the document (see Figure 3.140).

We will now enter our page numbers into the Footer area of the page. As we start to type in 'Page', Word will automatically prompt us to 'Autocomplete' with Page X of Y, which translated means: If you press 'Enter' now we will automatically place the page and the total number of pages in the footer. Click Enter and you will see appear the information shown on Figure 3.141.

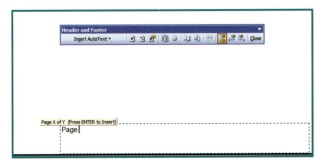

Figure 3.140

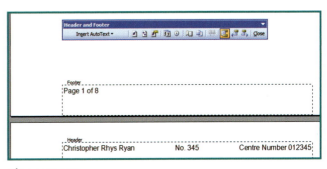

Figure 3.141

This shows the bottom of Page 1 (Page 1 of 8 pages) together with the Top of Page 2. This Header and Footer is 'running' across all pages.

Importing data from other applications

To import a previous Excel worksheet into our Word document, select Insert/Object/ Microsoft Excel Worksheet. Click the 'Create from file' Tab. This allows you to browse for a file that you already have stored on disk. In the dialogue box shown in Figure 3.142, the file has been selected by clicking 'Browse' and locating the file on disk. If you select the 'Link to File' checkbox you can effectively update your spreadsheet within Word every time the source spreadsheet is changed.

If your source spreadsheet has changed (as shown in Figure 3.143), Right on click on the embedded spreadsheet within Word and Select Update Link (see Figure 3.144).

Any changes in the original spreadsheet will be shown on the spreadsheet in your Word document.

This principle of importing other files can be demonstrated with a variety of applications within the Windows environment.

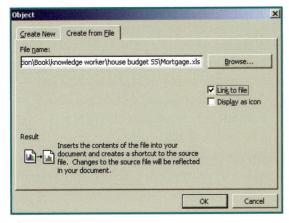

Figure 3.142

House Purchase Details		
Monthly Outgoings		
Food	£ 240.00	
Travel	£ 200.00	
Clothes	£ 60.00	
Miscellaneous	£ 150.00	
Council Tax	£ 120.00	
Savings	£ 100.00	
Proposed Mortgage payment	£ 650.00	
Total Outgoings	£ 1,520.00	
Monthly Income	£ 1,800.00	
Balance	£ 280.00	

Figure 3.143

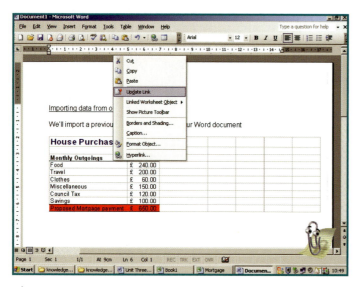

Figure 3.144

Formatting documents

A quick look at the Format menu will give an indication as to what's available within Word. All of these features are intuitive to use and work on the principle that you switch the feature on to start a process – e.g. select bullets and thereafter any text entered will be bulleted and will continue until you de-select it (double Enter will also switch it off). Alternatively, you can highlight text that you need to be formatted and then switch the feature on (see Figure 3.145).

In Figure 3.146 we have selected the text, right-clicked and selected 'Bullets and Numbering'. We then chose a bullet that would suit our document and clicked OK (see Figure 3.146).

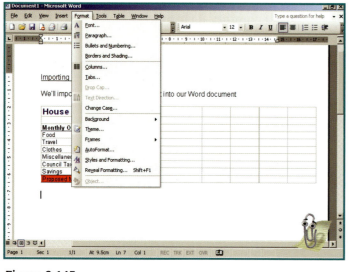

Figure 3.145

Creating document layouts

Let's try inserting a table to enhance the layout of our document. We can either do this by selecting the feature from the menu via Table/Insert/Table, then specify the table size, or we can click the 'Insert Table' icon and drag the cursor across the required number of Columns and down the number of Rows. We've chosen a 3 Row by 3 Column table (see Figure 3.147), which will be placed at the insertion point (the place where the cursor was when we issued the command) in our document.

Figure 3.146

All we have to do next is enter the appropriate data. Each border of the table has a 'handle', which may be selected and dragged in order to reduce or increase the column widths to suit our data.

In Figure 3.148, we have decreased the width of the right-hand column. We have highlighted the three cells on Row 1 in order to merge them so that we can insert text for a title.

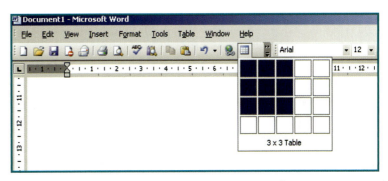

Figure 3.147

Everything you do in a Word document in terms of formatting text is also available within individual cells of the table. If you want to select, for example, an adjacent series of cells you could centre the text, apply bold and italic, select a different text colour and apply a shaded, coloured background, which would then be applied to these cells alone.

In the case of a long table that spans more than one page of your document – for example, your work plan for your portfolio – you can select 'Heading Rows Repeat'. This feature assumes that the first row of your table would contain labels and ensure that these are automatically repeated at the top of each new page thereby improving the documents readability (see Figure 3.149).

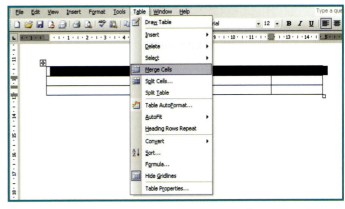

Figure 3.148

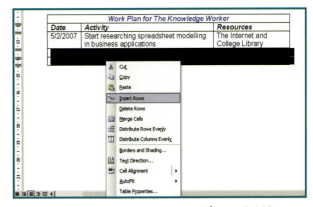

Figure 3.149

Checking documents

As you're probably aware by now, there's a variety of tools provided within Office to enable effective document checking. Spelling and grammar checking are probably the most used of these tools. However, a surprising number of documents fail the quality test as a result of this part of the process not being carried out effectively. To use the spelling and grammar checker select Tools/Spelling and Grammar (as shown in Figure 3.150).

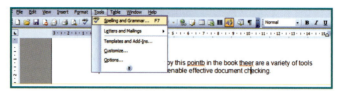

Figure 3.150

The Spelling and Grammar dialogue box will open together with a confirmation of the dictionary being used – in this case English (UK). Before you run the spell checker, Word will highlight spelling mistakes with a red line and grammatical errors with a green line. As soon as you run the checker it will highlight the first incorrect word it meets in the sentence (see Figure 3.151), presenting you with a list of suggestions (if the spelling is not recognised, you may not get any options).

If you want to correct spelling as you go, you can simply right-click when you see a word with the red underline and select from the drop-down list. In the case of a word which **is** correct but is presented as incorrect (because it is not in the dictionary) you may use 'Add to Dictionary' (see Figure 3.152). This will ensure that it is passed as correct the next time you use it in your document.

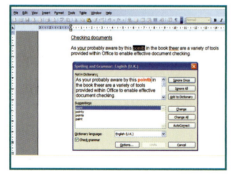

Figure 3.151

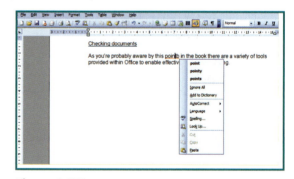

Figure 3.152

As you continue with the spell checker, Word will prompt you with suggestions as soon as it finds words that it thinks are incorrect (see the example in Figure 3.153).

Having completed this in a sentence it will then concentrate on the grammar. In Figure 3.154, Word has identified 'your' as being incorrect and presented 'you're' as a possible alternative. It has also presented a helpful 'commonly confused words' list from the animated paper clip.

Figure 3.153

Figure 3.154

Producing effective presentations

Creating and editing presentations

We have covered this element in reasonable detail in Chapter 1. The use of PowerPoint (or alternative application) is an essential tool for the knowledge worker and we'll provide some additional help throughout this section.

Formatting slides

You'll notice a menu of content layouts to the right of the active slide. These allow you to load pre-defined templates into each active slide. In Figure 3.155 we've selected a 'Title and Content' slide. This configuration allows us to insert: a table, graph or chart; Clipart, picture, diagram or organisational chart; or a media clip (sound or video files).

If you right-click and choose 'Slide Design' you are able to choose from a variety of preset templates that help us to gain a professional finish to our presentation. We'll choose 'Ripple' just to illustrate the feature (see Figures 3.156 and 3.157).

Inserting text, pictures and charts into presentations

The principle for pictures and charts is similar. Click the appropriate icon, browse to the object – e.g. an image or chart – and click OK. In Figure 3.158 the picture is inserted and the Picture Toolbar is highlighted ready for any further editing.

The difference with a chart is that a mini-spreadsheet is loaded with some sample data at the same time (see Figure 3.159).

You can then add in your data and the finished chart will appear on the PowerPoint slide; just add a title (see Figure 3.160) and that's it.

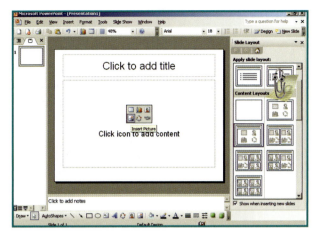

Figure 3.155

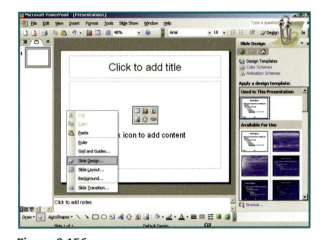

Figure 3.156

Figure 3.157

Figure 3.158

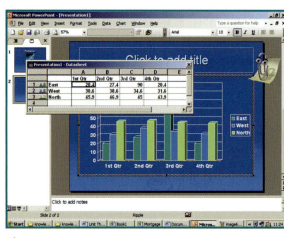

Figure 3.159

Figure 3.160

Importing data from other applications

Imagine you've been asked to set up a presentation for a company regarding your organisation's strategy for producing stainless steel tanks. As part of the presentation the company requires a Microsoft Equation Editor object to illustrate one aspect of the process. Select Insert/Object/Microsoft Equation 3.0 (see Figure 3.161).

Now it's possible to enter your formula, selecting the appropriate symbols from the symbol icons, as shown in Figure 3.162.

Using the equation editor is a little long-winded, but it does allow you to insert properly formatted equations into your presentation.

You may be asked to import data that is in the form of a text file. For example, you may have data that is essential for the model you are given in the examinable component of Unit 3. This is a fairly simple process. With a new worksheet open select Data/Import External Data/Import Data (see Figure 3.163).

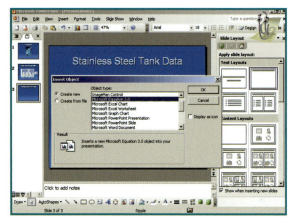

Figure 3.161

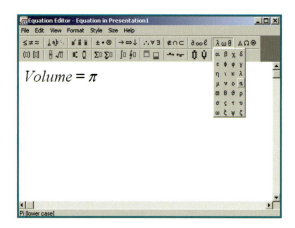

Figure 3.162

The Text Import Wizard will be displayed, as shown in Figures 3.164 and 3.165.

In this case the text file contains data that is 'comma delimited'. This means that each data item is separated by a comma. So every time Excel meets a comma, it knows it must place the data item in the next cell along in the spreadsheet. As soon as it comes to a 'carriage return or enter' it knows to move down one row.

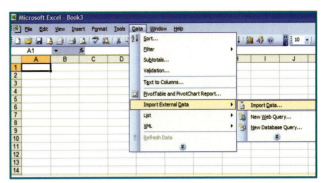

Figure 3.163

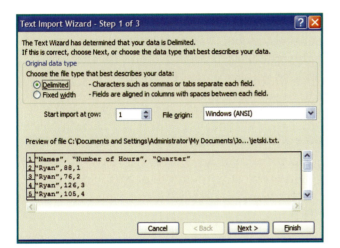

Figure 3.164

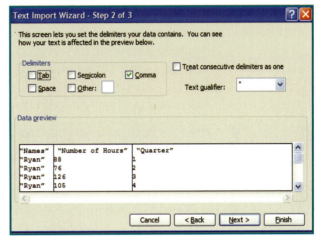

Figure 3.165

Figure 3.166 shows how you may choose the data type for each column. In this case 'Text' is chosen for the first column, which is the person's name. When you've finished highlighting each column and selecting the appropriate data types, click Finish and your data table will appear in your spreadsheet. All you have to do then is to Copy and Paste the relevant parts into your model.

Checking presentations

Checking presentations is often the part of a presentation that receives least attention. You've spent hours entering information, pictures, graphs and so on. You've checked and edited along the way. So why bother spell checking and proofreading when the presentation is complete? If you've been thorough in your proofreading and spell checking from the start, then it may be that you don't need to do too much more. However, most of us do leave things out and spell checking alone is not enough. As we've already seen, missing or additional commas can change the message. Even if it's spelt correctly, the wrong word can affect the meaning.

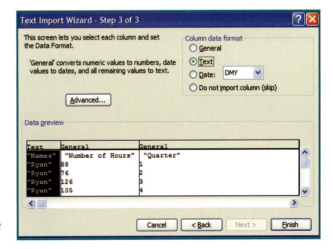

Figure 3.166

All of these issues may be resolved by effective proofreading and spell checking. We will also need to look for:

- unfinished paragraphs
- layout problems
- appropriate text size.

For some of these issues, you may need to try your presentation using an overhead projector or interactive whiteboard. This is always useful because you can see how the slide is going to look from the viewpoint of your audience.

And finally...

This chapter has shown you how spreadsheet models can assist with many of your business decisions. As you go through the modelling processes, don't be afraid to pick up a good maths book and refer to it as you try to build your formulae. Never rely on your spreadsheet calculations until you have manually completed the calculations. Then, and only then, can your spreadsheet formulae be relied on.

Always check your spreadsheet formulae when you've:

- inserted a new row at the end of a list
- copied cells containing formula
- added an absolute address.

Appendices

Standard ways of working

One of the most important habits to get into whilst using the computer is regularly saving your work. Power cuts, physical damage, fires and other mishaps can all combine to ruin your day, especially if you haven't saved your work. Some applications will even allow you to set-up an 'Auto-save' option which will allow you to instruct the computer to automatically save your files at regular intervals e.g. every ten minutes. Then if you have a power surge and you lose your work, the most you will have lost is ten minutes worth of data entry!

Figure 4.1

Using sensible filenames

New users often label their files with their own name and add a number to distinguish it from other files. Naming conventions such as Ellen1, Ellen2, Ellen3 etc. will soon have your head in a spin when you try to find a file you created sixty five 'Ellen's ago'. Whenever you save a file it is important to give it a meaningful file name. If, for example, you are working on a document about the Knowledge Worker, then that may be an appropriate file name. In fact, Word actually looks at the first line of text in a new document and suggests an appropriate file name based on the first line of text that it sees. Click File/Save As... from the menu of a blank document and you will see that the Default file name given by Word is 'Document ??', the question marks will hold a number based on the number of documents you have worked on. In my case it is 'Document2' which we won't use because it doesn't tell us anything about the contents of our document.

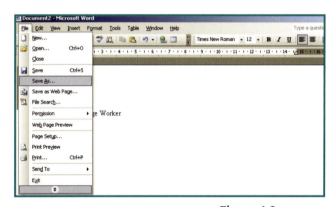

Figure 4.2

Notice however that the 'File Save As' dialogue box is suggesting the more meaningful (in this instance) first line of text as a possible file name i.e. The Knowledge Worker (see Figure 4.3)

In this case we will use this name, Click 'Save'.

File Management

When you first start using a PC there is a tendency to store files 'anywhere and everywhere'. Early on in your 'computer life' this won't seem to matter too much. However, as time

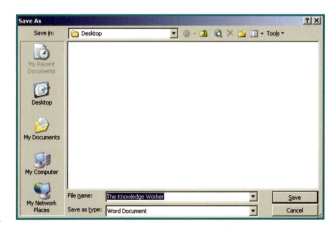

Figure 4.3

goes on and you accumulate more and more files so you will find it increasingly difficult to locate your work.

Working in this way is rather like taking a 4 drawer filing cabinet, removing the file wallets and placing documents straight into any drawer in any order. Pretty soon you will have a messed-up system which will take you hours to sort out.

Setting up directory/folder structures to organise files

Figure 4.4

Backups are an essential part of the process of file management. Disks can be delicate and are sometimes temperamental. Floppy disks are prone to being easily damaged. Magnets, water, dust, heat etc can do irreparable damage to the disks. Even though you may measure the actual cost of physical replacement in pence, the actual cost of data replacement could be in the order of thousands of pounds.

Backup systems allow us to keep additional copies of our data well away from the original source. Ideally you will keep your school or college files on a network drive and make your own backup copy on a Pen Drive for example. As a further safeguard you could register with Yahoo's 30 Mb Briefcase (see Figure 4.4) and store an additional copy of your file on their free, virtual internet drive.

Just log on to Yahoo, set up an account, go to the Briefcase page and Click 'Add Files'. Once you've stored your files in the Briefcase you will be able to access them anywhere in the world where there's internet access. This is helpful if you're working on large files in School or College and you want to work on them at home.

Choosing appropriate file formats

Figure 4.5

All files are made up of a file name and extension (separated by a full stop). Just to confuse matters we don't often see files represented in this way within Windows. The file name is 'user defined' and allows us to apply a meaningful label to our computer file. The extension is defined by the files originating application. That sounds complicated but basically means that if you create a file in Word for Windows then the extension will have the pre-defined **.doc** as its extension. When we view our files in Windows Explorer we will very often just see the file name with an icon representing the extension. Our Word files will show up as icons in the Tiles View in Windows Explorer:

We have the choice of various views within Explorer which gives us flexibility when we are trying to find files. For example, if we are working with graphics files it is easier to switch views to Thumbnails View (see Figure 4.5). This allows us to see a small 'thumbnail' of the actual image or video on our disk. In this case we have thumbnails of a PowerPoint presentation, a CD cover for a band called The Aftermath and two video files. This makes accessing these files very quick because of the additional visual view.

OK, back to appropriate file formats. If ever you want to change a file's type it must be achieved via the host application or a converter. It's not enough to; for example, rename the file and its extension. The underlying file type will remain unchanged.

Figure 4.6

Limit access to confidential or sensitive files

This may be achieved by 'attaching' a password to your documents which you deem to be of a sensitive nature or perhaps you don't want others to be able to open and read them. For example, you may want to stop the possibility of other people taking your ideas from any of your assignment work. To protect these files:

Figure 4.7

- click File/Save As

- then click Tools/Security Options

- The dialogue box shown in Figure 4.8 will open allowing you to enter a password to Open and (if required) a password to Modify your document.

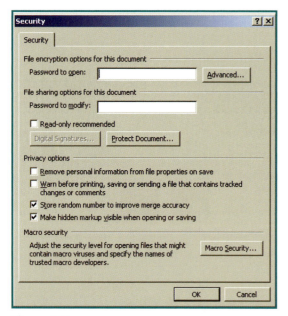

Figure 4.8

Use effective virus protection

It is imperative that you have an 'updateable' virus protection system. You must have a system that allows you to gain regular online updates in order to keep your PC protected. There are free versions available e.g. AVG Free which will keep your PC free from this type of problem.

Available from **www.grisoft.com** "AVG Free Edition is the well-known anti-virus protection tool. AVG Free is available free-of-charge to home users for the life of the product! Rapid virus database updates are available for the lifetime of the product, thereby providing the high-level of detection capability that millions of users around the world trust to protect their computers".

(Copyright **www.grisoft.com**)

Using 'Readme' files to provide technical information

When applications are designed there is usually a time lag between the final software version and the shipping date. As the testing process extends into the full working life of the application, very often there is information that the user needs that couldn't be incorporated within the application Help files. To overcome this difficulty most applications are shipped with the latest 'readme' file in a .txt format (no special applications are required to read it just Windows Notepad). If you look at Figure 4.9 you will see that my selected application group contains additional files for the user e.g. Uninstall and Readme. This Readme file gives additional help regarding the effective installation of the software. The logic being that if a Help file on installation is 'within' the application, it's in the wrong place! You can only read it once that application has been installed, which is what you needed the help with in the first place.

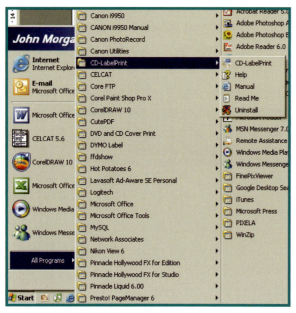

Figure 4.9

In Figure 4.10 there is a video file set in a directory together with a Readme file for users.

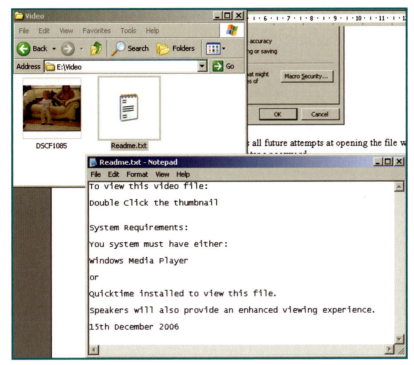

Figure 4.10

Personal Effectiveness

Much of the work you will be concerned with in an ICT environment will involve the use of computer applications to enable you, and others, to work more efficiently. It is always important to select the right tool for the job.

Early on in her career Allison selected a spreadsheet application to store the company name and address details. It soon became apparent that, although easy to use, this application lacked the functionality and power of a database. Fortunately Windows applications have various tools for resolving such issues and Allison was able to import her spreadsheet file into Microsoft Access and thereafter use all of the database features to manipulate her company details.

This is just a simple example of how we can start out with tools that we will soon outgrow. Whilst it is true that Excel can be used as a database, full functionality can only come by using the tools that were designed for the job.

There are many techniques that we use on a day-to-day basis which make our computing work very easy. The idea of Copy and Paste may save us hours of work over the years. Fortunately for us many of these techniques are available across a range of applications. For example, we may use Copy and Paste within Word, Excel, PowerPoint, FrontPage etc. We may also use these features between packages e.g.

Copying a paragraph from a report in Word and Pasting it into a web page in FrontPage, the opportunities are endless, and used properly, can save us a lot of time.

Select appropriate ICT tool and techniques

This topic could be the subject of a book in its own right. Choosing appropriate tools is all about getting the right tool for the job. Over the years software developers have tried to enable their applications to complete a variety of additional tasks. As computer hardware has increased in speed and memory capability, so has the profile of the software. Facilities are being added with every update, to the extent that the word processor of ten years ago is hardly recognisable.

Word processors are great for producing functional documents but if you want something that is fit for publishing then a Desktop Publishing program is the right tool for the job. Word processing software has many more features today than ten years ago, likewise DTP systems have moved on as well and are much more capable for this type of work. Word processing software can also lend a hand with Web Page Design, but if you want to create something impressive then go for something like FrontPage or Dreamweaver, these software tools have been designed for the job.

Yes, you can use your spreadsheet program for compiling a database, but further down the road this 'spreadsheet database' is going to need additional features which Excel just won't be able to manage. Do yourself a favour and start out with the right package in the first place, Microsoft Access.

Within applications there are many facilities that will help you to become more efficient. Store frequently used groups of key presses as macros. Once stored, a click of an icon will have the job done. Don't spend endless sessions typing your name and address for letters, save this information as a template and use this every time you need to write a letter. Spend more time on content and less time getting bogged down with the mundane.

Customising Settings

When you run any application, it will present the desktop with a variety of the most commonly used settings and icons. In the Word toolbar below (Figure 4.11) we have clicked on the additional toolbar icon to reveal further formatting tools. If we were to select the 'Add or Remove buttons' it would allow us to personalise the desktop further giving the option of displaying frequently used features for further use. If you are using Star Office or similar, you will have access to similar features that personalise your working space.

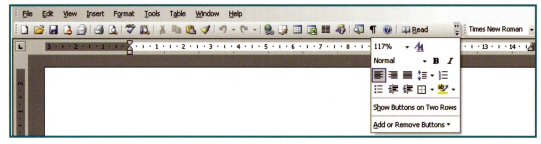

Figure 4.11

As we become more familiar with an application, so we may find the need to customise it so that it 'fits' our mode of working. For example, you may use the Drawing toolbar quite a lot in Word so it makes it easier if it's always available as a Toolbar button. To switch this on click 'Tools/Customise…' from the menu bar.

The 'Customise' dialogue box (Figure 4.12) will open and if we click the checkbox next to Drawing, we will always have this toolbar on the Desktop.

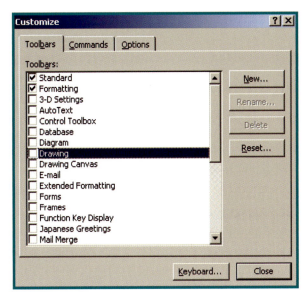

Figure 4.12

I often use the Menu to insert a Page Break by selecting Insert/Break, selecting the Page Break button, then clicking OK. Although this may seem simple enough, if you do enough of these operations it does become a pain! To overcome this we can add an icon to the tool bar which will accomplish all of these steps in 'one click'.

To switch this on click 'Tools/Customise…' from the menu bar.

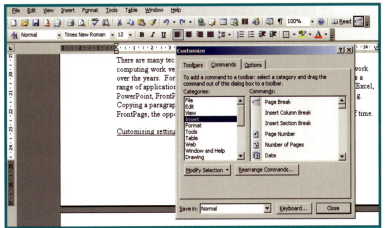

Figure 4.13

With the Customise dialogue box open, select the Insert from Categories then left-click 'Page Break' and drag it onto the main toolbar. You can see the icon in position on the main toolbar (next to 'Read') after we've completed this operation. From here on in, anytime we need a Page Break we just click this icon.

Creating and using shortcuts

If you are working on a project that is hidden in the depths of many directories on your hard drive, you can make this more accessible by temporarily dragging the folder to the desktop. The files will still be saved in the same place but the 'shortcut' will allow you to access them much more quickly.

For example, the 'Project.doc' assignment file stored in **H:/College Drive/AS Level ICT/Knowledge Worker/Assignments/Project.doc**, could simply be dragged to the Desktop so that thereafter a double-click would access it without having to navigate through the whole of the directory.

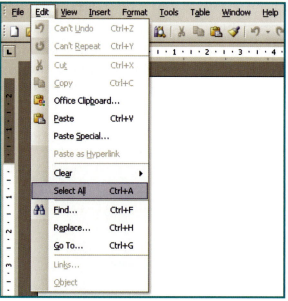

Figure 4.14

There are a variety of keyboard shortcuts that can save you time including Ctrl C to Copy and Ctrl V to Paste selected text. These shortcuts have been inherited from the 'olden days' when we were forced to use them on 'command driven' word-processing programs such as WordStar.

If you look at the menus you'll notice that these keys, where available, are 'advertised' next to the appropriate function e.g. Select All = Ctrl A (see Figure 4.14).

You'll notice a 'Keyboard' button on the Customise Dialogue box. If we click this we will be able to assign shortcuts to some of our keys. Let's suppose that we want to be able to surround our text with a border. There are a number of ways of doing this but one way would be to assign a keyboard shortcut as follows:

- select Tools/Customise

- click 'Keyboard'

- select Borders in Categories

- select BorderOutside in Commands.

In the 'Press new shortcut key:' box, choose the 'left arrow' (number 4) on the numeric keypad as the quick key (see Figure 4.15).

Click close on both Dialogue boxes.

The next time you have some text that needs a border, highlight it and press the number 4 on the numeric keypad and the border will be applied.

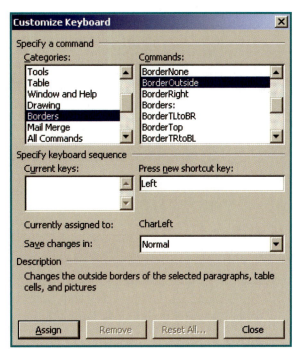

Figure 4.15

Using available sources of help

Within almost all applications there is a Help menu that enables us to gain additional assistance when we are struggling to make something work. Available by pressing the F1 Function Key or via the right hand side of the menu bar, these files can help when you're having problems. The internet also has a number of websites which give free tutorials on almost any application package you can think of.

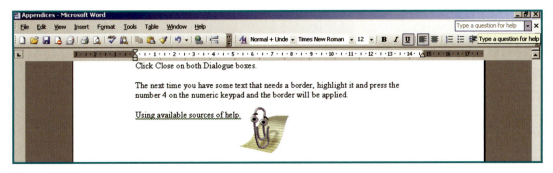

Figure 4.16

Choose Help from the menu bar will open the Assistance Pane to the right of your document (see Figure 4.17). We've typed in 'saving files'

Figure 4.17

Using a plan to help you organise your work and meet deadlines

Planning is one of the hardest disciplines to master. We always tend to think of it as a waste of valuable time and naively think that 'rolling our sleeves up' and getting on with the job is the better way. Sometimes this may be the case, but more often, and especially if you work with others, then you'll have to plan.

Just the process of writing tasks down will help you to focus your mind and be productive. A spreadsheet or a table in Word will get you started, using applications such as Microsoft Project will give you access to a wide range of tools built specifically with planning in mind. However, if you choose the Project route, then be prepared to pay the price in time spent learning this application. My advice, stick to a table in Word with a task description, target due date and a space for a ✓. This will give you a real sense of purpose as you see your table slowly filling up with tick marks representing completed tasks.

Quality assurance

A lack of quality in your work with spelling, grammar and other errors, may give the impression that it has other, more important inaccuracies. It is always important to eradicate, or at least minimise any errors which would detract from the overall quality of your work.

Using spell check, grammar check and print preview

We have covered spell checking in Chapter 3.12 so there is no need to cover this aspect again. Just remember that spell checking alone is not enough, words such as 'to', 'too' and 'two' will all pass the spell check test but have different meanings within a sentence. Having completed your pages, always see what they look like by using Print Preview.

Proofreading

One of the often forgotten essentials, and always noticeable if neglected, is proofreading. If you can, have someone else read your final submission, a fresh viewpoint will help you to clarify important points. Try not to proofread from your monitor, it will strain your eyes and you will lose concentration.

Seeking views of others

The more you are involved with a piece of work, the less likely you are to see its faults. Particular problems involve the overuse of certain words or phrases and even consistent use of incorrect words e.g. the confusion of their, there and they're.

You must seek the views of others if directed to do so by the assignments criteria. For example, in the assignment criteria for Unit One part (f), Mark Band 2, you are asked to incorporate feedback from others. You may decide to accomplish this by designing and issuing a questionnaire and then analysing the results. Mark Band 3 then asks you to prove that you've taken these views into account by making some improvements to your e-book. Seeking the views of others is an important aspect of being an effective knowledge worker.

Authenticating work

Don't believe all you read! Internet sites are notorious for content which is not authenticated and cannot be substantiated. It follows that you shouldn't fall into this trap by including elements within your work which you cannot substantiate. If you are quoting the work of others ensure that you reference this work properly.

Legislation and codes of practice

Acknowledging sources

The work of others can contribute to your own work if you are using it as supporting evidence. As you use this additional material it is important to acknowledge this.

Respecting copyright

Copyright has been designed to help protect people, for example authors, musicians and software designers etc. The law makes it illegal for us to copy such materials; if we want to use them we must make a purchase thereby providing the authors with their fees.

Avoiding plagiarism

Plagiarism is copying the work of others and thereafter presenting it as if it were our own. Examination boards are becoming increasingly strict on work that has been plagiarised and use special software tools to identify submitted work that is believed to be copied. If you copy someone's work you are in danger of losing your qualification.

Protecting confidentiality

In our electronic world it is very easy to write an email, click send and have confidential matters sent to the wrong person in your address book. Forwarding emails, using the 'cc' and 'bcc' features must all be used with care. Sometimes sensitive project details meant for one person, may be inadvertently sent to others!

> **Tip:**
>
> As you carry out your research copy and paste the source details of any websites you have used into a new document. This will make the creation of a bibliography much easier at a later point.

Safe working

Ensuring that hardware, cables, seating etc. are positioned correctly

It is very important that you observe safe working procedures as you use the computer. Your computer monitor and operator's chair must be positioned to minimise fatigue.

For example, your chair height should be adjusted so that your elbows are level with the table. Any reading materials should be held in a copy holder and level with your eyes. If you would really like to work more safely, then visit the following website where you will find a wealth of information on setting-up your working area correctly.

http://www.openerg.com/dse/index.html

Take a look at their informative 'Office of Horrors' set-up to see how not to do it!

Ensuring that lighting is appropriate

Avoid glare from windows or bright overhead electric lighting. Use a screen guard if you can to avoid unnecessary glare.

Taking regular breaks

Take a ten minute break away from the monitor at least every 50 minutes.

Handling and storing media correctly

In the 'olden days' when floppy disks really were 'floppy', the data stored was fairly vulnerable. One good 'chew' from a pet Labrador or wrongly placed disk in a college bag and your data would be gone forever! Nowadays we have storage media such as CD-ROMs and Pen Drives which are much more stable and robust. We still need to keep these safe however, because a lost Pen Drive is just about as good as a floppy disk which has been chewed by the dog! Avoid extremes of temperature, magnetic fields, liquids and direct sunlight.

E-portfolio

Creating an appropriate structure for an e-portfolio

Using appropriate folders for your work is a good start. This will pay dividends the further into the course you get when you will have more and more material to work with. Ideally you will set out your e-portfolio as a series of web pages which will contain your evidence. Don't forget that you will not need this type of portfolio for Chapter Three 'The Knowledge Worker' as this is the examinable component.

Collecting together all the required information, converting files to an appropriate format if necessary

We've already talked about collecting together your materials and storing them in appropriate folders. Some files you may collect may well be in the wrong format at this point and will require conversion. For example, you may have a very large picture file stored as an uncompressed Tiff file that must be converted to JPEG for your e-portfolio. Do this at the time you collect the file so that you can then delete the original Tiff, this way your student drive will not get full of large files.

Authenticating your work

We've already discussed this in detail and now is the time to ensure that all of your work is authenticated.

Providing a table of contents, using hyperlinks to locate information easily

One way of building your e-portfolio is to use Word to generate web pages (or you could use PowerPoint as we did for our e-book in Chapter One). If you choose Microsoft Word you may do this by 'Saving as Web Page' and as you do so the Toolbars will give you access to additional features such as 'Create Hyperlink' etc. We've already completed something similar in PowerPoint when we made hyperlinks for our e-book (we also created a sample structure with FrontPage in Chapter One). The basic concept here is to have an Index Page with links that will take you to the content.

Testing for size, compatibility and ease of use, making sure that the e-portfolio conforms to the technical specification

Having built your e-portfolio, you must test it to ensure that it works i.e. all of the links take the user to the appropriate sections. In addition you must ensure that the e-portfolio meets the latest Edexcel specification (your teacher or lecturer will give you up-to-date guidance on this aspect).

The following section shows how you may document some of your procedures as you construct your e-book. It has been written from the student, Christopher R. Ryan's perspective! Note: Your teacher or lecturer may require that you present this using the 'third person', without the use of 'I' or 'me' etc.

Creating my multimedia content

This part of my project illustrates how I created some original multimedia components for my e-book. I decided to use PowerPoint as my authoring package because I felt it was easy to use and I certainly had some experience of using it as I completed other projects in school. I thought it would be good to have a sound file play as soon as my e-book opened. To do this I decided to use the sound recorder provided with the Windows XP operating system.

I decided to make this recording at home and then transfer the file to the school system using my pen drive. I did this because I was unsure about speaking into a microphone with the background noise at school.

To do this I first had to run the Microsoft Sound recorder software.

This was achieved by: selecting Start\All Programs\Accessories\Entertainment\ Sound Recorder

> **Tip:**
>
> Please check with the latest version of the ICT specification on the Edexcel website to ensure you know everything that needs to be included in the e-portfolio.

The screenshot shown below (Figure 4.18) illustrates the steps followed to do this. As you can see there are quite a few steps to remember.

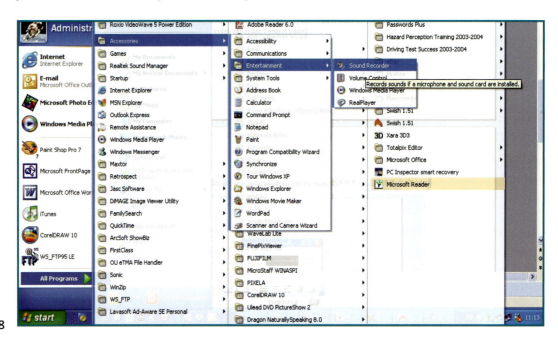

Figure 4.18

At this point the sound recorder then appeared on-screen and allowed me to record my own voice. As you can see from the screenshot below, the control buttons on the sound recorder look just like a video recorder control panel (Figure 4.19).

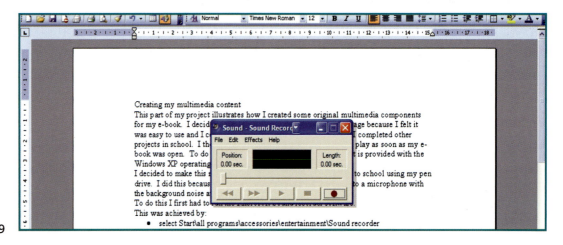

Figure 4.19

To create my sound file I clicked the record button (see Figure 4.20) and then, using a microphone, said "Hi, my name is Chris Ryan, welcome to my e-book".

I then pressed the stop button (see Figure 4.21) which finalised my recording. I then saved my file by:

Figure 4.20

Figure 4.21

- selecting File\Save As

- naming my file

- Then storing it in an appropriate directory.

After going through this process I found that I could have recorded my voice file directly into PowerPoint by Insert\Movies & Sound\Record Sound!

Evaluation

My first attempt at creating the sound file failed miserably. I stammered my way through the first part and almost forgot my name! I soon found that as I persisted with the sound recorder I became more confident. The great thing about working with digital tools is that if you make a mistake you can just delete it and start again.

Having successfully created a file, I played it back and it sounded just right for my e-book. I played the file to some of my group at school and they thought it sounded OK but felt my voice was a little quiet in places.

As a result of this feedback, I re-recorded my sound file, replayed it to confirm that it was to an appropriate standard and then saved it as my final copy. It was this file that I used for the opening page of my e-book.

Index

Index compiled by Indexing Specialist (UK) Ltd